# The 21st-Century Case for a Managed Economy

The role of disequilibrium, feedback loops and scientific method in post-crash economics

by Seán Harkin

**Hh**

HARRIMAN HOUSE LTD

3A Penns Road
Petersfield
Hampshire
GU32 2EW
GREAT BRITAIN

Tel: +44 (0)1730 233870
Fax: +44 (0)1730 233880
Email: enquiries@harriman-house.com
Website: www.harriman-house.com

---

First published in Great Britain in 2010

Copyright © Harriman House Ltd

The right of Seán Harkin to be identified as the author has been asserted
in accordance with the Copyright, Design and Patents Act 1988.

ISBN: 978-1-906659-54-7

*British Library Cataloguing in Publication Data*
A CIP catalogue record for this book can be obtained from the British Library.

Printed and bound in the UK by CPI Antony Rowe, Chippenham

To My Grandparents,
Francie and Molly Harkin

# Contents

# About the Author

Seán Harkin is a risk manager working in the City of London. He specialises in quantitative analysis of financial and economic data and has worked on structured finance, sovereign debt, bank capital and other areas. Seán was previously a research scientist working in the field of cell and molecular biology. He holds an MPhil from University College London and a BSc from the National University of Ireland.

# Acknowledgements

In writing the acknowledgements for any book, it is important to thank both those who played a direct role in getting it to print and those whose indirect contributions made the whole effort possible in the first place. Therefore, there are many people I need to mention. First, I would like to thank Fiona for all her love and encouragement and for keeping me company while I was writing and she was studying for her accountancy exams. Even though we sat at opposite ends of the living-room table, each focused on our own efforts, having her there made all the difference.

Next, I would also like to thank my good friend Daniel Mumzhiu for so enthusiastically agreeing to be my first reviewer and for giving me so many helpful comments on style and content. As someone who knows the financial world well, Dan's contributions were invaluable.

In the same way, I would like to thank all my close friends in and around London for always being ready to have a good debate on matters political and economic. These discussions have often taken place over a beer (or ten) and, while they usually give way to more frivolous matters, they have provided much food for thought. I won't name names because I will inevitably end up leaving someone out, but you all know who you are!

A special mention must also go to my publishers, Harriman House, for taking this project on and for their efficiency and professionalism in getting it to print. I am especially grateful to Chris Parker and Stephen Eckett for their astute comments on style and presentation, for their consistent ability to see how things will come across to the reader and for ensuring that I kept it all concise. I am also grateful to Suzanne Anderson for her efforts in making the whole process flow smoothly. In all of my dealings with Harriman House, I was consistently impressed with their approach and I would recommend them to anyone writing on a topic of a financial or economic nature.

Similarly, I would like to thank all those in London's financial industry who supported me when I first made the move from scientific research to financial risk management. Both Ryan Jong and Duncan Martin deserve mention here; without their input, I would have been much slower to make the links between abstract theory and practical reality that are crucial to any understanding of the economy. I would also like to thank Julian Morgan and Michael Hutchinson for more recent opportunities to continue this learning.

Finally, and most importantly of all, I would like to thank my mother, Mary Harkin, for all her sacrifices over the years and for giving me the commitment to hard work and education that is the most fundamental starting point in writing a book such as this. The need to ensure that values such as these are made reality for as many people as possible is one of the core themes I hope come through in what I have written here.

SEÁN HARKIN
LONDON, 2010

# Preface

On 16 July 2009, *The Economist* magazine carried the remarkable cover story: 'Modern economic theory, where it went wrong and how the crisis is changing it'. There was a striking image of a hefty-looking textbook halfway through the process of melting into a puddle, and the article that followed pointed out how

[m]acroeconomists, especially within central banks, were too fixated on taming inflation and too cavalier about asset bubbles. Financial economists, meanwhile, formalised theories of the efficiency of markets, fuelling the notion that markets would regulate themselves and financial innovation was always beneficial. Wall Street's most esoteric instruments were built on these ideas.

There were caveats but, to anyone who has been for or against market liberalisation over the years, the admission was nonetheless profound. The theories which previously supported triumphant market fundamentalism had now been shaken to their core. Not only disproved by events, they themselves had helped sow the seeds of a vast global economic disruption. In the years to come, we may hear much less of the idea that markets are so fantastically efficient that governments have little need to regulate them on our behalf.

More empirical perspectives on the economy – not tied to dogma but focused on the facts – can at last, perhaps, begin to gain a hearing. This matters a great deal. The economy is an area upon which we should bring to bear as much as possible of the scientific rigour that we apply to more fundamental areas of investigation, and in which we should insist on honest recommendations aimed at maximising the well-being of society. Indeed, as someone who entered into financial analysis from a background in science, this is how I had expected economics to be practised. But, as the writers of *The Economist* partially admit, things have not hitherto quite worked out this way. The subject of economics as it is presently taught often seems to be as much a barrier to understanding the underlying issues as it is a help.

## Long-run equilibrium

Perhaps the main reason for its shortcomings is that contemporary economic analysis has a tendency to focus relentlessly on those processes that draw the system back towards long-run balance and equilibrium, and to neglect the equally important processes that tend to disrupt this equilibrium and drive the system away from it[1]. Economists may make clear and explicit allowance for the level or position of long-run equilibrium to move or to drift over time, but they underplay the more chaotic nature of the short run and the non-equilibrium aspects of certain processes that are relevant in the long-run. The student thus comes away with the impression that little is permitted to vary; that all the ceaseless fluctuations and sustained trends of the real world must somehow be figments of their imagination.

It is not that modern economics pretends that the fluctuations of the real world do not exist; it is simply that the academics who first came up with the theories we use were not enthused by such things and instead viewed them either as minor processes occurring on the way to restoring long-run equilibrium, or as 'real' movements in the position of that equilibrium. To take just one example of this strange outlook, a spike and fall in the rate of unemployment playing out over two or three whole years is seen as being just a ripple as the economy is displaced from, and returns dependably to, full-employment equilibrium – or as the position of that equilibrium, for some obscure reason, itself undergoes a fluctuation.

A worldview such as this might be acceptable if the economy did indeed spend most of its time in a state of long-run equilibrium, but we know from our everyday experience that this simply cannot be the case. Indeed, as we shall see, long-run equilibrium should instead be viewed as some sort of anchor level that the economy cannot move too far away from, but which it never settles at either. To continue with unemployment, the level of joblessness never plots as a flat line at its long-run equilibrium level but instead takes the form of a wave, rising up above this level and falling back below it again in an endless succession of peaks and troughs with a rough periodicity of 7-10 years. In a US-style economy, this wave rarely falls below about 3.5% of the labour force and rarely rises above 10% (the long-run equilibrium for joblessness in such an economy seems to be about 6%)*.

---

* At this point, lest I inadvertently sound like a cold-hearted proponent of laissez-faire that just accepts periods of crushing unemployment as a fact of nature, I should point out that, for important things such as unemployment, we can exercise significant influence over the long-run equilibrium level, over the amplitude of fluctuations around this level and over the duration of these fluctuations. We can also redirect some of our economic output towards helping those who are out of work and towards swiftly getting them back into work again. These are themes I will naturally return to later in the book.

## Disequilibrium and the logic of feedback

Given such observations, it should be clear that study of what happens when the economy is out of equilibrium – and study of the forces that drive it away from equilibrium in the first place – should be at least as important as consideration of the equilibrium condition itself. To explain these things, and to explain their relationship with the processes that tend to restore equilibrium, one can put forward a simple thesis rooted in the principles of systems science. This is as follows:

1.  The market economy is a dynamic network system composed of millions of interacting units that show certain behavioural patterns.

2.  Like all such systems, it is driven by positive and negative feedback: processes that tend to either amplify or to attenuate themselves.

3.  Those processes that tend to restore equilibrium are forms of negative feedback.

4.  Those that tend to drive the system away from equilibrium are forms of positive feedback, and

5.  The system as a whole is driven by a mixture of positive and negative feedback, with each being dominant under different circumstances.

Simple examples of positive and negative feedback – as general principles that can apply to any dynamic system – are to be found in the burning of a piece of paper. Fire requires three ingredients: heat, fuel (in this case paper) and oxygen. But it also produces heat, while it consumes fuel and oxygen. The result is that, in the initial stages of combustion, where fuel and oxygen are abundant, fire produces one of its own key ingredients – heat – without yet depleting the other two. This heat produces more fire, which produces more heat, which produces more fire, and so on in a runaway process of positive feedback where the consequences of a given change drive that change yet further and which, in this case, manifests itself as the phenomenon of bursting into flames. Eventually, however, as the fire consumes both fuel and oxygen, one of these (or both) will begin to run short and the fire will have removed one of the conditions necessary for its own existence, causing it to flicker and die. This is negative feedback; a process where a given change sets in train consequences that tend to reverse that change, in this case restoring the absence of flame.

Applied to the economy, feedback explains the ups and downs of the system in a simple and elegant manner. In some settings, negative feedback is dominant and economic conditions corresponding to classical long-run equilibrium therefore prevail. For example, in the market for some core consumer item where conditions of supply and demand are highly stable in the long run, a cut in prices will lead to an excess of volume demanded over supply, causing retailers to swiftly increase prices back up again to their original level – leaving the system relatively unchanged.

In other settings, positive feedback is dominant and any change feeds upon itself until large movements occur – in either a desirable or undesirable direction depending on the nature of the process in question. A rise in share prices, for example, may convince potential buyers that shares are attractive, creating further demand, which causes prices to rise further, creating yet more demand and so on in a typical bubble phenomenon.

However, in many such cases, positive feedback cannot remain dominant forever – otherwise levels of activity would routinely explode towards infinity or collapse towards zero. Negative feedback must eventually take over and cause the system to pull back from whatever maximum or minimum it has reached. This change of direction then allows positive feedback to take over once more, albeit now operating in the opposite direction. It causes the system to once again power past its long-run equilibrium level, until it reaches another extremum on the far side and turns back again. In stock markets, for example, bubble conditions may cause prices to rise to a level where investors realise they are entirely out of line with the underlying earnings potential of the companies in question – causing them to begin selling, causing the market to turn and probably causing it to over-correct and crash far below its equilibrium level.

Dynamics such as these are clearly consistent with the wave-like fluctuations we observe in many aspects of the real economy. They therefore deserve to be a central part of our economic theory.

## Replacing a blinkered view

The feedback-based approach also shows that, until now, economists have focused on just half the story – negative feedback and equilibrium – making it inevitable that their theories sometimes seem oddly out-of-touch with reality. In particular, by arguing that the system has a strong tendency to quickly return to a desirable balance, the economics profession leads us to the conclusion that leaving markets to their own devices will produce beneficial outcomes in almost all cases. Recognising that positive feedback has as great a role to play as negative feedback, however, leads to very different conclusions. It shows that the markets can be chaotic, with imperfections that were initially minor leading to extreme dislocations – making government oversight necessary to ensure proper functioning of the system.

The idea of feedback also goes far beyond consideration of economic stability, which is just one of several aspects of the economy that matter to us. Feedback is a general principle of network science that has just as much to say about the dynamics underlying economic growth, and about the inexorable rise in inequality that always seems to occur in very free-market economies, as it does about stability. And in this, too, the feedback perspective leads to conclusions that are very much at odds with the classical view that growth is driven almost entirely by the free play of market forces, and that whatever level of inequality exists in a market economy is the level that is necessary for optimal performance overall. Instead, it argues that growth is built on a self-reinforcing interplay of state and private sector action and that the phenomenon of 'money going to money' in a free-market economy ensures that inequality builds up far beyond what is practically necessary.

## The necessity of a mixed economy

These observations show again that state involvement is pivotal to desirable economic outcomes. The state must reach beyond its basic functions of maintaining law, institutions and security and must provide essential links in the chain of events leading to growth – especially such links as education and long-term scientific research – if growth is to take place. Likewise, if excess inequality that reduces efficiency and overall well-being is to be avoided, the state must engage in progressive taxation and provide essential services that give the disadvantaged a firm base from which to compete.

All of this gives us two interwoven insights: that the scientific principle of feedback fundamentally changes key aspects of what classical economists tell us about the economy; and that this should lead us to favour a mixed economic system in which both state and market have essential roles to play – as opposed to the mainly-market system favoured by classical economics. These insights go to the heart of the fundamental questions in economic and financial theory: which economic system is best, what should be the role of government, and which modes of analysis enable us to answer these questions? *They are therefore the twin pillars around which this book is built; working out in more detail what the concept of feedback has to say about the economy and describing in depth what this implies for policy.*

This book cannot, of course, be a final elaboration of the feedback perspective on the economy. It is, rather, a first attempt at building the economic story around this idea, and at re-interpreting existing knowledge in this context. No other work has yet done so in as much detail.

For me, exploring these matters has cast light on social and political questions I have found fascinating since my school days. I hope it is equally useful to the reader and that they find it both enlightening and enjoyable.

# Part One:
# Foundations

# 1. Introduction:

# Disequilibrium and the Logic of Feedback

I n October 2005, as part of a speech to the US National Italian-American Foundation, Alan Greenspan, then Chairman of the US Federal Reserve, expressed the view that,

> [a]lthough the business cycle has not disappeared, flexibility has made the economy more resilient to shocks and more stable overall during the past couple of decades. To be sure, that stability, by fostering speculative excesses, has created some new challenges for policy-makers. But, more fundamentally, an environment of greater economic stability has been key to the impressive growth in the standards of living and economic welfare so evident in the United States.

Such views were common from the mid-1990s through to 2007. Economists and policy-makers believed that, either because of the flexibility inherent in deregulated economies, or because governments had finally stumbled upon the right combination of stabilisation policies, the problem of economic instability had been solved. In 2002, Harvard economist James Stock labelled our era of economic history the "Great Moderation", a label that was subsequently adopted by Ben Bernanke, Greenspan's successor as chairman of the Federal Reserve. And, in 2003, Nobel Laureate Robert E. Lucas declared that macroeconomics had solved its central problem of "depression-prevention" and should move on to other matters.

The dominance of such thinking was the outcome of a constellation of forces affecting politics and academic economics that were especially powerful in the US and UK, and which had roots going back to the 1970s. I will not, however, dwell on these intellectual currents here. I will instead adopt the view that such ideas have been fatally undermined by the events of 2007-2009, and that challenging and replacing the economic theories at their core is the best way to finish them off.

## Equilibrium Theory and its Limitations

In improving economics, or any other subject, the first step is to consider what analytical approach and mindset are most appropriate. In this there is a long-standing debate as to whether fields such as economics can qualify as science, and thus as to whether they are amenable to scientific methodologies. I would argue that they can qualify; science encompasses any area of inquiry where objective evidence can be obtained, and where this evidence can be analysed in a rigorous and methodical way to reach an understanding of underlying dynamics. As a consequence, a great many subjects can be included under the banner of science. Clearly, not all of these can achieve the same rigour as subjects such as physics, which are amenable to experiment or direct physical measurement. But, in pursuing them, we should nevertheless try to be as rigorous and methodical as possible.

However, when one applies the yardstick of science to the contents of the economics textbooks that confront us today, it forces observations that economists of a more conventional or conservative inclination are likely to find uncomfortable. One such observation is a striking mismatch between the pure and applied aspects of economics – the economics of the textbooks seems to fall far short of being able to explain the events of the real world.

The 'neoclassical'* economics taught today centres on the concept of equilibrium, and analyses all economic events in this context. To be precise, it invokes two kinds of equilibrium: short-run and long-run equilibrium. Short-run equilibrium is simply the combination of price and volume that tends to prevail in an individual market over a short period or, similarly, the average level of prices and overall level of output that prevail in the aggregate economy over a short period. Long-run equilibrium, on the other hand, is seen as some level of price, volume or both that either an individual market or, more commonly, the economy overall tends to return to when sufficient time has passed. In this framework, the 'long-run' is defined formally as a period of time sufficient for all variables in the system to adjust to new conditions; and, in the case of the economy overall, the position of long-run equilibrium is seen as itself changing in a directional way as the economy grows and prices inflate over the 'very long run' (i.e. historical time). Beyond this, when it comes to actually performing macroeconomic analysis, discussion of long-run equilibrium in the economy overall is usually closely

---

* The taxonomy of classical economics is complex. From the 1870s, the specific economic ideas of the late 1700s and early 1800s were revamped and were labelled 'neoclassical' in 1900. Keynes then referred to all foregoing economics as 'classical' in the 1930s. And, in the 1970s, a specific form of macroeconomics emphasising 'rational expectations' and 'rigorous microfoundations' of macro behaviour became known as 'New Classical Macroeconomics'. Since all of these modes of thought reach essentially the same conclusion – that the economy makes a quick return to long-run equilibrium – I usually just refer to all of them as 'classical'.

combined with discussion of long-run equilibrium in 'factor markets' (markets for natural resources, labour and capital) that inevitably have a tight relationship with aggregate activity)[2].

It is clear that short-run equilibrium must exist. In individual markets, when we construct a graph that places price on the vertical axis and volume on the horizontal, we find that demand (the amount people are willing to buy per day at a given point in time) must usually plot as a downward-sloping curve, and that supply (the amount firms are willing to sell per day at a given point in time) must usually plot as an upward-sloping curve. Likewise, on an equivalent plot of price-level versus output for the economy overall, aggregate demand must slope downwards and aggregate supply must slope upwards, at least in the short run. As a consequence, on any plot of this kind there must be just one location at which the supply and demand curves intersect and the intentions of buyers and sellers coincide – a point that is described as the short-run equilibrium or 'market clearing position' associated with the set of supply and demand conditions we are considering (Figure 1).

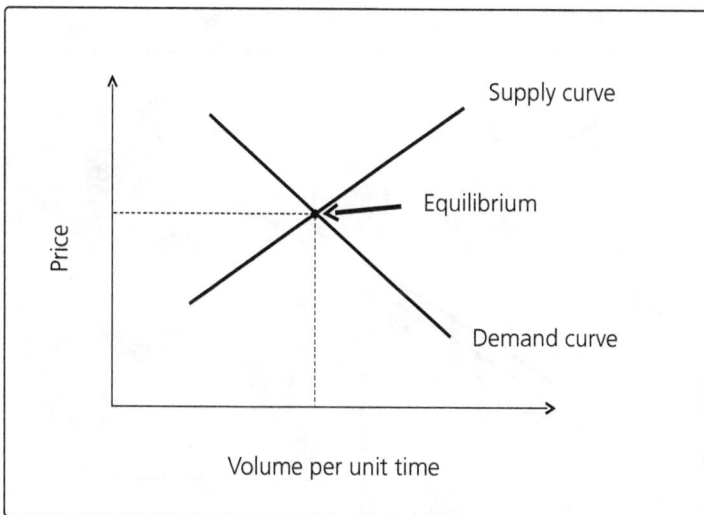

**Figure 1 – The classical model of short-run supply and demand in an individual market.** Price and volume are determined by the intersection of the supply and demand curves.

This short-run equilibrium is established and held in place by negative feedback effects. If suppliers try to increase prices above the equilibrium determined at that time by the logic of the market, they will find that unsold stock accumulates, and they will be forced to reduce prices again. Conversely, if they cut prices below their equilibrium level, queues and waiting lists arising from excess demand will develop, and they will find themselves in a position where they can increase their prices again. And, moving from the micro to the macro level, since these forces preserving short-run equilibrium prevail in individual markets, they must also prevail in the economy overall.

However, the implications of short-run equilibrium can be over-stated. Just because short-run equilibrium exists, it does not imply that its position remains in the same location on our plot of price versus volume or that it has no systematic tendency to move about from one location to another. Indeed, in the case of asset markets, as we have already alluded to, most movements of the demand curve to the right (reflecting an increase in the price investors are willing to pay for a given volume), lead to a further movement to the right. And most movements to the left, lead to a further movement to the left. The position of equilibrium swings thus wildly through a range of prices and volumes under the influence of these positive feedback effects (Figure 2).

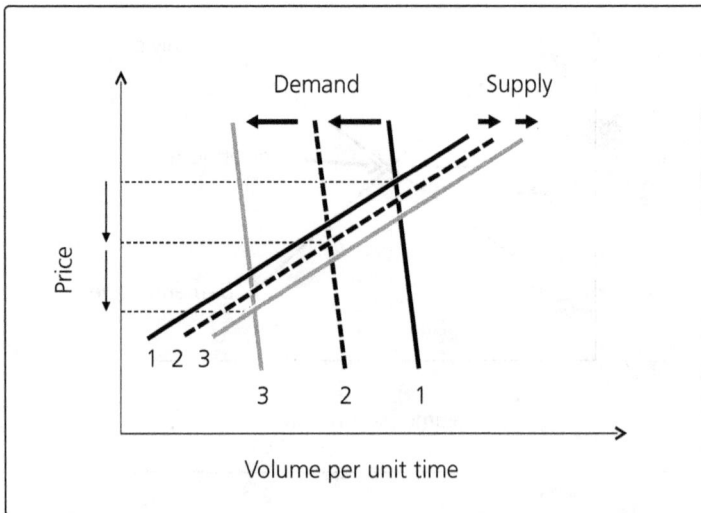

**Figure 2 – Stylised behaviour of supply and demand in a falling-price asset market.** Each movement of the demand curve is likely to cause further movement in the same direction (with an eventual reversal, probably after many moves, that causes the same process to begin again in the opposite direction). At the same time, because interest in making transactions often increases both when prices are sharply rising and when they are sharply falling, the supply curve moves to the right in a less stable market and to the left in a more stable one. When prices are rising, this supply-curve behaviour attenuates the rise, though not to completion, as some investors possessing the asset will want to hold for a period in anticipation that the trend will continue, while there may also be physical or practical limitations in bringing more assets to market (especially in the early stages of a price movement). And, when prices are falling, as here, supply-curve behaviour intensifies the fall.

On the slopes of the curves the demand curve is shown as being near-vertical because it could be argued that both high and low prices attract buyers (probably different sets of buyers), but still has some downward slope so that supply-curve movements can affect volume in an intuitive way. The supply curve, meanwhile, is shown as upward-sloping because higher prices attract more suppliers into the market (developers building houses when prices are high, companies issuing new shares when the price is high etc). These slope choices are debatable, showing that this classical model is weak for asset markets, but similar overall dynamics result whatever slope assumptions are made.

Nevertheless, provided we understand that equilibrium and stability are not the same thing, we can analyse even rapid economic change in terms of the model of short-run equilibrium. Such change must, after all, be driven by rapid changes in supply and/or demand, and the result of these changes must be what we observe when we see rapid change taking place in the real economy. The only question is whether the underlying movements of supply and demand are due to changes in factors, such as tastes and technology, which are exogenous to the particular market we are considering; or whether they are due to endogenous positive feedback effects.

Long-run equilibrium must also exist. At just a glance, we can see that most macroeconomic variables do not routinely spiral towards infinity, or implode towards zero. This suggests that there must be some sort of mean level (or range) to which they tend to revert when enough time has passed, and which must be equivalent to some sort of long-run equilibrium.

To be more precise, economists view long-run macroeconomic equilibrium as being something that is maintained by events in the factor markets, and especially in the labour markets. In this analysis, aggregate demand plots as a downward-sloping curve on our plot of price level against output and, in the short-run, aggregate supply plots as an upward-sloping curve. However, in the long run, aggregate supply plots as a vertical line – indicating that real output maintains a constant value, independent of price level, over the long-run. We shall see why this is in a moment.

Over brief periods of time, fluctuations in aggregate demand can shift real output away from its long-run equilibrium level but, in the mainstream model, these changes quickly reverse themselves. For example, if a surge in demand causes output to rise above its long-run equilibrium level, more workers must be employed and unemployment must fall to such a low level that the increased bargaining power of workers pushes up wages. This creates an extra cost to firms, which causes short-run aggregate supply to fall (the short-run aggregate supply curve moves to the left) and causes the position of equilibrium to move back to its long-run level (Figure 3). Alternatively, if aggregate demand falls, unemployment must rise; enhancing the bargaining power of firms, enabling them to cut costs, and causing short-run aggregate supply to increase, so that output again moves back to its long-run equilibrium level.

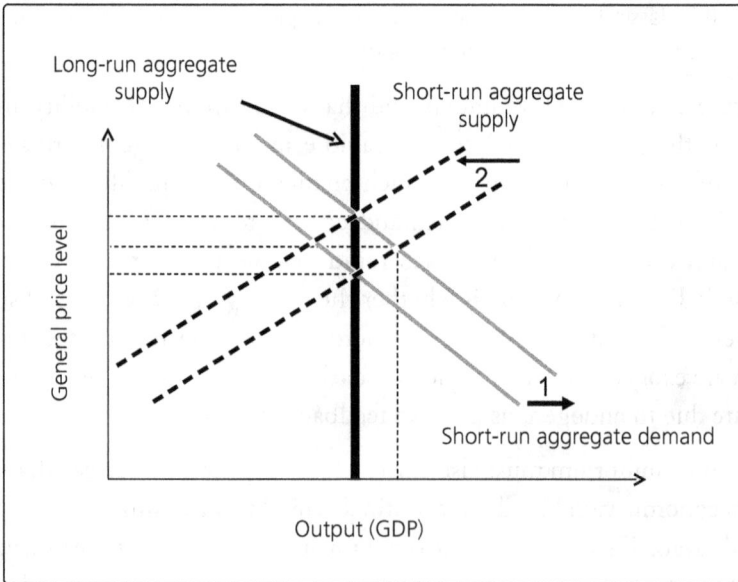

**Figure 3 – The classical model of long-run equilibrium in the aggregate economy.** In this example, aggregate demand has increased for some reason (step 1). This causes both output and the general price level to increase. However, since a rise in output is associated with a fall in unemployment, workers acquire bargaining power and wages rise. This is an extra cost to companies and it causes short-run aggregate supply to fall (step 2) so that output and employment return to their original level. The general price level will have increased but this has no real effects as the relative prices of different things (including wages) will have remained unchanged.

However, the time period over which this process plays out is generally several years and many additional complications arise over this period. In addition, long-run aggregate supply moves to the right over the 'very long run' as technology advances.

In this analysis, the position of long-run equilibrium is defined purely in terms of output – it is any point along the long-run aggregate supply curve – and the price level is basically irrelevant. After each dislocation, the economy returns to long-run equilibrium at a different price level to that which prevailed before but, while the transition to this price level may have real economic effects, the end level itself is arbitrary. If, for example, the price level were twice, or half, as high, the prices of different items relative to one another would remain constant and the incentives of buyers and sellers would remain unchanged. In addition to this, the vertical line representing long-run aggregate supply and long-run equilibrium, to which the economy always returns, is seen as moving to the right over the very long run as the economy grows. Likewise, the price level is seen as gradually inflating as growth in the money supply and enthusiasm for spending lead to repeated positive demand shocks.

This model of long-run equilibrium captures many essential features of how economic fluctuations work themselves out, but it still leaves a great deal unanswered. In essence, if there is a powerful condition of long-run equilibrium to which the economy tends to quickly return, why then is analysis of real-world economic events dominated by observations of unceasing volatility, of sudden dislocations and of slow movements back to trend? Classical economists typically respond to this question with the view that these dramatic events are just minor undulations that happen on the way to restoring long-run equilibrium. But as the great 20th-century economist John Maynard Keynes famously put it, "The long run is a misleading guide to current affairs. In the long run we are all dead. Economists set themselves too easy, too useless a task if in tempestuous seasons they can only tell us that, when the storm is past, the ocean is flat again."

# Introducing Feedback

To meet Keynes' demand that we understand what happens when the economy is not in long-run equilibrium, and to properly and systematically explain the unceasing fluctuations that we observe on both a micro and a macro level, we must note that there is a phenomenon that is observed again and again in analysis of the real economy, and of other physical systems, but which is not given a central role in the theory of economics. This phenomenon is that of *feedback*. It consists of *any process operating in a network system whereby a change in some element of that system leads to a further change in the same element at a subsequent point in time*[3].

Different kinds of feedback occur in the economy. Some are negative feedback – changes that set in train consequences that tend to reverse the original change – and these are the forces that maintain short-run equilibrium, and which tend to draw the system back to long-run equilibrium when it is displaced. Other forms of feedback are positive feedback – changes that set in train consequences that tend to amplify the original change, leading to multiple cycles of self-reinforcement – and these are the forces that tend to disrupt equilibrium. Positive feedback causes the position of short-run equilibrium to move about in systematic ways; it drags economic systems away from long-run equilibrium; and it causes secular trends in the position of long-run equilibrium (such as economic growth) that play out over the very long run.

As we shall see, both kinds of feedback play a central role in familiar processes such as the asset price cycle, the wider economic cycle, runaway inflation and deflation, economic growth and the rise of inequality. Indeed, as we shall see, an awareness of feedback allows us to construct a complete explanation of economic change that is consistent with many existing ideas, but which is more realistic than the current synthesis.

This approach eliminates features of the classical model that are most at odds with reality. Most notably, it does not rely on the unrealistic assumption of consistently rational human behaviour. Take asset markets, for example. The classical model assumes that investors perform a rational calculation based on projecting future cash flows resulting from ownership of a given asset; on discounting these returns by a given annual percentage based on the returns achievable from a lower-risk investment (such as a bank deposit); and on then summing discounted returns to arrive at a proper value for the asset in question. In this theory, some investors will overestimate, some will underestimate but, on average, they will produce a rational valuation based on all available information. And, because they will be willing to pay up to this price but no more, this calculation will define the market price of the asset.

What this model ignores, crucially, is that, in most cases, *the data needed to perform a calculation such as this simply do not exist, and cannot exist.* As a consequence, investors must instead base their buying and selling decisions on perception and on the price movements they have observed thus far – leading to the wild fluctuations in price (unrelated to new information on real prospects for earnings) that we have already mentioned.

Likewise, in the aggregate economy, the classical model assumes that rational wage bargaining quickly reverses the consequences of any fluctuation in aggregate demand, and that the economy is therefore stable. But, in reality, changes in employment associated with a given change in output can lead to a further change in aggregate demand in the same direction as that which happened initially, because the ability of the public to spend naturally moves in line with the level of employment. This provides the basis for a positive feedback process, which sets the system on a trajectory of wild undulations that can play out over periods as long as a decade.

## The Inescapable Logic of Feedback

When we think about it for a while, it becomes clear that an interplay of positive and negative feedback must unavoidably determine economic events. For starters, it could never be just positive or negative feedback alone. If it were just negative feedback, then nothing would ever change. And, if it were just positive feedback, economic variables would either quickly collapse to zero or forever explode towards infinity.

Beyond this, because humans are social animals, and because high productivity relies on extensive division of labour, our economy naturally takes the form of a network of interlocking supply chains and other structural connections. Directly connected nodes in this network must, by virtue of how we define a connection, be linked by relationships whereby a change in the upstream node has either a positive or negative effect on the level of activity at the downstream node. And, because of the sheer number of connections in any such network, there must be loops where a node that is one or several steps downstream of another node itself affects, at a later point in time, the level of activity at that upstream node. In symbolic terms, where letters denote system elements and numbers denote time indices, we could say that A1 affects B2 affects A3, or that A1 affects B2 affects C3 affects A4.

These loops may take the form of positive feedback loops where it happens that a change in the level of activity at A leads to another change, in the same direction, in the level of activity at A. In other words, an increase in A at one point in time leads to a further increase in A at a subsequent point in time, while a decrease in A at one point in time leads to a further decrease in A at a subsequent point in time (Figure 4).

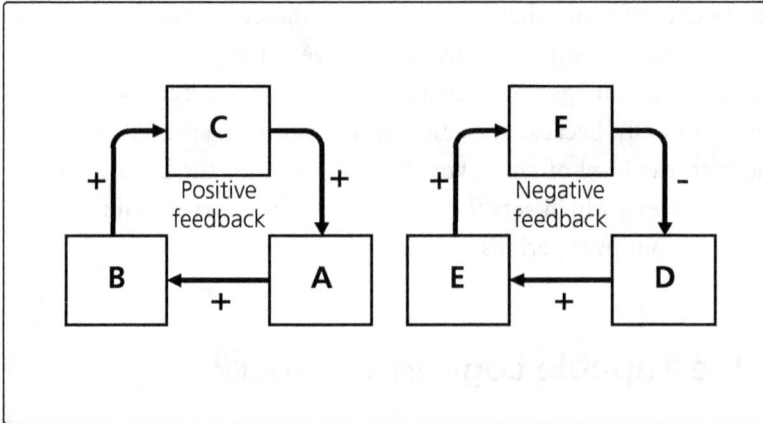

**Figure 4 – Simple positive and negative feedback loops.** Each of elements A to F correspond to the level of activity at a specific node in a network. The arrows show direct connections between nodes whereby the level of activity at one node influences the level of activity at another. And the signs show the directionality of the influence. If a change in activity at the upstream node causes a change in activity in the same direction (an increase or a decrease) at the immediate downstream node, then the sign is positive. If the changes are in opposite directions, the sign is negative. In the positive feedback loop, an increase in A leads indirectly to another increase in A, and, in the negative feedback loop, an increase in D leads indirectly to a decrease in D.

Alternatively, such processes may take the form of negative feedback loops where it happens that a change in activity at A leads to another change, in the opposite direction, in the level of activity at A. In other words, an increase in A at one point in time leads to a decrease in A at a subsequent point in time, while a decrease in A at one point in time leads to an increase in A at a subsequent point in time.

And, in a dense and complex network such as the economy, it is a simple matter of chance that a mixture of positive and negative feedback loops will occur. In some cases, a downstream element will happen to have a negative effect on the level of activity at an upstream element and there will be negative feedback. And, in some other cases, a downstream element will happen to have a positive effect on the level of activity at an upstream element and there will be positive feedback.

Positive feedback loops may be capable of operating in two overall directions – a self-sustaining increase or decrease in the level of activity at some reference node – or in just one direction (an increase or a decrease) if the reference node is capable of changing only in that one direction. Positive feedback that can operate in either direction gives rise to cycles where periods of increasing activity sustain themselves for a time, before changing direction and giving rise to periods of decreasing activity, which also sustain themselves for a time. The turning points in these cycles come about either as a result of external forces or as a result of negative feedback effects that build up and eventually overwhelm the positive feedbacks that usually drive the system.

By contrast, positive feedback that can operate in only one direction gives rise to secular trends in activity, possibly overlaid with undulations around the trend if the same reference node is affected by both kinds of positive feedback (secular and cyclical). And, finally, systems that are dominated by negative feedback tend to produce stability in the reference node over long periods of time – economic equilibrium of the kind that classical economists focus on, even though it is a rare occurrence in its pure form.

Given all of this, the principle of feedback can be said to represent a complete paradigm for explaining the dynamics of economic change. Feedback is, after all, nothing more than a principle explaining the logic of change in any dynamic network system, and it must therefore be as applicable to the economy as to any other such system.

# Further Aspects of Economic Feedback

## Trends and cycles: superimposition

Two of the positive feedback processes that can be observed in the economy at the macro level are essentially secular – meaning that they are usually capable of operating in just one direction when left to their own devices – and play out over time periods of decades to generations (the 'very long run' in macroeconomic terminology). One of these processes is the tendency towards GDP growth that occurs in a mixed economy with access to technological innovation (as we shall see in Chapter 10). The other is the tendency for inequality to rise far beyond what is necessary in an economy with a very free-market orientation.

The other positive feedback processes that can be observed in a market economy are cyclical – meaning that they alternate between activity-increasing and activity-reducing phases – and play out over time periods of months to years (the short run in macroeconomic terminology*). These consist of cycles in asset prices, credit, overall price levels, employment and general economic activity that interlock with one another to produce the overall business cycle with which we are so familiar.

These short-run cycles are essentially superimposed on the very-long-run processes that drive growth and inequality. Technology-driven growth increases the productive capacity of the economy, while short-run cycles cause the economy to rise up to the limit of this capacity, to fall away again and to rise back up in an endless succession of peaks and troughs (Figure 5). Because of growth, each time the peak of the cycle is reached it occurs at a higher level of output than the peak before, and the expansionary phases of the cycle therefore tend to be longer in duration than the recessionary phases[4].

---

* Very approximately, the macroeconomic short run corresponds to time periods of months to years, the long run corresponds to periods of years to a decade and the very long run corresponds to periods of decades to generations.

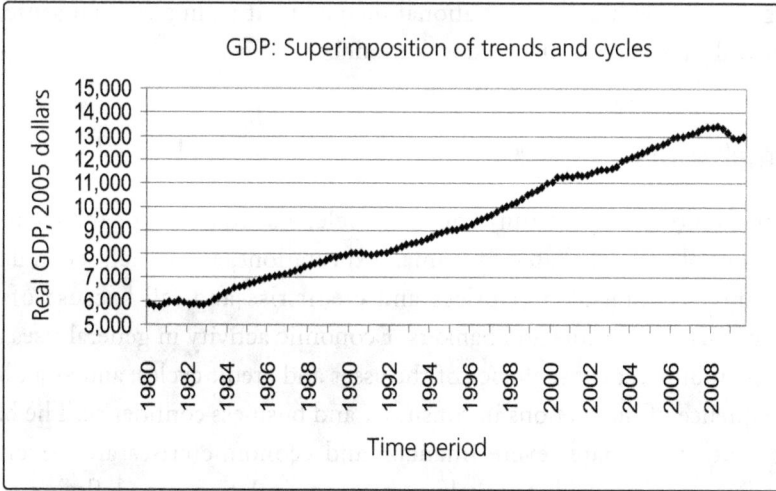

**Figure 5 – Quarterly Real GDP in the United States, 1980-2009.** The plot shows the kind of undulating trend which is characteristic of variables that are subject to both secular and cyclical positive feedback effects operating over different timescales. This, in itself, does not prove that such feedback effects are at work but, taken together with the fact that we can identify such feedback mechanisms in how the elements of the economy interact with one another, it represents powerful evidence for the feedback perspective. The data also show that lost GDP in recessions is not usually a severe cost to society – as we shall see later, the real cost is unemployment. [Data from the United States Bureau of Economic Research.]

When the economy is lightly regulated, distributional inequality tends to behave in a similar fashion to GDP and rises steadily over time – but with changes in its pattern as the economy moves from expansion to contraction and back again[5]. In a recession, as the number of unemployed rises sharply, so too does the number of people on a very low income (in the form of unemployed persons). At the same time, as business profits fall and speculation slows, the number of people on a very high income also falls. However, on balance, because the number of unemployed during a recession is generally much greater than the number of high earners during an expansion, a recession usually causes real material inequality to rise. Thus, without policy action, inequality rises steadily over time but with faster increases during the recessionary phase and transient falls as recovery begins.

In essence, feedback predicts that trends and cycles will be superimposed on one another in the economy. And, since this is exactly what we observe with things like growth and distributional inequality, it is, in a general sense, an empirical validation of the feedback model.

## Animal spirits

In the case of the short-run economic cycle, essentially all of the feedback that takes place is mediated by human expectations, as we shall see in detail in coming chapters. Asset prices and credit rise and fall because of the perceptions of investors and bankers. Economic activity in general rises and falls as an indirect consequence of the asset and credit cycles, and as a direct consequence of fluctuations in consumer and business confidence. The bank runs that can initiate severe financial and economic crises are driven by depositor panic. And the self-sustaining inflation or deflation that occasionally besets economies operates through general expectations of future price movements.

All of this corresponds to what Keynes, and the authors of a recent book written in a similar vein to Keynes[6], referred to as the "animal spirits" of market participants. It is very different from the kind of 'rational expectations' described by classical economists – based on cool-headed calculations of the future. It instead recognises that forward calculation with any precision is usually impossible, and that people instead rely on perception and gut instinct. This, of course, leaves them vulnerable to either excessive pessimism or to excessive optimism. And, because they are each aware that economic outcomes will depend on the collective behaviour of all market participants, their feelings tend to reinforce one another and to produce alternating waves of exuberance and hysteria over time.

# A Broader Keynesianism

Because it recognises irrational fluctuations as an inevitable feature of the economy, the feedback model is especially useful in explaining serious dislocations of the kind we have experienced over the past three years in the developed world, and over the past 30 years in the developing. Faced with events such as these, it is natural to ask what constitutes economic stability and how it can be achieved. The answer, according to the feedback model, is that stability, in the guise of any kind of stable long-run macroeconomic equilibrium, does not exist. Instead, the economy is driven by a series of interlocking feedback processes and is intrinsically prone to fluctuations over time, as we shall see in more detail in Chapter 3. These fluctuations are not usually as destructive as the global recession that began from 2007, but the cycle of expansion and contraction does always carry a substantial risk that the downturn phase of the cycle will develop into a self-perpetuating slump in activity. *This risk can, however, be minimised through government policies designed to dampen out the feedback processes giving rise to instability, while supporting those that lead to economic growth.* Thus, because such policies are needed, we should view government as an intrinsic part of the economic system.

The feedback-based view of the economy presented here is informed by principles governing similar processes in other physical systems, but it leads to conclusions that are essentially a refinement of the Keynesian perspective that was dominant from the 1940s through to the 1970s. Keynesian economics centred on recognising that instability is an intrinsic feature of the market economy and that government involvement is needed to keep this under control. It also involved the concept of a *multiplier effect*; in essence a particular example of positive feedback affecting jobs and output that operates when an economy is slipping into recession, when it is pulling out of recession again, or when government policy is being used to hasten the latter process*.

In terms of policy details, some aspects of the Keynesian consensus were clearly undesirable. The misconception that desirable multiplier effects could be achieved even when the economy was near capacity led to over-use of 'stimulatory' fiscal policy. The idea that currency stability was essential for international trade, and for general economic stability, led to an unhelpful preoccupation with exchange-rate management. And the combination of these policies, together with an inadequate understanding of inflationary dynamics, left the system vulnerable to sustained inflation after a number of shocks in the early 1970s, especially the price shock of 1973.

---

* These ideas were set out by John Maynard Keynes in his landmark 1936 book, *The General Theory of Employment, Interest and Money* and are often interpreted as a multiple-equilibrium model in which the economy can find high or low employment equilibria. However, Keynes' core ideas can be just as easily interpreted as a no-equilibrium model in which the economy is driven by self-reinforcing positive feedback processes and nothing resembling a persistent long-run equilibrium can exist on the macro level.

However, it seems clear that an economy organised along classical lines would have performed just as badly in the face of an exogenous shock such as this – probably undergoing a deep slump instead of the combination of inflation and recession that actually materialised. Likewise, it seems clear that, in less troubled economic times, the Keynesian-activist paradigm delivered superior economic performance, and did so with greater stability and more justice than the aggressively free-market consensus that has dominated since the early 1980s[7].

This book, in essence, takes a new intellectual approach – one based on feedback – that leads back to conclusions like those recommended by Keynes. However, because it is more general, and because it has more historical evidence to draw on, it has the potential to avoid some of the pitfalls of that earlier era. It is then, if you will, a 21st-century case for a managed economy.

# 2. From the Old to the New

The British Marxist historian Eric Hobsbawm, in his 1994 book *Age of Extremes*, compared the economy of the 1980s to that of the 1930s by saying "those of us who lived through the years of the Great Slump still find it almost impossible to understand how the orthodoxies of the pure free market, then so obviously discredited, again came to preside over a global period of depression in the late 1980s and 1990s".

At first glance, this comparison seems exaggerated. But, if we bear in mind that unemployment in the UK and a number of other OECD countries remained well above 10% for a significant period in the 1980s, and that the economy of the former Soviet Union underwent a 40% nose-dive in GDP following the failed reforms of the late 1980s and an abrupt transition to the free market in 1991-1992, then we can see what he is getting at. The experience of the UK in the early 1990s (as opposed to the 1980s) actually had more to do with its maintaining an over-valued currency peg against the German Deutschmark, and therefore pursuing deflationary monetary policies, than with the 'orthodoxies of the pure free market'. But this is a small modification of Hobsbawm's point[8].

In any case it is indeed difficult to comprehend how a viewpoint that is so starkly at odds with reality (the litany of bubbles, crises and recessions experienced in the first decade of the 21st century is evidence enough of this), and which had seemed near-dead in the 1950s and 1960s, once again became so dominant. It is equally difficult to avoid the conclusion that, because the free-market principle is deeply embedded in the minds of economists, and because it naturally gains much political support from business and from the wealthy (and from certain conservative cultures), it may have a tendency to come back again and again.

Given this, it is necessary to ask: why does the economics profession think as it does? This is the key question. Because the theorising of classical economists lends credibility and respectability to the free-market chattering of vested interests and conservative cultures, it is more important to explore this than to explore such vested interests and conservative cultures themselves. In essence, if we are to clear the way for something better, we must first expose the absurdity of classical economic thinking.

This chapter aims to do exactly that; to explain why classical economists think as they do (and to look at some aspects of the classical consensus that are actually salvageable), before moving on (in the bulk of the chapter) to look at the new, more promising research that is being performed.

# Mainsprings of the Classical Theory

## Rationality and self-interest

One of the two most fundamental factors underpinning the classical macroeconomic paradigm, especially in its current guise of "New Classical Macroeconomics"[9], is the assumption that all economic actions must be rational. Individuals, it is thought, are relentlessly self-interested and are capable of quickly developing a complete understanding of their economic surroundings. They will combine these two things to produce a set of actions designed to get them exactly what they want in the environment they face. In its purest form, this perspective assumes that all participants in the economy must quickly exhaust the optimal set of mutually-beneficial interactions available to them, that large deviations from long-run equilibrium must therefore be impossible and that all attempts by government to influence the system must either be futile (because people will adapt to them) or lead to suboptimal outcomes.

This view is held to different extents by different economists who could all be said to deserve the label 'classical'. The real purists hold that effects such as these operate instantaneously and that the economy is therefore always at full-employment equilibrium. This, apparently, is true even when unemployment stands at 10% or more. Those who are a little less adamantine, by contrast, accept that some deviations from optimality do occur when circumstances have changed and people are in the process of adapting, but they still believe that these are very transient and that the economy therefore never strays from full-employment equilibrium by much distance, or for much time.

It is clearly very questionable as to whether individual behaviour is rational in the way classical economists imagine. Firstly, people do not behave by calculation, but rather by rules of thumb that are based on innate psychology, cultural inheritance, past experience and observation of what others are doing.

These modes of behaviour are clearly approximately rational – otherwise they would not have developed – but they are not as rigorous as classical economists imagine or as capable of quick adaptation. Secondly, the human brain simply does not have the computational speed needed to understand its complete economic surroundings on a continuous basis. Indeed, if economists themselves struggle to achieve this understanding, how can they possibly think that ordinary people have it?[10]

In any case, even if people did behave in accordance with the conception of rationality held by classical economists, stability and general prosperity would not be the result. It is, for example, clearly rational for an individual to dump assets in a falling market, to withdraw funds in the midst of a bank run and to hoard cash in a deflationary environment. But, as collective social choices, these actions produce painful results and are deeply irrational. And, even though individual participants in the economy may be aware of this collective irrationality, and perhaps of the fact that they themselves will come to grief because of it, they still tend to take part because they expect that others will do likewise.

Similarly, while it may be rational for an individual to find a roughly optimal set of economic relations from amongst those available to them in a deeply disadvantaged social position, the existence of entrenched social stratification in the first place is clearly suboptimal in terms of overall societal well-being.

Classical economists sometimes respond to the differences between their predictions and what is actually observed in reality by saying that there has never been a true free market and that, if there were, it would behave as they predict. But this ignores the fact that their underlying assumptions about human behaviour stand in sharp contrast to everything that evolutionary biologists, psychologists, sociologists, and indeed common sense, tell us is true. It amounts to saying that, if only people would behave as classical economists say they must, then the model would be correct.

The unreality of the classical model also shows us that economic policy is neither futile nor bound to be counterproductive. For starters, and classical economists do accept this, if policy measures enforce hard changes in economic activities (such as by re-directing funds to social investment), then it is self-evident that they will affect economic outcomes in the long run. And, contrary to the theorising of classical economists, provided that such policies are targeted at major weaknesses of the market and are based on a realistic conception of economic dynamics, it is equally self-evident that the effects should generally be beneficial. Beyond this, even policies that have direct real effects in the short run but not in the long run (such as monetary policy changes) are still effective because the macroeconomic short run lasts a number of years and because repeated changes can be implemented to achieve a continuous effect.

## Abuse of mathematics

Closely related to its obsession with rational behaviour, the second factor underpinning the classical paradigm is an insistence that economics should rely near-exclusively on advanced mathematical reasoning as an analytical approach. This seems to be motivated by a desire for economics to resemble a certain perception of the natural sciences; with equilibrium conditions similar to those which occur in classical physics and with mathematical equations that are as precise as those of Newton or Einstein[11]. This, however, is a kind of precision that economics can only achieve through the inappropriate means of assuming that individual behaviour is strictly rational, and predicting consistent patterns of behaviour from there in the style of a mathematician. It would be impossible to achieve similar results by starting from the messy evidence of the real world, or by assuming behaviour that has a component of unpredictable or inconsistent irrationality to it.

As a consequence, mathematical models* constructed in classical macroeconomics draw on the concept of 'rational expectations', they involve a 'representative agent' whose behaviour is supposedly reflective of all market participants and, in this way, they attempt to build up a model of macro-level behaviour based on a set of 'rigorous microfoundations'. In many ways, this approach consists of carrying over to macroeconomics the high levels of abstraction found in the theory of classical microeconomics – which was less changed through the Keynesian era – but without recognising the much greater complexity of the macro domain.

---

*This is a good moment to note that, in academia, the term 'model' has varying connotations. In science, it is simply an alternative word for 'theory' – an understanding of the world that has been built up through observation, hypotheses and further observation to test these hypotheses, and which may or may not be mathematical in nature. In economics, by contrast, while the term may be used in the exact same way as in science (as it often is in this book), it more often refers to idealised mathematical representations that are built on assumptions with only the loosest connection to reality, and which produce outputs that are only cursorily checked against this reality.

In modern times, the quest for mathematical rigour in macroeconomics began in the late 1960s, it gained momentum in the 1970s when the New Classical school coalesced and, since then, it has distorted academic thought away from seeking a realistic description of the world in which we live and has instead built up a theoretical world in which conceptually idealised market participants interact with one another in perfect rationality and relentless self-interest. Inevitably, this quest has led to policy recommendations that would be valid only in such a world and it therefore bears much responsibility for the regulatory loosening that was the ultimate cause of the current economic crisis.

## Relaxing standards to preserve the theory

To give some idea of how thoroughly its originators believe in this approach, Nobel Laureate Robert E. Lucas – the same man who insisted that macroeconomics had solved its central problem of "depression-prevention" – is quoted as having said that the statistical tests normally applied to scientific theories should be relaxed for economics, because they lead to the rejection of "too many really good models"[12].

This latter perspective is actually part of a more generalised viewpoint known as the 'Lucas critique', which essentially argues that, because the relationships underlying observed economic trends may break down over time or change as soon as they are observed and acted upon, we should often place more faith in models based on *a priori* reasoning than on empirical observation[13]. This view, however, contravenes the basic scientific principle that observation of reality must be the ultimate arbiter of truth. And it also neglects the millennia-old pitfall of philosophy that, as soon as you loosen your grip on the evidence of reality, it is possible to convince yourself that almost anything is true.

Beyond this, modes of thinking such as the Lucas critique are really only applicable to naïve analysis that takes simple macro-level empirical relationships at face value and attempts to make immediate practical use of them. Such criticisms would, for example, be applicable to any attempt to conclude that, since there is an inverse correlation between inflation and unemployment, we should be able to have less of one if we are willing to induce more of the other. But this is not how empirical science actually works.

Instead, scientists take as many empirical observations as they can perform on both a micro and macro level, use these to work out what the underlying dynamics are and then recommend practical measures based on this – measures that might be very different from what would be recommended based on one or two naïve observations.

In a biological context, for example, a simple empirical observation might be that a given chemical compound kills tumour cells in a dish and the naïve conclusion from this might be that the same compound would also kill tumour cells in humans. But a more comprehensive set of empirical results might show that the compound in question works by blocking a molecular process that is also essential to the survival of normal healthy cells, and that it is anyway altered by enzymes in the liver into a form that has very little potency on either tumour or normal cells – a picture of the underlying dynamics that would lead to very different recommendations in terms of practical action than the initial naïve analysis.

Similarly, in economics, comprehensive empirical observation must necessarily represent a more reliable means to get at underlying dynamics than *a priori* reasoning, and it should therefore be treated as the main tool of economic research. As we shall discuss later, there must still be a place for mathematical methods in analysing empirical data and in reasoning through economic processes, but it must be more circumscribed.

## A closed intellectual universe

Despite all this, and despite the resurgence of a Keynesian strand in macroeconomics in the wake of the 2007-2009 crisis, there remains a hard core of classical economists who are committed to the assumption of rationality and to the unrealistic mathematical models linked to it. They have constructed a closed intellectual universe where reason and evidence cannot enter. This universe rests on an insistence that their subject must be a highly mathematical one – because this is perceived as a precondition for qualifying as scientific – and it clings steadfastly to the idea of rational behaviour since this underpins all their mathematics, and because it is what they have drawn from the economists of earlier times. In essence, the main reason that classical macroeconomic theory is so strangely at odds with reality is that it is propagated by thinkers who are more interested in a strange kind of intellectual purity, and in mathematical rigour, than in providing empirically-based answers to economic questions – answers which society badly needs.

## Points of Agreement

There are some principles that the classical and feedback perspectives have in common, principles, in essence, which can be 'salvaged' from the classical consensus. These constitute the very foundations of economics; the essential features of the economic network that are constant over time, regardless of what feedback effects are operating at any given moment. They provide the context within which feedback effects operate.

The most fundamental of these is the basic principle that all output requires an input of labour, and probably other resources, by someone, and that everything of value therefore has an associated cost – as a popular economic saying has it, 'there is no free lunch'. Similarly, when it comes to understanding the economic choices that people make, we must understand that they act on the basis of the individual motivations and incentives they face. However, this does not mean that these motivations are entirely selfish or that they are based on an unremitting calculation of rational self-interest, in the way that classical economists assume. They can just as easily be based on inherited culture, on an estimate of self-interest that is constrained by social norms or on something else.

A further set of core principles in economics relate to the division of labour and the clustering of related tasks. The most basic of these is that, because people are much more productive when they focus on just a few tasks than when they try to do a little of everything, division of labour along with extensive exchange are essential for high levels of productivity to be achieved. Indeed, this system works even better if clusters of related activities are combined within a single organisation under one management. It is for this reason that the economy consists of a collection of firms and other productive units, as opposed to isolated workers trading with one another. Firms also need to be within a certain size-range – the efficient scale – in order to operate effectively. The exact size-range in question varies with the nature of the activity they are engaged in, and firms that are within the efficient range for their area of activity are said to have achieved economies of scale.

Following on from this, the size of a given market compared to the size of the efficient scale for that market will, through competitive forces, determine the number of firms in that industry – which can vary from one to millions depending on the activity.

Carrying the principle of clustering yet further, it is often efficient for firms that are engaged in similar activities to congregate in the same geographic region. This allows a better service infrastructure to be built up; enables customers to have one place to go; and facilitates the diffusion of skills and workers from one firm to another. This effect explains the existence of industrial parks, specialised financial and technology districts, cities and even whole economies with some sort of specialism.

Within an economy where there is division of labour, it is also vital to somehow coordinate the composition of output with what people want to consume. This can be done through central planning, but it is in many cases much more simply and effectively done through the price mechanism, as it is described in Chapter 1. The price mechanism enables people to simply vote with their feet. It provides producers with a powerful incentive to give people what they want, and avoids any problems relating to the agents of central planning having to find out what millions of people desire, before forcing firms to comply. Because it avoids the need to create a single all-powerful body to run the economy, the price mechanism is also more consistent with the separate good of human freedom than is central planning. And, in a society that is both complex and anonymous, the nature of market exchange protects us from the danger that we will not be reciprocated for services we have provided.

Related to all this, the price mechanism only functions properly when there is competition in an industry. Competition gives firms an incentive to be productive so as to maintain or expand their market share, and it prevents them from charging consumers more than a certain margin above that which it cost them to provide a given good or service. Competition, as we have seen, also drives firms to conform to an efficient scale, and it contributes to the formation of clusters of firms that achieve greater productivity by being in proximity to one another.

A further consequence of the price mechanism is that it creates an essential need for banks and financial markets. Banks can maintain payments systems that are safer and more efficient than using cash. And they funnel financial savings into physical investment in a way that provides a return to savers and also supports economic growth. Likewise, financial markets provide a means of storing the funds placed in pension, insurance and mutual funds and they provide an alternative means of funnelling these funds into real investment. In both of these areas, the financial services sector achieves efficient scale in a way that private individuals simply could not[14].

This, however, is where agreement between the classical paradigm and the feedback perspective comes to an end. Classical thinkers hold to a view of the economy in which negative feedback and rapid return to long-run equilibrium are the dominant features whereas, in reality, most dynamics in the economy are driven by an interplay of positive and negative feedback.

## Building a Better Theory: Feedback and Allied Ideas

Many people already know what a better version of economics would look like. They know that it would involve a synthesis of empirical methods (including a focus on economic history), of behavioural science, of institutional analysis, of systems theory and of mathematical methods whose role is more carefully delineated. All of this would naturally involve a role for the concept of feedback – which is a central concept of systems theory – and it is highly compatible with the idea that all economic events can be understood in terms of an interplay between positive and negative feedback.

In this new paradigm which may take hold, empirical observation of behavioural and institutional factors identifies for us the connections in the economic network; the systems concept of feedback allows us to predict what kind of dynamics will emerge from different parts of this network; and empirical observation again allows us to test these predictions against reality, leading us to revise our ideas if they are found to be inaccurate. At the same time, mathematical tools are needed to facilitate data collection, to support theoretical reasoning and to express predictions in a form that can be tested against the data.

The following box provides a summary of these key elements in a better form of economics. The remainder of the chapter is organised in line with this, with a section for each of the points it contains.

---

### Elements of a better approach to economics

1. Empirical/scientific methods, including a focus on economic history

2. Behavioural and institutional foundations

3. Systems theory: seeing the economy as a dynamic network and applying the concept of feedback to linkages identified through behavioural and institutional analysis

4. Empirical methods again, to test theories arrived at through feedback analysis

5. Judicious use of mathematics at all of the above steps

---

## The Scientific Method

The cornerstone of any research that aims to be scientific is the simple empirical principle that the evidence of reality must be the ultimate arbiter of truth. In essence, since our aim is to understand the world in which we find ourselves, rigorous observation of this world must be our constant guide[15]. Pure theory, experienced judgment, blind faith and random guessing are poor substitutes by comparison.

The essence of the empirical approach is that we separately observe the workings of different parts or aspects of whatever system we are examining; we apply our reason to the results of this observation; we check the conclusions of this reason by further observation; we refine our conclusions if necessary; we integrate our work with that of others and we thereby gradually build up an understanding of the whole. Through this approach, we sidestep the limitations of human reason – imprecision and finite capacity – and, in effect, allow the universe itself to guide us as to its own workings, as we never proceed except by what is evident and verifiable.

In this process, the observations that are performed should be as careful and exacting as possible, and the reasoning that is performed should be as thorough and methodical as possible. These are the elements of methodological rigour and they obviously ensure that the conclusions we ultimately reach hold much closer to reality than would otherwise be the case.

This whole approach is also referred to as the scientific method and it has the important feature that, in it, the search for knowledge becomes an ongoing cycle with alternating phases. Initial observation leads to tentative hypotheses, more extensive observation leads to either the rejection or the acceptance of these hypotheses, those hypotheses that are accepted are elevated to the status of theory and these theories then raise new questions that cause the whole process to start over again. There may be paradigm shifts along the way where a new theory radically departs from some elements of the theories that went before, but the replaced theories were still progressive in that they explained some aspects of reality. In this way, we converge over time on the truth in each area that we investigate, but we never quite achieve perfect understanding either.

In terms of the observation that is involved in the scientific method, including in economics, there are, in principle, two ways we can proceed: controlled experiment and passive observation. The former is superior because it allows us to isolate one aspect of a system, to change just one variable, to see how this change affects the rest of the system and thereby to clearly see how this factor feeds into other features of the system. However, there are many areas of investigation (such as astrophysics, geology, ecology, and social sciences like economics), where this is usually impossible and where passive observation must therefore be the main tool.

Because such passive observation involves looking at the system as it moves and changes of its own accord and as it is open to external influences – meaning that many things that can be considered inputs to the system will be changing simultaneously – it is impossible to ever achieve the same certainty that one change is causing another as can be achieved with the experimental approach. For example, observing that a combination of a young population, investment in education, EU grants, transference of workers from agriculture to industry/services, measures to attract foreign multinationals and more cooperative labour market structures led to an economic boom in Ireland in the 1990s (the 'Celtic Tiger') might seem conclusive. But which of these factors was most important? Did any of them merely happen, by random chance, to occur at the same time as the boom? And was there any unquantified factor – perhaps a general feeling of 'newness' and progress sweeping the world after the end of the cold war – that was just as important? Without being able to go back in time and do the experiment of removing factors to see the result, it is hard to know for sure.

Such problems are, however, not intractable. By applying some combination of experimental knowledge from more fundamental fields, of directly observing one thing leading to another (process tracing), of observing and quantifying correlations in large sets of numerical data, of observing patterns where one event follows another and of observing instances where it happens that only one significant input has changed (natural experiments); we can build up sufficient data to arrive at reasonably robust theories, even in social sciences like economics. In essence, where we can see a correlation through several methods, where we can either directly observe a causative mechanism or can postulate one based on experimental knowledge, and where no better explanation is available, we must accept the theory proposed.

In the above example, we can note from time series analysis that rapid economic growth came to Ireland soon after a period in which targeted tax cuts were introduced and labour markets were reformed; a package that attracted foreign multinationals, brought wage costs under control and ensured peaceful industrial relations by giving workers a fair sense of participation – all of which might suggest that these were the only important factors in spurring development. However, we can also observe that the foreign firms which arrived (in IT, the biomedical sector and other areas) depended on young, well-educated, English-speaking graduates, and on infrastructure that had been funded by the EU. We can therefore conclude that tax and labour market reforms actually acted as a trigger that unleashed existing potential*. Thus, we have revealed, by combining analytical approaches, that the Irish experience in the 1990s was a truly multifactorial situation where most of the factors we identify above were independently necessary.

Beyond the need to largely rely on passive observation, social sciences such as economics face other specific difficulties. Society is the area where the precision of basic physical laws is most distant. It is naturally more complex than the individual personalities who are part of it, making it hard for us to understand it. It is an area where we are far more likely to have ingrained

---

* Ireland's especially poor showing in the global recession that began in 2007 does not change this picture. Until about 2002-2003 Ireland experienced sustainable growth. It was only after this time that lax banking laws, eurozone monetary policy that was too loose for Ireland and global capital flows caused development to give way to speculation, focused on housing, and laid the seeds of an 11% contraction in GDP in 2008-2009. This, however, only put output back to where it had been earlier in the 2000s – leaving the growth achievements of the 1990s untouched. (A separate matter is unemployment, which is not progressive in the same way as GDP and where the 2009 level of 12% was a record for the country.)

prejudices about how things work than in other areas. And it is the one topic where the conclusions we reach, by leading to changes in collective or individual behaviour, can potentially change they system they apply to.

However, there are also counterbalances or solutions to many of these problems. The fact that society is based on our innate and learned behaviours gives us a more natural understanding of it than other areas. At the same time, our ingrained prejudices can be negated by looking at multiple clashing prejudices drawn from different cultures, so that they tend to neutralise one another, and by making a simple commitment to objectivity.

Likewise, the problem of social dynamics changing in response to people acting on their discovery is mitigated by a whole range of factors. Firstly, some social dynamics are broadly invariant and occur again and again over history. Secondly, thorough empirical analysis on multiple levels allows us to get at the true invariant micro-level drivers of social dynamics. Thirdly, sufficiently diverse observation on the macro level gives us knowledge of how the system behaves under a range of possibilities for those micro-level behaviours that are variant. And, fourthly, it is possible to update our analysis so as to keep our understanding approximately current. In essence, arguments such as those discussed earlier in the context of the Lucas critique – that empirical methods break down in face of the changeability of social systems – are applicable only to very naïve analysis that is based on simple macro-level observations.

In practice in economic and financial research, empirical methods must be used in two stages. These were mentioned in the preceding section of this chapter, but they are worth reiterating. Firstly, empirical methods must be used to observe the micro-level behaviours and institutions present in the economy. And, as a subsequent step, after reasoning through the conclusions of the first phase, empirical methods must be used again to test macro-level predictions derived from theories that make use of the initial observations. Both of these steps must necessarily involve making extensive use of the evidence of economic history, which is after all a much more extensive source of information than contemporary observation, and which is especially useful in later periods for which we have official statistics.

# Behavioural and Institutional Foundations

The dynamics of any social system must necessarily be an emergent property of the behaviour of individual actors in that system, together with the behaviour of forces from the environment that can also be thought of as micro-level components of the system. Our starting point for understanding such dynamics must therefore be to understand the behaviour both of the individual actors in the system, and also of the environmental forces that interact with them.

## Limitless rationality or behavioural reality?

The behaviour of environmental forces is the province of the natural sciences and is not usually a contentious issue within economics. By contrast, the behaviour of human actors in the economy is a matter of much debate. One approach to understanding this behaviour is that of classical economics; assuming that people have limitless capacity to rationally adapt to new circumstances and assuming that they are governed by unremitting self-interest. This approach, however, flies in the face of all that we know about human neurology and psychology and, in any case, its predictions are so startlingly out-of-synch with reality that it must be rejected.

Instead, we must turn to various categories of behavioural scientist to tell us how people actually behave in the economy. And, since our basic biology programs the deepest layers of our behaviour and also establishes the neurological framework within which all the more adaptive layers above this are established, it is with evolutionary biologists and behavioural ecologists that we must start. Such investigators tell us, for example, that instead of unremitting self-interest, most people are programmed to behave in a fashion that consists of self-interest constrained by a strong fixed instinct to support the group and other members of it (indeed those few individuals who do show unrelenting self-interest are considered to be sociopaths)[16].

Beyond this, psychologists and sociologists can tell us how people tend to behave as a result of inherited culture, life experiences and observing the actions of others. Amongst the findings of these researchers are the conclusions that economic behaviour is less ruthless in countries where economic structures are designed to compress income differentials[17] and, startlingly, that economic behaviour is more ruthless amongst those individuals who have studied classical economics.

Clearly, much of the behaviour discovered by behavioural research must be approximately rational – if it were not, humans would not have survived the process of natural selection – but there is also much that tends to be irrational. One prominent example of such irrational behaviour relates to our tendency to over-consume foods high in fat and sugar and therefore to develop health problems such as obesity, diabetes and coronary artery disease later in life. A strong affinity for such foods made sense for our ancestors when they evolved as hunter-gatherers and such foods represented a rare and valuable source of high-energy nutrients. But it makes little sense today in a world where such foods are abundant and where incessantly consuming them is virtually guaranteed to shorten our lives, to reduce the quality of those lives and to impose great medical costs on society.

## Institutions – behavioural patterns and building blocks

Society has long recognised that some patterns of behaviour are rational while others are irrational (either individually irrational, collectively irrational or both). It has therefore tried to encourage the former while discouraging the latter, and has put in place various arrangements designed to achieve these objectives – arrangements that are referred to by economists as 'institutions' and which represent core building blocks of the economy. People think of institutions as being solid objects – like a public building or the head office of a major corporate – but, at root, they are just highly cohesive patterns of human behaviour that tend to persist over long periods of time. Obvious examples of economic institutions are stock exchanges set up to create a market in corporate ownership, and stock-market regulations designed to prevent manipulation of prices on these exchanges through the spreading of false information and other malicious practices. However, while institutions are just a special kind of behavioural pattern, it does make most discussion and analysis simpler if we separate institutions from behaviour in general as building blocks of the economy[18].

Taking the institutions that exist in the economy at any given point in time, together with the ways in which people behave within these institutions and the other non-institutionalised patterns of behaviour that are observed, we can define an economic network that can then be subject to further study. Compiled correctly, information on this network consists of data on both the nature of its connections and on the approximate strength of these connections. As parts of it will be variant (especially data on the strength of connections) while other parts are basically invariant, such information must also be updated regularly in order to be valid in the face of changes in the make-up of the economy but, provided that this is the case, it is the natural starting point for economic analysis.

## Microfoundations

In fact, as we have alluded to, the network mapped out in this way constitutes a set of micro-foundations for understanding macro behaviour. Establishing such foundations constitutes part of a complete analysis in the manner of an empirical scientist, and it avoids the pitfall that naïve analysis based purely on a few relationships observed at the macro level may not hold true over time because it is not based on an understanding of underlying dynamics. In effect, the behavioural and institutional approach offers a better way to get at the microfoundations that classical theorists seek than the *a priori* reasoning of which they are so fond.

But this is where any similarity with classical economics ends.

Microfoundations based on analysis of behaviour and institutions are more realistic than those based on assumptions. And, at the same time, such foundations do not pretend that they can ever be 'rigorous' in the mathematically precise manner of the representative-agent approach found in classical models. However, by accepting this limitation of the behavioural-institutional approach, we actually enable ourselves to build up theories that are more powerful in terms of their ability to reflect the real world.

Seeking microfoundations for macro behaviour also touches upon a debate that has sometimes occurred between economists and sociologists in which the economists have argued that causation flows entirely from the individual to the whole, whereas the sociologists have argued the opposite with patterns of individual behaviour (as opposed to the behaviour of specific individuals) being shaped largely by social forces[19]. The resolution to this conflict is that both camps are right; in a given instant, aggregate behaviour is determined entirely by the behaviour of individuals but, over time, patterns of individual behaviour are shaped by aggregate experiences (in the form of biological evolution, cultural evolution or individual learning, depending on the timescale). This conclusion allows us to seek meaningful microfoundations but, at the same time, to recognise that some of these microfoundations were shaped by macro outcomes at earlier time points.

## Some recent advances in behavioural economics

Adopting this as an implicit part of their make up, the disciplines of behavioural economics and behavioural finance are already making significant progress in taking the established knowledge and investigative methods of fields such as psychology and sociology and applying them to economic questions[20]. Indeed, these disciplines have already produced a number of striking results that have the power to significantly alter our economic theories.

One such result relates to 'anchoring'; the tendency of decision-makers to focus on one particular piece of information, or category of information, in making choices, leading them to take systematically skewed actions. Another is the 'sunk cost fallacy'; the observation that people will expend further resources on a course of action that they have already initiated, even though they no longer believe that this course represents the best option available to them. This observation directly contradicts the assumption of classical economics that sunk costs will be ignored, and it is based on the fact that people seem to be programmed to believe that not following through on something always constitutes waste.

Further results of behavioural economics relate to various biases exhibited by market participants. One such bias is confirmation bias, where only information consistent with a pre-existing view is taken into account. Another is self-serving bias, where the causes of success are attributed to internal personal factors while the causes of failure are attributed to external situational factors. Yet another is status-quo bias, where people do not change patterns of behaviour unless there is a very compelling reason to do so. These findings may not be radically new for psychologists, sociologists or canny market participants but they do represent something new for formal economics, which has generally relied on simpler assumptions about human behaviour.

## A molecular basis for market movements?

Beyond such findings, perhaps the most interesting results of all to emerge from this whole area have combined pure behavioural methods with biochemistry and have looked at the levels of different hormones in financial market participants as events unfold. This research has found that levels of testosterone rise in traders experiencing good results and that this facilitates further good results by stimulating aggression, but, as soon as performance drops for whatever reason, testosterone falls and levels of the stress hormone cortisol rise instead[21]. Given that testosterone is associated with aggression and overconfidence, while cortisol is associated with fear, these findings may actually constitute a molecular basis for the way in which movements in market prices reinforce themselves on both the upwards and downwards legs of the cycle. In practical terms, this suggests that such markets would work better if they were populated by a mixed demographic that included more women and older men, not just the usual young men who have the highest levels of testosterone*.

In any case, all of the results outlined here are very different from what classical economics tells us about human behaviour. In some ways this is not surprising; whenever the tools of empirical science are brought to bear on a new area of investigation, the results are usually quite different from what assumption and theory alone would predict. As a consequence, we can see that foundation stones are being laid for a much better style of economics than that which currently prevails.

# Systems Theory

Despite the wish of many economists for their subject to be more like physics, with robust equilibrium conditions and deterministic equations, many areas of science have moved on from such simple early models in the time since economics emerged as an academic discipline in the 1800s. Indeed, the simpler models of physics have always been understood as being model systems that capture individual interactions which occur in nature, but which do not predict the complex behaviours that arise in networks of such

---

* One young male trader I discussed this finding with interpreted things another way and wondered if he should use testosterone patches to help him stay at the forefront of "bull markets".

interactions. Over the past few decades, science has gone further and has come to understand that complex networks can behave in ways that are far more unpredictable than anyone imagined and which do not correspond in any sense to a simple extrapolation of the behaviour of individual components.

This realisation is manifested in the area of research known as systems theory and it has proved instrumental in understanding phenomena such as cellular metabolism, biological regulation, food webs, weather, climate, traffic flow, the internet and many others[22]. And, since the economic network must necessarily have many of the same general features, economics too stands to benefit immensely from applying this approach to its traditional questions.

On a basic level, doing this simply entails analysing all economic events in terms of an interplay of positive and negative feedback – the main recommendation of this book – and this may be all that is needed in most cases. However, systems theory also makes it possible to study certain broad features of particular systems and, while the programmes of research that have sought to do this in relation to economics (such as that of the acclaimed mathematician Benoit Mandelbrot[23]) have yet to establish a wide consensus, it is possible to see the outlines of some of the conclusions that might be reached.

## No thermodynamic equilibrium

One general feature of complex systems that is relevant to the economy is that such systems never attain a state of equilibrium in the thermodynamic sense of the word. Thermodynamic equilibrium represents a condition where the lowest-energy state available has been achieved and, in the case of a complex system such as the economy, this only occurs when all complexity has been lost – that is, when the system has collapsed. Thus, when we speak of equilibrium in economics, we are actually referring to what natural scientists would call a *steady state*; a situation where physical equilibrium has not been achieved (fortunately in this case) and where there is still much dynamic activity going on, but where some aspects of the system are in a condition of stasis.

## Tipping points

Another recurrent feature of complex systems is that, when examined on certain dimensions, they are often found to have two or more discrete alternative states; such as the expression or non-expression status of a self-inducing gene in a living cell, or the cyclonic or anti-cyclonic nature of a weather system. In the economy, dichotomous pairings such as these are found in growth versus contraction, in inflation versus deflation and so on. Each branch of these pairings can be said to be discrete in that it corresponds to a state that tends to reinforce itself and which therefore tends to separate cleanly from its polar opposite.

Dichotomies such as these generally entail tipping points at specific moments in time where the system may or may not shift from one state to the other and the system is therefore said to undergo bifurcation at these points (or multifurcation if there are more than two possible states). In economics, this might correspond to the possibility for an economy to tip or not tip into recession at various points during the economic cycle, and it might likewise correspond to the possibility for it to fall or not fall into a deflationary slump when in recession.

## Sensitivity to initial conditions

Complex systems also show sometimes intense sensitivity to initial conditions at the moment of bi- or multifurcation. In pathobiology, for example, the outcome of a single immunological event can determine whether or not a tumour subsequently develops and, in meteorology, the beating wings of a single butterfly at the right time and place can famously determine whether a hurricane subsequently develops or not. In essence, points of bi- and multifurcation each represent a set of conditions where the tiniest difference can determine which way the system turns.

This also holds true in economics. For example, the actions of a single investor at a crucial moment can determine whether a bank run or a stampede out of a given asset class gets going or not. Likewise, the words of a single central banker can determine whether the economy gets through a sensitive patch comparatively unscathed or whether that period of time gives way to a self-reinforcing fall in activity. Indeed, it is precisely because of this property of sensitivity to initial conditions that the consequences of economic events sometimes seem to be entirely out of proportion to that which caused them. In fact, the event that appears to have been the cause was often not really a fundamental cause at all but was actually just something that 'nudged' the system at a moment when it was already prone to significant change.

## Self-organisation

Complex systems also exhibit self-organisation. That is, so long as the components of such a system behave by consistent rules, coherent patterns of macro-level behaviour will emerge even if the system was functionally shaped neither by design nor by natural selection. This property is demonstrated by the economy in the case of such things as business cycles and the emergence of certain industries as a coherent whole, even though no one planned them.

This ability for the economy to develop 'spontaneous order' was first noticed, independently of systems theory, by the conservative Austrian economist Friedrich Hayek in the first half of the 20th century, and was taken by Hayek to mean that a market economy would produce desirable outcomes independent of any centralised coordination. However, while we should be impressed by Hayek's insight, there is nothing in systems theory to show that the results of self-organisation need necessarily be beneficial. Indeed, as asset market volatility and bank runs show, it is possible for the spontaneous order that emerges from individually rational decisions to be collectively irrational.

## More exotic ideas

Further strands of systems thinking see economic dynamics in terms of Darwinian evolution, with different kinds of economic arrangements (such as different categories of firm) competing to replicate themselves and survive over time. Alternatively, some see the economy in terms of neuroscience and the collective behaviour of insects, with the economy constituting a single learning engine that can refine its activities and composition over time. This work, however, extrapolates very far from the basic principles of systems theory and makes heavy use of analogy. Much more research is needed to know how useful, or not, it might be.

On a more definite note, the application of systems theory also creates a dichotomy between two modes of scientific investigation. The poorer approach is *linear causal reductionism* and it assumes that all macro-level behaviour is the result of a simple extrapolation of micro factors. This approach can explain simple systems quite well but it fails profoundly in the face of greater complexity. The richer approach, by contrast, might be called *integrated reductionism* and, while it still starts from the proposition that, in order to understand the whole, you must first understand the parts, it does recognise that the connection between one and the other is rarely straightforward. Given the complexity of social dynamics, all economic research should be conducted in the latter spirit.

# Testing Our Theories

How should we test economic theories based on feedback or other systems concepts? Answering this question inevitably entails much overlap with what I have said above about the scientific method, and its applicability to social systems. However, I will here focus more narrowly and briefly discuss the kind of approaches we might take to validating economic theories based on feedback and other systems concepts.

## Patterns and past data

For starters, we should recognise that the goal is not to forecast specific events or to predict economic patterns in precise quantitative detail. Rather, it is to predict general patterns that can be tested against past data. For example, an understanding of some aspect of the economy based on feedback may predict, say, a stable equilibrium, a cycle with symmetric peaks, a cycle with asymmetric peaks of some shape, a secular trend that is continuous (monotonic) or a secular trend that features periodic changes of some specific kind. If the patterns that are observed for the relevant economic indicator are as predicted, then the model should be accepted. If they are not, it should be revised or rejected.

Similarly, if given differences in economic arrangements would, under a particular hypothesis, be expected to have particular effects on economic outcomes, instances should be sought where arrangements changed along this axis and it should be determined whether the effects were as predicted. As before, if they were as predicted, the theory should be accepted and, if not, it should be revised or rejected. In a slight modification of this approach, if instances of such changes cannot be found, then countries that have different arrangements along the axis in question should be compared instead.

## Micro-level predictions

Beyond predicting overall macro-level patterns, specific theories based on systems principles might also make predictions for the behaviour of individual system elements, other than those on which the theory was originally based. To take a simple example, a theory that financial markets are speculative and volatile might predict that the cash balances of certain kinds of market participant would surge periodically as the system goes through speculative falls (which precipitate a 'dash to cash') and, if this is found to be the case, then the theory is supported.

To take another such example, a theory of hyperinflation based on self-reinforcing rises in the velocity of circulation might predict that the behaviour of spending money early in the expectation that it will lose value would cause average individual cash holdings to quickly fall to zero after any pay days that are synchronised across segments of the workforce. Again, if this is found to be the case, then the theory is supported.

# Getting the Numbers Right

Basic mathematics is essential in all science. In order for the most fundamental laws of nature to be precise, as they must be for the universe to be coherent, these laws have to be quantitative and it must therefore be possible to express them mathematically. It must also be possible to use mathematical manipulation to reason through the ways in which laws identified by observation interact with one another and the ways in which they play out in different contexts.

Likewise, while higher levels of organisation in the universe do not show the precision of basic physics, the relationships observed at these higher levels must still be approximately quantitative because of the precision that lies beneath them. It is thus meaningful, alongside purely descriptive observations, which are equally vital, to enquire as to the strength of the relationship between any two connected factors in any system. And, in order to answer this question, it must be necessary to quantify, in some way, the extent to which a change in one factor causes a change in the other. This, in turn, creates the need for statistical methods to process quantitative data, to assess whether there is a relationship between two factors or not and to ascribe a strength to those relationships that are proven to exist.

All of this is as true of economics as of any other area that attempts to be scientific. Statistical methods are needed to validate and quantify behavioural and institutional relationships detected on a micro level. Mathematical manipulation of various kinds may be needed to help in reasoning through the consequences on a macro level of interaction between micro factors. And statistical methods are again needed to test such predictions against actual macro-level observations.

The first and third steps in this process consistently call for fairly straightforward statistical methods, but the level of mathematics required in the second step – reasoning from micro foundations to macro outcomes – varies significantly. In some cases, mathematics is not needed at all and intuitive reasoning is enough. In many others, simple equations (such as the quantity theory of money, which we will encounter in Chapter 3) or simple diagrams (such as the supply-and-demand graphs of classical economics) are called for. And, in a few cases, more complex mathematical reasoning, or computer modelling, is needed. However, regardless of which approach is taken, the results of economic reasoning are only valid if they are then found to predict reality, and they are much more likely to achieve this if their starting point is also empirical. Recognising a place for mathematics in economics takes it as implicit that these conditions are met.

## How much math is the right amount?

This is a difficult question. On the one hand, mathematics, because it removes ambiguity, yields a degree of objectivity, in seeing that conclusions follow premises, that verbal reasoning alone struggles to match. It allows us to test whether different ideas are logically consistent with one another. And, in cases where we must reason through to a concrete number that is needed for some practical purpose, and which cannot be measured directly, some form of mathematics is indispensable. On the other hand, mathematics makes an argument harder to follow for most people. It can disguise the fact that conclusions are just initial assumptions processed into a very different form. And, in economics and other social sciences, it entails gross simplification of the relations between factors.

The reason for the latter is that, while the presence of quantifiable price and volume information may give the illusion of economics being a precise mathematical science in the same way as physics, the underlying realities of the two subjects are quite different. While the quantitative coefficients of basic physical laws must be precise and stable over time, those of economic 'laws' are imprecise, they show many kinds of dependencies, and they vary over time as the social context changes – even though the 'law' itself may be basically invariant. Thus, although simple chains of mathematical reasoning interspersed amongst verbal and visual reasoning may approximately reflect reality, and may therefore be of some use, more complex chains are likely to be highly unrealistic and can easily lead us astray (unless of course they are simply a means to transform expressions so that they can be tested for mutual consistency)[24].

Alongside these drawbacks of mathematical economics stands the fact that the great virtue of mathematical methods – their objectivity – can often be replicated, without the serious drawbacks of un-realism and un-transparency, through the empirical approach of sticking as closely as possible to the evidence of reality.

The only acceptable conclusion, therefore, is that there should be a bias towards using as little mathematics as possible in economics. Basic statistical methods are clearly necessary to identify valid microfoundations, and to test theories. But, in the middle step of reasoning from foundations to theories, we should treat verbal and visual reasoning as our first port of call, we should use simple math only if such reasoning fails, and we should use advanced math only if there is no other option. And, throughout all of this, we should use assumptions only in cases where there is no hope of getting empirical inputs but where we can still empirically test outputs; or where the assumptions are so obvious or so innocuous as to not substantially affect the conclusion.

In summary, there are two kinds of mathematics in economics: the kind that starts from wild assumptions, with little regard for empiricism, just to achieve intellectual elegance; and the kind that acts as a servant to the empirical approach. We need the latter. We do not need the former.

# Part Two:
# Feedback in Action

# 3. The Business Cycle:

# How Feedback Drives Economic Volatility

**W**hen it comes to understanding the ups and downs of the economy, economists have traditionally thought in terms of long-run equilibrium. In individual markets, they have seen the forces of supply and demand keeping price and volume at an equilibrium level that changes only when the factors underlying supply and demand – things such as tastes and technology – themselves change. And, in the aggregate economy, they have seen changes in the prices of factors of production (natural resources, labour, capital and other inputs) bringing aggregate supply and demand back into line with one another at a level equal to long-run equilibrium output – albeit probably at a different average price level to that which prevailed before.

In so far as they go, these insights are essentially correct, and represent forms of what natural scientists would call negative feedback; processes whereby a shift away from equilibrium sets in train consequences that ultimately restore equilibrium. However, economists have underestimated the extent to which the economy is also subject to positive feedback; processes whereby a given dislocation amplifies itself and drives the system through a continual process of change, with no stable equilibrium. Instead of equilibrium, positive feedback produces either cycles (semi-regular up- and down-fluctuations in activity) or continuous secular change – both of which are very familiar in macroeconomics, and which can actually be said to represent a complete perspective on the dynamics of the economy. Cycles occurring as a result of positive feedback may have some central tendency that they fluctuate around, and which can be meaningfully referred to as a long-run equilibrium, but they never actually flatten out at this level.

In this chapter, I will present an overview of the feedback processes that drive economic cyclicality and I will show that positive feedback is generally dominant over the time frames we are considering (months to years).

# The Credit-Asset Cycle

## Rises…

One example of the positive feedback that drives cyclicality in the economy affects asset prices and credit[25]. In this process, a rise in the price of certain classes of investment assets*, such as housing or shares, creates the expectation that prices will rise further; an expectation which increases demand, drives prices up again and creates further expectation of rising prices. This expectation of rising prices also increases the amount that banks are willing to lend to buyers of the asset class in question, thereby creating yet further demand, driving prices up still more and producing yet more 'favourable' expectations that, as before, fuel both further demand and further lending. All of this constitutes a set of self-sustaining positive feedback loops, which drive prices and debt levels ever upwards with no stable equilibrium (Figure 6).

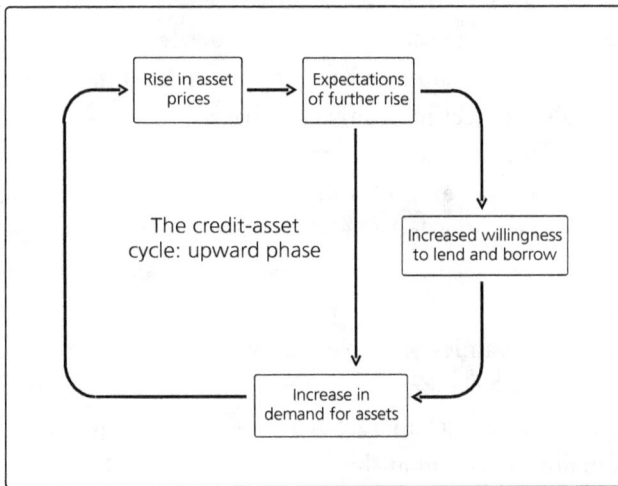

**Figure 6 – The upwards (price-increasing) phase of the credit-asset cycle.** This self-reinforcing process operates until some external shock causes it to reverse, or asset prices and debt levels become so high that market participants realise they are out of line with real economic prospects.

---

* Assets purchased as a store of wealth, possibly in addition to having some real physical use. This stands in contrast to assets purchased or built purely in order to generate real output or serve some other material purpose. Throughout the book I refer to the latter as 'business investment', 'real investment', 'physical investment' or 'investment in capacity' in order to underline the distinction between this activity and the mere exchange of investment assets – financial terminology in the English language unfortunately uses the same word for both activities.

## ... and falls

The converse process, however, can also operate. If asset prices fall, expectations are then of further falls; demand reduces and further price reductions do, in fact, take place. At the same time, borrowers become less willing to borrow, as they have lost the certainty that the wealth they hold in the form of assets will rise in value. Banks become less willing to lend, because they see prices falling, and because they may be taking losses when existing borrowers move into a state of negative equity and default*, forcing lenders to make recoveries *via* assets that are now worth less than originally expected. This situation creates a further downward pressure on prices and this, in turn, drives lending and demand down still further – a set of positive feedback loops operating in the exact opposite direction (Figure 7) as those which operated when the market was rising (Figure 6). In the wake of what happened in the US and UK economies at the end of the first decade of the 21st century, readers ought not to be at all unfamiliar with these phenomena of interlocking rises and falls in credit and asset prices – or their fallout.

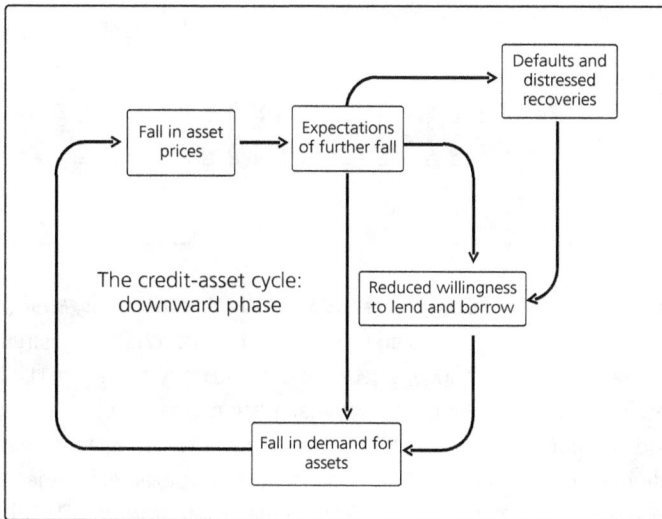

**Figure 7 – The downwards (price-decreasing) phase of the credit-asset cycle.** This self-reinforcing process operates until some external event causes it to reverse, or asset prices become so low that market participants realise they are out of line with real economic prospects.

---

* 'Negative equity' is a state whereby the value of an asset has fallen to the point where it is now worth less than the remaining balance of the loan used to purchase it. In this situation, the borrower may have no incentive to continue repayments and may default on the debt. However, in the many [contd. overleaf]

## The ubiquity of the cycle

These two alternative processes of a self-sustaining rise and a self-sustaining fall in asset prices and credit tend, as we shall see, to alternate with one another over time, giving rise to what can be called a credit-asset cycle. This cycle has been extant in market economies from events such as the Dutch tulipomania of 1634-1637 (they were actually speculating with tulip bulbs as the asset class), through to the share bubble of the late 1990s/early 2000s (Figure 8) and the housing bubble of 2002-2007. It is one of the main drivers of economic volatility[26].

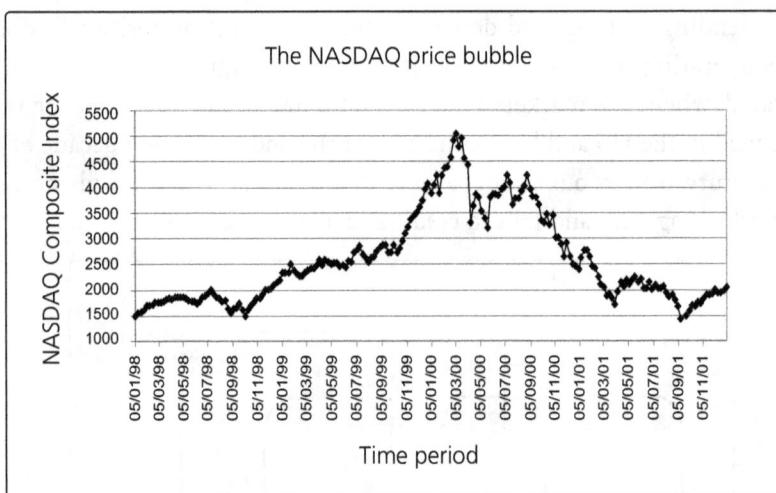

**Figure 8 – The NASDAQ Composite Index at Weekly Intervals, 1998-2001.**
The NASDAQ Composite Index is an index of all shares and related instruments traded on the NASDAQ exchange, a decentralised trading system in the US. Given this diversification, there is almost no way that a rational market calculation could lie behind the pattern shown. Instead, because the NASDAQ was heavy on information technology stocks, it was the most dramatic example of the bubble that affected investment in this sector at the time. [Data from NASDAQ.]

---

[contd.] cases where the asset in question is a home and the owner still needs somewhere to live, and in the cases where they wish to preserve their credit rating, there is still an incentive to continue repayment. Thus, as we shall see, wider economic stress is often a more significant cause of borrower default and therefore a more significant driver of a falling credit-asset cycle.

## Intensifying the cycle

The upward part of this credit-asset cycle can be made more prone to speculative excess by banking structures that encourage reckless lending. One such set of structures is securitisation and the originate-and-distribute model of banking. In this model, banks sell-on debt they hold, in the form of securities (contracts that give the holder the right to receive a given income stream, in this case income from the loan) so that the bank obtains funds to engage in further lending, and can thereby earn more income from fees and interest. Adopting this model, however, both increases the amount of borrowing in the economy, and also dilutes the incentive of banks to ensure that their loans are responsible. In theory, the buyers of debt-backed securities should perform the necessary due diligence themselves but, because they are at least one step removed from the actual lending, such buyers find it difficult to carry out this function. Instead they can either come to place excessive trust in what they view as 'responsible lenders' (or on rating agencies working with those lenders), or can simply be swept along in a wave of euphoria at economic prospects.

Likewise, the downward part of the credit-asset cycle can be especially violent if banks have the ability to call-in lines of credit to certain classes of investor. Exercising this option may make it necessary for the investors in question to liquidate some of their holdings in order to meet their obligations. If this happens, it can lead to a further fall in the price of the assets in question, and thereby intensify the downward tendency of the system. This process can also cause a collapse in the price of one class of assets to spill over in to other classes, as investors sell these in order to meet their 'margin calls'.

## International effects on the cycle

International effects can also intensify both the upwards and downwards parts of the cycle. Funds can flood into a jurisdiction when a speculative bubble is underway, driving asset prices up even more steeply – as well as pushing up the relative value of the national currency, in a process that inevitably attracts yet more investors. And, when the bubble eventually bursts, foreign funds can flood back out again in a self-reinforcing fashion, thereby intensifying the asset-price collapse.

## Sovereign and corporate bonds: exceptions but not invulnerable

Markets in the asset class of sovereign and corporate bonds are not as susceptible to internal feedback effects of the kind described here. This is because the future cash flows from these instruments are precisely defined by legal contract and their real value, ascertained by a rational investor calculation of the kind described in Chapter 1, is therefore approximately knowable. In the case of corporate bonds, due to the fact that the borrowers in question may be less creditworthy, there may be more room for fluctuations in price (compared to sovereign bonds) as a result of risk- and confidence-related effects. But this still takes place within a relatively narrow margin, unless the borrower is close to default. In addition, sovereign bonds can be susceptible to spillover effects from other asset classes such as shares and housing: investors rush to the safety of such bonds when the prices of other assets are collapsing, and they trickle back out of them again when other asset classes are recovering.

## Inefficient market hypothesis

Notwithstanding the special characteristics of bonds, all of the dynamics presented here argue strongly against the efficient market hypothesis (EMH)*; a piece of classical economic theory that effectively states that asset prices are, at all times, based on a rational calculation of real economic prospects performed by market participants on aggregate. This calculation supposedly uses all available information and is carried out in something like the manner described in Chapter 1. However, while the EMH may contain some truth when we consider average asset prices over very long periods of time, it is clearly inconsistent with the bubbles and collapses that can play out in investment markets over periods of up to a decade.

The unpredictability of market movements is often cited as evidence in favour of the EMH. This argument holds that, since all information has already been priced-in, and since truly new information must, by definition, be random, then it is impossible to know in which direction the market will move next. However, it is equally possible that the unpredictability of asset markets derives simply from the sheer number of real and speculative forces

---

* This is also known as the theory of 'informationally-efficient capital markets'.

that are at work, and from the fact that the arbitrary nature of speculative herd effects makes them intrinsically unpredictable. That this is the case is strongly suggested by the bubble effects we routinely observe in these markets.

Indeed, statistical analysis also supports this idea. The EMH holds that, unless asset prices are very close to zero, an upward movement is as just likely as a downward movement at any given instant, and the size of the movement is random. It therefore predicts that the size of daily price movements should map out as a statistical bell-curve over time. However, this is not what is actually observed; in reality, the distribution shows 'fat tails', reflecting the fact that extreme self-reinforcing price movements (bubbles and crashes) occur frequently in the system.

Further evidence against the EMH comes from the observation that market participants expend significant sums trying to predict future trends in asset prices (as opposed to just estimating the effect of current information). If assessments of asset prices were based on rational calculations incorporating all already-existing information, this would be a futile effort and, being rational, market participants would know not to engage in it. Thus the fact that this behaviour is observed refutes the EMH.

An alternative, and much milder, version of the EMH states that asset prices incorporate all information that investors hold at a given point in time, regardless of whether this is based on precise calculation, approximate judgment or pure emotion. However, this amounts to the simple statement that investors generally act out, in full, whatever perceptions they have at any point in time – and even this is open to question. Instead, when market sentiment is moving in a particular direction, investors often follow it incrementally, waiting to see if others will do likewise and gradually being egged-on by analysts who progressively convince themselves and others that observed trends are based on real factors.

A corollary of the likely invalidity of any form of the EMH is that a superior analyst who understands the speculative dynamics of the system (without participating in them) can, very occasionally, earn a better return than the rest of the market. However, since understanding that the market is speculative is not the same thing as being able to foresee the turning points of this speculation, this is rare[27].

# Cycles in Prices, Output and Jobs

A similar set of positive feedback processes to those which operate in banking and asset markets affect economic activity overall[28].

## Rise…

In this case, a rise in economic activity enables businesses in general to make more profit, and creates favourable expectations amongst the business classes. This leads to investment in capacity, to payment of higher wages, to a rise in consumption demand and to a further rise in output – possibly combined with a rise in the average price level. Increased real output, in turn, gives a further impetus to profits and to business confidence, and this leads to the establishment of a positive feedback loop that drives economic activity ever upwards with no stable equilibrium.

## … and fall

Conversely, a fall in output leads to reduced profits and to a loss of business confidence. This leads to a reduction in physical investment, to staff layoffs and/or wage cuts, to a fall in consumption and to a fall in output that may be combined with a fall or stagnation in the average price level. This, in turn, leads to further falls in profit and confidence, and to the establishment of a positive feedback loop driving the system in the exact opposite direction as the loop which operated when the economy was in its expansionary phase.

## The quantity theory of money

A good theoretical model for understanding these processes is actually the quantity theory of money, $MV=PY$. Here M is the money stock after operation of the deposit expansion multiplier (explained below), V is the velocity of circulation expressed in terms of how many times an average unit of currency is used per year, P is the average price level and Y is real output expressed either as a monetary amount (adjusted for inflation) or as the number of transactions made for cash[29].

The 'deposit expansion multiplier' mentioned above is the process whereby a given amount of money injected into the economy by the central bank expands into a variable multiple of that sum as a result of this money being deposited with commercial banks, loaned out by these banks and deposited again. Since the original deposit retains its full nominal value to the depositor even when the funds have been loaned out, this process creates several times the original amount in terms of the total sum of deposits. It therefore expands the money supply because people trade based on the level of their bank balances.

A simple proof of the quantity theory can be given by imagining an economy where the money supply (M) is £10bn, where the average pound is used 10 times per annum (the velocity of circulation, V) and where the average price (P) is £20. In this situation, it is clear that total spending (M x V) must be £10bn x 10 = £100bn. It is also clear that the real output, expressed as a number of transactions, must be Y = MV / P, which is £100bn / £20 = 5bn transactions. Thus, the quantity theory must, by definition, be true.

This theory was much abused by monetarists in the 1970s and 1980s, economists who argued as part of the broader free-market revival of those years that responsible control of the money stock, M, was one of the few roles government should play in the economy. However, provided that it is combined with a number of critical realisations about how the economy actually operates, then this model represents a powerful way to look at the feedback mechanisms that affect spending, prices, output and employment.

The key realisations needed here are:

1. That all of the components of the above equation are instantaneous measurements applicable over a single very brief period of time.

2. That all of these components, including the velocity of circulation, can change over time.

3. That the economy has a physical capacity for annual output beyond which activity cannot readily increase in the short run.

4. That physical investment causes this capacity to increase continuously but very gradually.

5. That any significant fall in real output shows up largely as unemployment in the short run (as opposed to a fall in average earnings and output share for those in work), and

6.    That both real-economy purchases and investment asset purchases must be included in this model since they both use the same currency and that, while these two sectors tend to move in synchrony, the model will not hold perfectly if either sector is viewed in isolation*.

Taking these insights into account, the quantity theory shows, for example, that an increase in the velocity of circulation leads to an increase in output alone if the economy is operating far below capacity. It leads to an increase in both price level and output if the economy is operating somewhat below capacity. And it leads to an increase in price level alone if it is already at capacity. This pattern holds because, if there is a great deal of spare capacity, producers will respond to an increase in demand mainly by producing more, and refraining from price increases in order to remain competitive; but, if there is no spare capacity, they will respond entirely through price increases.

Beyond this, in an economic boom, because a significant portion of the increased spending that occurs under these conditions goes on investment in capacity, increases in the velocity of circulation arising from increased confidence can continue for a prolonged period before the economy reaches the limits of its capacity. The upward phase of the wider economic cycle therefore operates – in simple terms that exclude interaction with the credit-asset cycle and changes in the money stock – through an increase in the velocity of circulation leading to an increase in output and this, in turn, leading to a further increase in the velocity of circulation. The downward phase, conversely, operates through a fall in the velocity of circulation leading to a fall in output (expressed mainly as a fall in employment, rather than in the wages of the average worker) and this, in turn, leading to a further fall in the velocity of circulation. These are two positive feedback loops operating in opposite directions.

## Cycles in Commodity Prices

The fluctuations in credit, asset prices and overall activity described here are standard processes that operate in all economic cycles. There are, however,

---

* Using CPI measures of inflation for the UK economy, for example, will produce this kind of imperfect fit. CPI is not even a comprehensive measure of prices in the real sector of the economy.

additional positive feedback effects that may operate in one cycle of expansion and contraction, but not in another.

## Self-sustaining bubbles

If, for example, real economic forces cause the price of some raw material commodity to begin rising sharply, and there is significant uncertainty as to just how high prices might go, then a self-sustaining bubble in this commodity that drives prices far above what they would otherwise have been may be the result[30].

This process operates as follows: the price of some widely-watched commodity increases sharply, market participants come to expect further increases, and this causes sellers of the commodity to demand higher prices at the same time as buyers become willing to pay such prices. This, in turn, drives prices up further, and this creates yet more expectation of rising prices: a positive feedback loop that can sustain itself over periods of weeks or months.

In this process, sellers of the commodity in question demand higher prices because this is necessary to make the sale attractive when there is the alternative of just hoarding the commodity and selling it later, when prices are expected to be higher. At the same time, buyers become willing to accept higher prices, because they expect things will be even worse for them in the future when prices have risen more.

## The role of the wholesale buyers

The latter effect of buyers becoming willing to accept higher prices may be mediated partly by the expectations of end-consumers, but it is likely to be mediated mainly by the expectations of wholesale buyers who either use the commodity themselves or sell it on to the public. These organisations watch economic trends much more closely than ordinary people. They have an incentive to pay somewhat more in the short run when they expect prices to keep rising, in order to maximise the spread between input and eventual output prices. And they also have the collective ability to pass price increases on to the consumer. This latter ability exists because the overall process described here is one where all wholesale intermediaries simultaneously face rising costs – meaning that the 'floor' to which competition drives prices down is raised – and it does not come at the cost of much of a loss of volume, because demand for most raw-material commodities is relatively price-inelastic (meaning that volume is relatively insensitive to movements in price).

## Price bubbles without inventory movement

It is also noteworthy that, because all this means that the demand curve is moving to the right at the same time as the supply curve is moving to the left, the price of the commodity in question can rise significantly while the volume remains relatively constant. This explains why commodity price bubbles of this kind are not necessarily associated with evidence of large-scale shifts in inventories of the material affected (Figure 9).

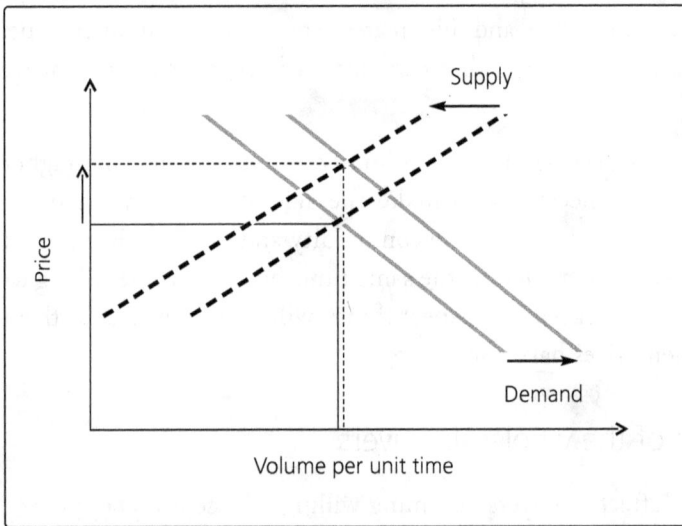

**Figure 9 – The behaviour of supply and demand in a commodity price bubble.** Because the supply curve moves to the left at the same time as the demand curve moves to the right, there can be little or no shift in volume (or inventories), even as prices soar.

## Commodities' susceptibility to bubbles

The fundamental reason that raw material commodities are more susceptible to bubble formation than other traded goods is that they each represent a single broad class of good that is essentially identical everywhere in the world. This means that there is a single clear price upon which the commercial world inevitably focuses a great deal of attention. For example, the existence of wholesale buyers who give a great deal of attention to economic trends may actually make the market more volatile; if it were somehow possible for suppliers to sell directly to end consumers, who have less of a tendency to analyse the wider economy, prices might be less prone to expectations-driven increases.

## Futures markets

The intrinsic propensity for bubble formation inherent in commodity markets may also be compounded by the existence of active markets in commodity futures.

In order to make this clear, the mechanics of the futures markets should be briefly explained.

Futures contracts play the vital role of enabling producing and consuming firms to manage commodity price risk by, in effect, locking-in a price for materials that will be delivered in the near-future. They do this by obligating those who are holding such contracts to take delivery, from sellers, of a specified amount of a given commodity, with a specified quality, at a particular place, on a specified date (typically three to twelve months from the date of original issue), and for an *un*-specified price. The price is then determined, as we shall see, by supply and demand in the futures' market, with the price that a buyer must pay for the underlying commodity being locked-in as equal to the futures price at the time of the futures transaction*.

Another important characteristic of futures obligations is that buyers have the right to sell them onwards, by various mechanisms involving a central clearing house (mechanisms we shall not delve into here). They can do so at whatever the current market price happens to be for a contract with a given set of terms, and contracts are then settled with whoever is holding them at maturity. In addition, futures contracts are standardised and each individual contract covers some small volume of the commodity it relates to – meaning

---

* The actual date of cash settlement can, in principle, be on the date of the futures transaction, on the delivery date, or on some other date.

that a purchaser must buy multiple contracts to cover whatever commodity volume they wish to purchase, and also that there are clearly identifiable prices for contracts with each standard set of terms that exist.

To be specific, the price of a futures contract is usually roughly equal to what market participants expect will be the price of an equivalent amount of the underlying commodity at the maturity of the contract. And, as with any traded item, this price is held in place by short-run market forces. If the contract is selling for less than the expected future price of the underlying commodity, perhaps after a rise in this expected price, people will rush to purchase it in order to get cheap materials; and this will cause the contract price to rise. Conversely, if the contract is selling for more, people will refuse to buy it, sellers will have to offer a more reasonable price; and this will cause its price to fall.

## Futures markets and commodity bubbles

So what does this mean for economic cyclicality? One effect of having an active futures market is to create a highly visible signal as to the consensus opinion of market participants on what commodity prices in the near-future will be. If this suggests a significant movement from where prices stand at present, it can cause the behaviour of participants in the market for the underlying commodity to change and can therefore actually bring about the outcome it suggests. For example, if the futures market is signalling a substantial price rise, this can amplify the dynamic whereby sellers of the underlying commodity demand higher prices while buyers become willing to pay such prices. And, if this movement in the price of the underlying is sharp enough, it can cause another rise in the futures price. This establishes an additional positive feedback loop beyond that which would have operated anyway for the relevant commodity, and drives the price of that commodity substantially higher than it would have been in the absence of futures trading.

At times, those transacting in obligations to take delivery of some commodity may include only potential users of the real commodity, some of whom are selling because they no longer intend to take delivery on a particular date, and some of whom are buying because they do now intend to take delivery on that date. At other times, it may also involve many speculative investors who take on exposures simply to 'bet' on expected price movements. These investors may purchase large numbers of futures contracts when they have a strong expectation that they will rise in value (with the intention of selling the obligation onwards before the delivery date), and this can, as we have just seen, actually cause such a rise to take place. In effect, investors adopt the view that commodity futures, as well as being a means to manage price risk, are also a class of short-term investment asset, and the trading activity that results from this view can indirectly affect the price of the underlying commodity[31].

## And in reverse…

As well as causing commodity prices to rise in a typical bubble phenomenon, the various positive feedbacks described here (both those involving futures and those not involving futures) can operate in the reverse direction, and cause them to fall. In this situation, when perceptions of real economic prospects become less optimistic (possibly as a result of the idea that high commodity prices are weakening the economy), people come to expect that commodity prices will fall, sellers of the underlying commodity become willing to accept lower prices, buyers become less willing to pay high prices and prices do, in fact, fall. At the same time, holders of commodity futures may begin selling in the expectation that the contracts will lose value – causing futures prices to fall and accelerating the whole process.

## Special characteristics of commodity bubbles

However, the symmetry between the speculative dynamics of a rising and falling market in something like oil is not as perfect as in the case of something like shares. In the case of commodities, there are substantial production costs and, as with any good, producers will not normally sell below cost – meaning that there is a certain floor below which speculative forces cannot readily drive prices. Instead, downward pressures of this kind are significant only after there has been a bubble in prices and they seem to act, in effect, to bring prices back to the level dictated by real costs and needs. Something similar could be argued for housing, where there are significant real costs in building the asset that might act as a price 'floor'. However, several factors weaken this effect in housing – the asset has a much longer lifespan and historic construction costs therefore weigh less on decisions, future rental income (a main determinant of value) is hard to know, and transaction volume is much more elastic in the short run than for essential commodities like oil – all of which mean that housing can transiently trade below cost, especially in major asset market crashes.

A more direct parallel between commodity and asset markets is that feedback effects in the market for one commodity can spill-over into the markets for others, as also happens between classes of investment asset. For example, when a bubble in one construction material is interpreted (as it is likely to be by many market participants) as meaning that demand for that commodity is surging due to increased real need (another possibility is reduced real availability), it implies that demand for other construction materials will also surge and can therefore instigate a bubble across all such materials. The same applies within the realm of foodstuffs, which are all partial substitutes for one another, giving them correlated real-world demand and giving traders the expectation that they will track one another in terms of price movements. Such effects can even extend to spill-over between entirely different classes of commodity, such as when a rise in the price of construction materials is seen as being linked to rapid economic growth in some major economy and this spills-over into foodstuffs.

## The human and economic impact

The human and economic effects that follow from a bubble in commodity prices can be serious[32]. Unnecessary surges in the prices of materials such as domestic fuel and, most of all, food can have a devastating effect on the world's poor, being directly responsible for significant excess morbidity and mortality. More indirectly, self-fulfilling surges in commodity prices can have a disruptive effect on the economy overall and can thereby have an adverse impact on the total material wealth that is produced. The ways in which this can happen are topics I will return to in the next section.

# Explaining Boom and Bust

## The boom

The two sets of positive feedback loops described at the outset of this chapter – in credit/assets and in the wider economy – interlock with one another. If the credit-asset cycle starts rising, confidence rises because people feel wealthier as their houses, shares and so on rise in nominal value. Businesses borrow more for physical investment. The money supply rises because the deposit multiplier effect becomes stronger as banks lend more aggressively, and because the central bank (sensibly) engages in 'accommodating' monetary policy that allows the money supply to rise in line with economic output. All of this results in increases in investment, wages and consumption and sets the wider economy on an expansionary trajectory. Equivalently, if the wider economy starts expanding first, asset prices subsequently pick up because of increases in confidence and real wealth and the asset-credit cycle is sent on an upward trajectory.

## The bust

Conversely, when either cycle is in its downward phase, this also sets the other on a downward trajectory and thereby indirectly reinforces itself. This includes an additional positive-feedback mechanism whereby economic stress may induce borrowers to default on their debts, forcing banks to make recoveries at depressed asset prices and thereby causing them to reduce their lending – a phenomenon that causes both further falls in asset prices and further economic stress[33].

## Synchronisation and momentum

All of this means that, even if they start out being out-of-phase with one another, the credit-asset cycle and wider economic cycle quickly become synchronised and thereafter reinforce one another as part of a generalised economic cycle. It also means that, once this economic cycle is set moving in a particular direction, it has a great deal of momentum and keeps moving in that direction for an extended period of time (Figure 10).

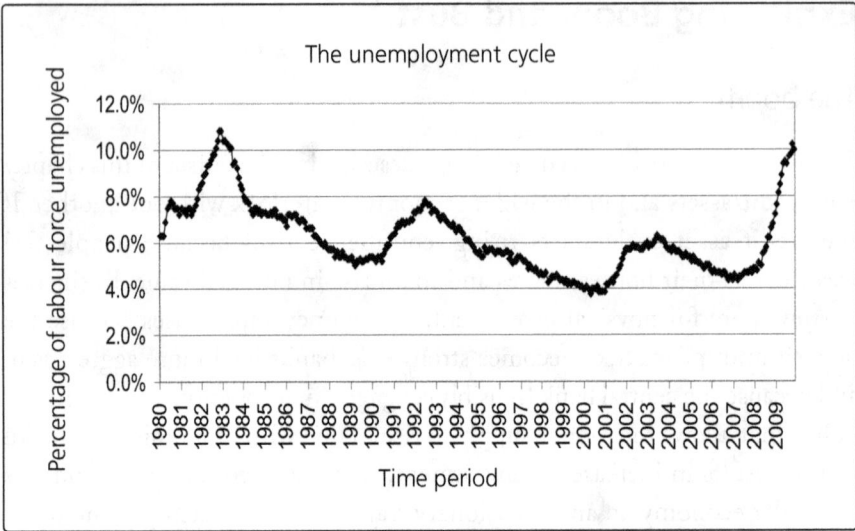

**Figure 10 – Monthly unemployment data for the US since 1980.** These data are both a clear demonstration of the business cycle, and of why it matters. In relation to the latter, it should be borne in mind that those who are unemployed at the time of the peaks are likely to find it much harder to get work than those who are unemployed at other times. We should also note that they are generally accompanied by many people who are under-employed because of the economic situation, a status that does not show up in this data. [Data from the United States Bureau of Labor Statistics.]

## Turning points – into recession

However, even if it is left to its own devices, a market economy will generally not keep moving in one direction forever. Expansions usually contain the seeds of their own destruction and so, too, do recessions. The peak of an expansion may, for example, come when asset prices have climbed to an improbable ratio of annual earnings, and of rental or leasing rates for the same asset. Similarly, it may come when debt levels are approaching the limit of what can be supported by annual incomes. The existence of either of these situations causes borrowing to slow, asset prices to stop rising, confidence to become less certain and investment to fall. These shifts quickly become self-reinforcing and, eventually, expansion tips into recession.

Alternatively, an expansion may come to an end when excessive enthusiasm amongst consumers causes growth in the velocity of circulation to begin outstripping growth in the real capacity of the economy, and therefore causes price levels begin rising sharply. This, in turn, causes the central bank to tighten monetary policy in order avoid the dangers of runaway inflation; a policy that causes credit expansion to halt and the credit-asset-economic cycle to tip into its downward phase.

Crude oil and other primary commodities can play an important role in setting limits to capacity growth of the kind that that can then allow consumer spending to outstrip capacity. The rate at which production capacity for minerals can rise is generally limited by physical factors and by the inefficiency of state-run oil and mining companies in certain exporting jurisdictions. These forces can cause the crude oil sector and other similar industries to reach capacity limitations before other areas of the economy and can therefore cause commodity prices to rise sharply once these limitations are reached. This is a direct component of higher inflation (petroleum products are part of the 'basket' of goods that people buy and statisticians monitor), it pushes up the price of goods made or transported using oil, and it can cause a spillover effect whereby people try to maintain their standard of living by spending faster, thereby pushing up the velocity of circulation along with the average price level and necessitating a tightening of monetary policy that causes economic expansion to end.

Even in the absence of a tightening in monetary policy, capacity limitations in primary commodities would cause expansion to end anyway. In this situation, the slowdown would take longer to come about, but it would be deeper – both because the economy would be contracting from a position of greater excess and because of the disorderly effects of a crunch in economic inputs. Such an outcome would involve high inflation in commodities and across the board; it would entail a hard barrier to growth because inputs of energy and raw materials could not be increased (efficiency gains cannot circumvent this over time frames of months to years) and it would feature the bankruptcy of a great number of firms that were especially vulnerable to high commodity prices (airlines and haulage firms are obvious examples).

In addition to real capacity limitations in the production of raw materials, commodity price bubbles of the kind described in the preceding section can also be important in bringing about the end of an economic expansion. When capacity limitations in the production of raw materials are compounded by such bubbles, it obviously makes the rise in prices that takes place more extensive, and therefore increases the risk that the economy will fall into a disorderly contraction. This either necessitates more aggressive monetary policy action by the central bank, leading to an abrupt downturn in economic activity, or, if the central bank does not realise that commodity prices are undergoing a bubble, monetary policy might not be tightened enough and some of the disorderly effects of very high commodity prices might be realised. In either of these scenarios, the downturn comes about earlier than would be the case in a similar scenario without an expectations-driven commodity bubble, but the potentially beneficial effects of this hastening are likely to be outweighed by the dangers of very high commodity prices.

## Turning points – out of recession

In the obverse of all these events, when a recession has gone on for some time, indebtedness may fall as people and businesses either pay down their loans or default on them; meaning that they may then become capable of borrowing again once banks have regained the confidence needed to provide the funds, and once enough time has passed for default cases to be rehabilitated. At the same time, assets may start becoming attractive as their prices fall to a low enough level to seem cheap. Likewise, businesspeople may find themselves unable to resist investing in efforts to exploit the many gaps in the economy that have opened up as a result of other businesses having gone bust. These shifts, if they take place, have the same tendency to become self-reinforcing as those which bring the boom phase to an end; and expansion therefore eventually resumes.

## Inventory in a recession

A further set of feedback effects that are important when the economy goes through a recession are related to the holding of inventory. For some period of time when the economy is entering a slowdown, outstanding inventory orders continue to be delivered and existing production plans continue to be acted upon. However, because consumption is falling, inventories delivered or created in this way tend to accumulate unsold. Businesses in general respond to this by scaling-back orders and production to a level below that which is needed to meet demand, something that brings inventories back down to the desired level. When this has been achieved, they then adjust both orders and production upwards again in order to stabilise inventories at the desired level. In most cases, this has the effect of initially accelerating the recession – a positive feedback effect – but then, after a few months, it has the effect of providing a negative feedback mechanism that causes the contraction to slow. In a severe recession, however, the positive-feedback phase may continue for much longer, as the process of inventory liquidation leads to the failure of upstream suppliers and thus to further falls in overall activity.

Conversely, when an economy pulls out of recession, rising consumption may cause inventories to begin running low and may therefore trigger a wave of ordering and up-scaled production. This initially accelerates the recovery and then, when this pulse ends, causes the pace of expansion to slow down again. And, in an exact mirror image of what happens in a deep recession, when the economy is undergoing powerful recovery from a deep low, or a sudden upwards surge of some other kind, the initial positive-feedback phase of this inventory effect may persist for much longer than would otherwise be the case.

## Conclusion – a new integrated understanding

Considering all of the feedback effects that drive the economic cycle, the conclusion we must reach is that the negative feedback processes traditionally emphasised by economists (that is, the forces that supposedly maintain classical long-run equilibrium) do not take effect immediately but operate only as the economy approaches the peaks and troughs of its cycle – after the behaviour of the system has been dominated by positive feedback for some time. The mechanisms driving negative feedback – expansion creating price pressures, cheaper assets appearing more attractive after a market fall and so on – must still operate when the economy is not near a peak or trough, but they are clearly overwhelmed by positive feedback mechanisms such as the self-sustaining fall in confidence that operates after a peak. That this is the case is clearly demonstrated by the cyclicality we observe in the real economy.

Because of this inherent cyclicality, the phrase 'no stable equilibrium' or some variation thereof, is one I use several times throughout this book. But it is important to be very clear about exactly what this means. What I mean by this phrase is that there is, by definition, a short-run equilibrium in all markets, but that the position of this equilibrium moves about in systematic ways under the influence of positive feedback. In the case of cyclical movements in the position of short-run equilibrium, it fluctuates on either side of some long-run equilibrium position and, as we consider further in Chapter 10, in the case of secular trends it moves in one direction with no equilibrium position at all in the 'very long run'. For economic variables such as aggregate output where a cyclical fluctuation is superimposed on a secular trend, we can marry classical and feedback terminology. We can say that there is short-run cyclical fluctuation around some long-run equilibrium position, but that the position of this long-run equilibrium itself moves under the influence of positive feedback, meaning that there is no equilibrium at all in the very long run. This terminology may be somewhat convoluted, but it is necessary to make a bridge between the equilibrium and feedback models.

A further point that needs to be made in relation to the economic cycle as it is depicted here is the difference between a feedback loop and a cycle. In an economic context, a loop is the actual series of steps that takes place in a feedback process – an increase in velocity of circulation leading to an increase in output leading to an increase in velocity of circulation, for example. A cycle, on the other hand, is the up-and-down change in activity that occurs as a result of the operation of the loop. In non-economic contexts, by contrast, the series of steps that take place can sometimes be referred to as a cycle, and the variation in activity that results can be referred to as an 'oscillation' or as 'hunting'. It is therefore important to be careful with terminology when discussing these processes.

Everything I have said in this chapter about the intrinsic volatility of the market implies the need for public responses in the form of fiscal, monetary and regulatory policy, to flatten out the amplitude of the economic cycle and to reduce the waste, pain and danger associated with recessions. Indeed, given that capitalism is dependent on the assumption of individual incentives being aligned with the social good, and given that this assumption does not always hold true – such as when firms abuse their power or when investors panic-sell assets or hoard funds in a recession – it should be no surprise that such economic management is needed. This conclusion comes out even more starkly when we look at the more extreme outcomes that can sometimes arise from the intrinsic volatility of the economy: situations of depression or of hyperinflation followed by collapse. Extreme dislocations such as these are the subject of the next chapter.

# 4. Depression and Hyperinflation: Extreme Examples of Feedback

n his influential 1962 book *Capitalism and Freedom*, Milton Friedman, an intellectual leader of the free-market revival that took place after 1980, commented that, "[t]he Great Depression, like most other periods of severe unemployment, was produced by government mismanagement rather than by any inherent instability of the private economy." This view reflects a prejudice – popular amongst conservatives – that government is the root of all evil, and it is closely linked with the assumption, inherent in classical economics, that all economic upheaval must result from shocks that are exogenous to the market system. These shocks may take the form of a conflict, natural disaster or resource crunch, or they may take the form of misguided government intervention.

Some notable economic downturns do fit this mould. The 43% decline in output that occurred in Russia between 1989 and 1998, following the mishandled transition from communism to capitalism, definitely fits the exogenous-shock model. So does the 23% fall that occurred in Saudi Arabia between 1981 and 1985, after a major spike and fall in the oil price that was initiated by geopolitical events elsewhere in the Middle East, and which was ended by monetary policy decisions in the United States. But the same is definitely not true of the 29% fall in output that occurred in the United States itself between 1929 and 1933, the 19% fall that occurred in Argentina between 1999 and 2002, or the rapid 12% fall that occurred in Indonesia between 1997 and 1998[34].

In each of these cases, the economic architecture set up by governments may have been the distal cause of the downturn and, when the crisis did strike, policy responses may have been imperfect or even negligent. But, in each case, the original policy error was to give excessive freedom to the market, and it is clear that the actual motor of the crisis, the forces that drove it, were very much of a private-sector nature. Details of some crises of this kind are provided in the next chapter, but we will here focus on general principles of how they can come about, and of how they are driven by private-sector forces.

# Falling Off a Cliff

At its most basic level, the central contention of classical economics is that a market economy has the ability to regulate itself, and that little government intervention is necessary. In relation to recessions, it is indeed true that the downturn phase of the economic cycle does usually have a tendency to reverse itself, and to this extent the market economy clearly does have some ability to manage its own direction. If this were not the case, modern capitalism would not have survived the 200-odd years before active macroeconomic management became the norm in the 1930s. However, management is still needed to control normal recessions and, as we have just commented, more adverse kinds of economic contraction where the economy cannot right itself without government action are very much possible.

## Deflation

If, for example, a recession is serious enough, significant falls in the average price level can occur as a result of falls in circulation and falls in the money supply that arise as reduced bank lending causes the deposit expansion multiplier to weaken. Since a severe recession is likely to have a sudden onset, or at least to have more momentum than expected, these effects can overcome the gradual money expansion that the central bank engages in at almost all times, together with the more aggressive action it takes in the face of a recession. They can therefore occur even in a jurisdiction that sets policy so as to achieve price stability.

Falls in prices such as these can lead those people who do still have an income to begin hoarding their money in the expectation that its buying power will continue to rise. This represents a damaging fall in the velocity of circulation. It prevents the real debt burden from shrinking because, even if debt is being paid down, average incomes are falling – causing real debt levels to remain constant. And it also discourages further borrowing, because people can see that the real burden of a given amount of debt may rise. These are additional positive feedback loops beyond those which operate in a normal recession, and they are of such a nature as to prevent the mechanisms that might give rise to recovery from operating. Once a deflationary spiral of this kind takes hold, the logical consequence, without government action, is outright economic collapse[35].

## External crisis

Recessions in less-developed countries can lead to extreme downturns in other ways too. As foreign investors (the main source of funds needed to purchase capital goods from abroad) lose confidence, they may begin to withdraw their wealth to stronger jurisdictions. This causes the currency of the affected jurisdiction to fall and this, in turn, accelerates the process as investors see the currency movement destroying their wealth and withdraw their funds even faster (Figure 11). Further acceleration may come if government or private sector borrowers in the country have foreign-currency debt that they cannot service because of the currency depreciation that is taking place and defaults begin to occur, frightening investors even more. There may even be contagion from one emerging market country to another, as investors lose confidence in all risky jurisdictions and start a generalised withdrawal.

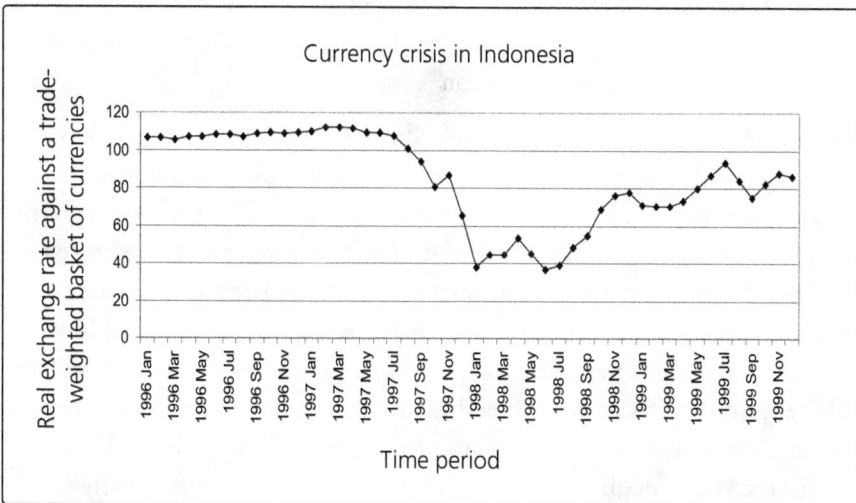

**Figure 11 – Monthly values of the Indonesian rupiah against a trade-weighted basket of currencies.** As part of the broader emerging markets crisis of 1997-2002, Indonesia was hit by capital flight in the second half of 1997. At the lowest point, the currency had lost more than half of its buying power on international markets. [Data from the IMF.]

The consequences of this for the countries affected are serious. They have no access to foreign currency with which to buy inputs and capital goods for their industry. Their weakened currencies prevent them from importing goods that are not made at home and upon which the population may be reliant. And, despite their falling currencies, they may lose export volume if their trading partners are also in recession. All of this leads to business failures and layoffs and tips the domestic economy even further into recession, probably leading to a deep depression.

A currency crisis of this kind can even lead to a surge in domestic consumer inflation in less-developed countries, just as the economy is on the verge of falling into a slump. In essence, as the domestic currency prices of key imports surge, there is a direct effect on consumer price indices. This may have real effects as people increase their rate of spending in order to try and keep purchasing these things and maintain their standard of living. However, as other forces (effectively a fall in economic capacity due to loss of external funding) lead to business failure, unemployment, loss of income and loss of confidence, this is rarely sustainable, and inflation usually falls away as the economy slides further into recession[36].

External crises of this kind generally do not affect advanced countries to anything like the same extent as they do less-developed countries. This is because advanced countries are generally less dependent on net external investment, because they are perceived as being stronger, because borrowers within them can borrow in their own currency and because there is, in any case, no rank of more attractive countries for investors to flee to. However, since the vast bulk of the world's population lives in less-developed countries, and because they are more vulnerable to downturns as a result of their low absolute levels of income, such events are of profound importance. They have not been given enough attention by leading economists, who mostly live in advanced countries.

## Disaster strikes when you least expect it…

In both developed and emerging economies, the dangers to the economy can be greater than usual after the peak of an especially exuberant boom. In this situation, the onset of the downturn may be especially sharp as confidence may collapse very suddenly when people realise the extent to which asset prices and debt levels are misaligned with real economic prospects. This may lead to a sudden halt in borrowing, to a sudden fall in asset prices and to significant losses for banks on their secured lending – all of which drive another sharp fall in confidence and cause an equally sharp fall in overall economic activity. In this scenario, the economy can go from boom to deflation in a period of just a few months, and the social and political effects can be equally jarring.

# When Banks Have No Money

Indeed, when a sudden reversal such as this takes place, depositors (and money-market investors – who are essentially larger, more sophisticated depositors whose support must be rolled-over on a regular basis) may begin to pull funds out of banks they view as being dangerously exposed. In this situation, the most dangerous of all economic feedback loops can take hold: a bank run. This scenario unfolds as follows in an unregulated banking system: once depositors see even a handful of their compatriots pull out of a given bank that has experienced defaults in its loan portfolio, they conclude that the bank in question must be unsafe and that, if they do not act soon, it will run out of money, ensuring that the first depositors to withdraw get the only funds available. This is a plausible outcome because of the fractional reserve nature of banking, and the prospect of it taking place causes depositors to rush to withdraw their funds – leading to a sudden, self-fulfilling collapse of the bank in question[37].

## The contagion of bank runs

To make matters worse, a contagion effect can operate here too. If depositors conclude that one bank is unsafe, they may conclude that others are also unsafe – and start a generalised withdrawal. This outcome is made more likely by the fact that banks tend to act as counterparties to one another in various kinds of complex financial transaction that were originally intended to dilute risk, but which can actually intensify it. These transactions may cause a bank to suffer losses if one of its compatriots fails and, since depositors will be aware of this exposure, it increases the chances that they will initiate a generalised withdrawal. Thus, when a bank run develops, it puts all banks in danger, causes lending to halt altogether and, if enough banks fail, may even damage or destroy the basic payments system that underpins the economy. All of this intensifies an already steep downturn, both through the loss of credit and through the likely layoffs of bank staff (who were probably comparatively big spenders). It is one of the darkest nightmares of those who make economic policy.

## CDOs and CDSs – infectious uncertainty

Modern examples of the kind of inter-bank transactions that can trigger contagion effects of the kind described above are securitisation products such as collateralised debt obligations (CDOs) and financial derivatives such as credit default swaps (CDSs). CDOs are debt instruments that are based on a pool of mortgages or other loans, that offer a return to investors based on loan repayments and which are separated into tranches whereby the most junior tranche (which offers the highest return) absorbs all default losses first and where the most senior tranche only suffers losses if all subordinate tranches have already lost all of the income to which they were entitled. Prior to the current crisis, it was thought that this structure would always confer a very high credit quality upon the more senior tranches and, in many cases, it did. However, as recent evidence has shown, by leaving depositors and money market investors uncertain as to where losses would be distributed within the banking system, CDOs and other securitisation products undermined confidence in the system as a whole and thereby precipitated, in 2007-2008, a series of money-market bank runs that left many major banks in a position where they could only survive with state support*.

CDSs, by contrast, are essentially forms of tradable insurance that give their holder the right to receive a payment if a designated company defaults on its debt obligations – even if that holder has no exposure to the company in

---

* This outcome happened to be compounded by technical errors that caused quantification of the risk associated with CDOs to be too optimistic (specifically underestimating correlation between defaults and having excessive confidence in estimates of default probabilities for the underlying loans in a context where, to quantify the risk of CDO tranches, the mathematics requires that these probabilities are raised to a power, magnifying any error). However, by leaving investors uncertain as to which banks the risk had even gone, and by raising at all in the minds of worried investors the question as to whether such complex calculations as those required by the CDO structure had been carried out properly, these instruments were almost guaranteed to be destructive.

question*. These instruments were issued by investment banks and major insurance firms in huge quantities over the past decade (reaching a notional value of $62tn by 2007, roughly equal to global GDP) as a means for various creditors to hedge their exposures. But they were sold at excessively low prices because they were an innovation that gained traction during the benign years prior to 2007, when it was perceived that risk would always be low. As a consequence, the issuers of these instruments were left facing substantial losses when the downturn came about and corporate borrowers began to default. This further weakened the position of a number of major banks and also left at least one major insurer in the US needing government support in order to survive. If such an insurer had been allowed to collapse, it would have further weakened confidence in banks and other assets insured by the firm, and would have left businesses in the real economy facing the risks and costs of finding a new insurer[38].

## What constitutes a bank

An important point in relation to all this is that, in the context of economic theory, a bank should be seen as any organisation or structure that borrows with short maturity (as in the case of deposits, which can be withdrawn instantly) and lends with long maturity. This clearly includes traditional commercial banks. But it also includes such things as auction-rate securities†; special-purpose vehicles (SPVs) set up to allow corporations to issue commercial paper‡; and the pairing of investment banks with the money market funds that finance them by taking deposits from corporations and wealthy individuals.

---

* Insurance proper, by contrast, is not tradable and must be held by the party that is directly exposed to the insured risk.

† An auction-rate security is an instrument where a borrowing institution issues bonds, where these bonds can only be transferred at auctions organised by the borrower, where the rate of interest established at the auction holds until the next auction, and where, if the auction fails so that not everyone who wants to offload the bonds is able to do so, the rate of interest goes up to a penalty level.

‡ An SPV is any commercial entity set up to carry out a single activity and which is ring-fenced so that its liabilities do not create recourse to any parent entity. There are many kinds of SPV and the ones I am referring to in this section are only those set up to facilitate the financing of corporations. The commercial paper issued in this fashion is just a form of short-maturity corporate bond but it was not floated through an investment bank as other bonds are.

All of these structures, if they hold reserves at all, generally operate on a fractional reserve basis: holding only a percentage of depositors' funds at any one time and lending out the rest, in the same way as a traditional commercial bank. Those structures that permit withdrawals are therefore susceptible to bank runs in the same way as commercial banks and those, such as auction-rate securities, that do not permit simple withdrawals, can still undergo a contagion effect that involves 'freezing' – an inability for companies to raise new funds because existing investors cannot sell their holdings onwards, as they would normally be able to do. Because of the shared fragility of these structures, and because any of them can be used to fund business investment or asset purchase, they can all be thought of as 'banks' and, when the term 'bank' is used anywhere in this book, it is in this broad sense that it is intended[39].

# When Money is Worth Nothing

## The feedback loop of inflation

As we have already seen, the time period around the peak of a boom may feature a significant rise in inflation, as consumer spending begins to outstrip the ability of business to bring new capacity into operation. This inflation usually falls away as the economy tips into recession, but it may instead lead to a form of economic collapse that is an alternative to that involving price deflation: runaway price inflation. In this scenario, people spend their money more rapidly because they expect it to lose value, and this causes price levels to rise even further. This, in turn, induces people to spend even more rapidly and to demand higher wages (which employers can afford to pay because of faster circulation); a state of affairs that causes prices to rise even more, and establishes a positive feedback loop that makes the entire process self-sustaining.

## Corrosive effects

This process benefits anyone who has borrowed, as the real value of their debt is eliminated; but it devastates lenders, and those, such as pensioners, who are on a fixed income. It also discourages businesspeople from investing in capacity, because prospects are so uncertain. And this, together with the unavailability of credit, causes capacity and real output to fall, even in the midst of rapid spending and price increases. In essence, while there may be a lot of spending going on, very little of it is on investment in capacity. As the process of runaway inflation continues, the practical consequences for shoppers, retailers and accountants of constant large price changes become highly disruptive. Eventually, the financial quantities used in everyday transactions may become so improbably huge that the use of currency becomes impractical and, if this takes place, spending stops, barter trade takes over and economic activity quickly collapses.

As a consequence, while this process starts out being very different from the process whereby deflation and possible financial collapse at an early stage ruin an economy, it leads to many of the same outcomes. Economic activity stagnates and then implodes, banks may collapse as the loan repayments they are receiving fall far below the interest they must pay on deposits, and the government may lose the ability to deliver basic public services. In Zimbabwe, for example, a process of hyperinflation initiated by government incompetence over recent years eventually led to the failure of sanitary systems, as the public workers who operated them could not be paid money that was worth anything, and a wave of cholera subsequently swept the country[40].

In considering inflation and growth alongside one another, it is important to think about the movement of economic capacity. If we look at the totality of transactions in a currency (including both the real economy and investment asset markets), or if we look at just the real sector in the case where it and the investment asset sector are tightly correlated, then it is clear that rising prices and a falling volume of cash transactions (roughly equivalent to falling GDP) can coexist only if the money supply is rising, or if the capacity of the economy is falling. This is because of the quantity theory of money, $MV=PT$. Capacity can fall if some external force pushes it down (as in the case of a resource crunch) or, in the case of runaway inflation, because of the corrosive effects of high and uncertain price level changes both on the banking system (which finances real investment), and on the position and actions of businessmen (who engage in such investment).

## Rolling Recession

Severe economic disruptions – of either the deflationary or hyperinflationary kind – can lead to persistent sluggishness in the economy for years after the supposed moment of recovery. This happens, in effect, because a deep slump can damage the structure of the economy. Workers can become deskilled as a result of long periods of unemployment, they may lose the will to work, and they may even engage in self-destructive behaviours that damage their health and consequently reduce their ability to work. Likewise, businesses can be affected for years by the under-investment that takes place in a recession. And if enough firms go under, the economies of scale, clustering effects and established supply-chains that underpin commercial productivity can be degraded. Since things such as these take years to build back up again, and are likely to have to be rebuilt in a different form to that which existed before, the consequences can persist for a decade or more.

Effects such as these lead to a reduced rate of growth and make the economy vulnerable to repeated downturns in the years following a major slump – aftershocks of the original earthquake, as it were. Economists refer to a situation such as this by the somewhat counterintuitive term of a 'growth recession'; a state of affairs where the economy is actually growing on the average, but where it is achieving much less than an economy of its kind should be able to achieve. Japan, following its property market bust of 1991, went through a process such as this and, up until the onset of the current crisis, it experienced both slow overall growth and a series of more minor slowdowns that prevented a full structural recovery from taking place[41].

In addition to the structural damage done by a major recession, such an event is likely to be followed by a heavy debt burden that acts as a drag on the economy for years afterwards. A major bust is likely to come at a moment when the private sector has accumulated large amounts of debt and, as a result of its vital efforts to support demand through the crisis, government is likely to also emerge with substantial debts. As a consequence of both this and of the more fundamental structural damage wrought by a collapse in activity, we can see that it is likely to take several years, at minimum, for the economy to fully recover from the events of 2007-2009.

## A mild recession or a deep slump?

All of this raises the question as to what makes the difference between the comparatively mild recessions that normally follow expansions, and the violent disturbances that can sometimes occur instead? In some cases it is simply that the boom has continued for a long period of time without any endogenous or exogenous shocks to bring forward the tipping point into recession. At other times, it is that people have lost awareness of the cycle of boom and bust. They may have instead come to believe that, as a result of a prior structural change of some kind, the economy has entered a new state of permanently elevated growth and frenetic activity in the banking sector and asset markets. In both of these scenarios, confidence remains high for longer than normal and, by prolonging the boom and allowing asset prices and debt levels to build up to even more excessive levels than is usually the case, this creates the conditions for an especially severe bust to follow.

More fundamentally, however, it is government policy that determines whether or not the economy has a tendency towards bubble and collapse, instead of the milder undulations of a more normal business cycle. Policies that give the market excessive freedom lead to greater instability, while those that involve responsible management and oversight lead to reduced instability. Detailed consideration of the kind of policies needed to achieve the latter of these two outcomes is the subject of Part Three.

# 5. Two Modern Crises as Feedback Loops

**H**istory is replete with financial ups and downs that conform to the feedback model. One could focus on the panic of 1907, on the depression years of 1929-1939, on the 'great inflation' of 1973-1979, on the third-world debt crisis of the 1980s, on the stock market crashes of 1987, on Japan's lost years of 1991-2003, on the emerging markets crisis of 1997-2002, on the global credit crisis and recession of 2007-2009* or on a host of other dramatic events. Here we will focus on just those events which culminated in 1997-2002, and on the distinct events which came to a head in 2007-2009. These are sufficient to put some more flesh on the bones of the feedback perspective and to draw everything we have looked at so far into something more concrete.

In looking at these or at any other episodes of market turmoil, it is important to be aware that the crises which history remembers most vividly are just the second part of the story; they are the falls that inevitably follow the excesses which went before. So, to fully understand the second stage – the crash – we must also seek to understand the first stage – the excess. The only complication is that the people affected by the crash are not always the same as those who benefited from the excess.

## The Emerging Markets Crisis, 1997-2002

This was a serious financial and economic crisis which affected many emerging market economies – causing a great deal of hardship for the people affected[42].

### Trouble in Bangkok

The crisis began in Thailand. Strong economic performance over many years prior to 1997 had led to an influx of foreign capital and this had caused asset prices, including real estate prices in the capital Bangkok, to surge. This, in

---

* I date this latter crisis to 2009 simply because I am editing the final version of this text in January 2010. The full story will take many more years to play out.

turn, attracted more capital, which caused asset prices to rise yet further, and so on in the kind of positive feedback loop that is typical of asset markets and which can be especially pronounced when it is difficult for excited investors to distinguish the effects of structural change (the rapid development of the Thai economy) from those of pure speculation.

This tendency for more and more capital to be drawn into Thailand was compounded by lax banking regulations and by a fixed exchange-rate policy that, because it had to prevent currency appreciation in face of the capital inflow that was underway, entailed a loose monetary policy to depress the value of the currency. The Thai authorities did attempt to maintain some controls on the cross-border flow of capital, and to target their loose monetary policy primarily at the foreign exchange markets, while they also tried to run a tighter monetary policy at home to offset the effects of foreign funds surging in. But their controls were insufficiently robust and the higher interest rates that monetary tightness at home induced simply created a further attraction to foreign investors. (Monetary policy will be described further in Part Three.)

Eventually, capital inflows drove up wages in Thailand, making its exports less competitive (especially in comparison with China, which had devalued its currency in 1994), while at the same time driving imports higher because people had the means to purchase them. This combination created a large trade deficit; the sure sign of a situation where capital flows or monetary policy have made a currency overvalued*. (The Thai currency was, because economic conditions had changed since the Thai peg was established, overvalued for the productivity and terms of trade of the country – exchange-rate policy merely kept it from appreciating further.)

The trade deficit created in this way signalled the end of the Thai bubble economy and the flow of funds into the country slowed, causing the upward momentum of asset markets to ease. Guessing that a reversal was imminent, and that they could benefit from it by precipitating it, a number of hedge

---

*The international transactions of a country are recorded in its balance of payments accounts. If a currency is over-valued, imports will tend to be higher than exports as foreign goods will be cheap and domestic goods will be expensive to foreigners – producing a current-account deficit. At the same time, regardless of whether the currency is being held up by private capital flows, or by monetary policy, there will be a net capital flow into the country – producing a capital-account surplus. This flow tends to bring the accounts very close to balance overall and, in practice, the accounting is contrived so that exact balance is always achieved.

funds chose this moment to leverage themselves highly in the Thai baht and to begin aggressively selling the currency. The Thai central bank thus found itself switching from a situation where it had to hold the currency down in order to maintain its peg, to one where it had to hold it up – using foreign currency reserves (originally accumulated by printing and selling baht) to buy-back their own currency. And, because other foreign investors, apart from those behind the original speculative attack, saw this and realised what happening, they began to abruptly withdraw funds from the country.

This caused asset prices to tumble and official foreign currency reserves to shrink – both signs of pressure that caused further investor panic, leading to further withdrawals, further falls in asset prices and reserves, and further panic. On 2 July 1997, the authorities in Thailand, now running out of foreign-currency reserves, were forced to concede defeat and float the baht. This led to massive currency depreciation and to a wave of defaults amongst corporate borrowers holding dollar-denominated debt that they could no longer service at the new exchange rate, an outcome that made foreign investors even more wary of Thailand than they were already.

At this point, domestic firms were being starved of foreign capital for real investment and for the purchase of inputs – a situation that led to layoffs, firm closures and a surge in unemployment (in a context where there were few social protections for those without work). This, together with the effect on business and consumer confidence of what was happening, caused domestic demand to plummet and kept the downward momentum going.

## Guilt by association

And the effect was not limited to Thailand. Investors who had been stung by the Thai crisis jumped to the conclusion that any emerging market economy with even minor issues (as they all necessarily have) might be too risky and they began a generalised withdrawal from the periphery of the global economy. They began to withdraw from Indonesia – which actually had a reasonably well-balanced economy at the time – from August 1997 after hedge funds initiated the process there in much the same way as they had in Thailand. This led to a currency collapse, to a wave of corporate defaults, to a series of sovereign bond defaults, to firm failures, to job layoffs and to widespread hardship for the Indonesian people as GDP shrank by 12% between 1997 and 1998 and unemployment soared.

Similar processes occurred, with varying degrees of severity, in South Korea, Malaysia, Hong Kong, the Philippines, Russia (whose economy had already been deeply troubled throughout the 1990s) and other places over the years 1997 and 1998. Indeed, in September 1998, the crisis reached US shores when the large New York hedge fund, Long-Term Capital Management (LTCM), which had been heavily exposed to Russian sovereign bonds, was almost felled by the contagion. Because the risk to counterparties of LTCM was, in essence, as great as if a significant bank was on the verge of failure, it had to be rescued and unwound by the Federal Reserve in order to prevent devastating systemic effects on the financial markets of the developed world.

## Slow-burn in South America

The crisis originating in Asia also had effects on Latin America over the years running up to 2001, as foreign investors became cautious about the region and as global commodity prices fell because of reduced demand in Asia and elsewhere. The effects of investor sentiment on Latin America were initially gradual because, although investors were concerned about government debt in the region and were cautious after what had happened in Asia, Latin America seemed in better shape than Russia and financiers were reassured by the exchange rate regimes that were then operating in Brazil and Argentina. In Brazil, this consisted of a quite flexible regime while, in Argentina, it consisted of a rigidly-fixed exchange rate that was maintained under a currency board system that had been introduced in 1991, after a domestic banking crisis (the details of currency board systems will be discussed in Chapter 9).

The Brazilian system created the impression that there was less cause for a fundamental imbalance, while the Argentine system created the impression that the peg would not be broken even under significant pressure and that there was therefore little prospect of a currency fall that would damage investors. Two diametrically opposite systems producing the same result might seem counter-intuitive but, from the point of view of foreign investors, the likely outcomes looked the same, and therefore were the same – at least for a time.

## Argentina defaults

Eventually, however, the withholding of capital by foreign investors hurt the Argentine economy at the same time as the fall in commodity prices cut into its export revenues and the rigid dollar peg caused its currency to fluctuate inappropriately against the currencies of its main trading partners elsewhere in Latin America and in Europe. In Brazil, by contrast, while there was some pain, the weakening of the *real* (amplified by a deliberate devaluation in January 1999) supported exports; keeping the economy closer to health but harming Argentina further in the process because it lost out competitively.

At this point, capital withdrawals from Argentina accelerated and domestic savers actually joined in as they anticipated currency devaluation, converting pesos to dollars and depositing them abroad. Eventually, in the last week of 2001, the government itself was under sufficient financial distress that it defaulted on its debt, and, in January 2002, it was forced to attempt the anticipated currency devaluation to regain competitiveness and convince investors that imbalances were resolved. This, however, merely triggered yet more capital flight, during which the peso tumbled to a quarter of its previous exchange value. And, even as the economy slid into depression, there was rampant consumer inflation through to September 2002 as the peso prices of essential imports surged – a consequence that compounded the situation yet further. Ultimately, Argentine GDP shrank by 19% over the years 1999 to 2002.

## Anatomy of a crisis I

From the mid-1990s in Thailand through to the end of 2002 in Argentina, the feedback aspects of the process we have outlined are clear. In the initial bubble, each flow of capital into Thailand had effects that attracted more capital from abroad; a positive feedback loop that created a self-fulfilling boom in asset prices and gave the currency a tendency to appreciate even as it was becoming over-valued in relation to the real trading position.

Eventually, negative feedback did take over when a persistent trade deficit built up and caused investors to belatedly realise the folly of what was going on, making them stop pouring capital into Thailand. However, this negative feedback dominated for only the briefest of periods because, as soon as any capital flowed out of the country under these circumstances, more tended to follow; a positive feedback effect operating in the reverse direction to before, that this time caused the Thai economy to 'over-correct' and to fall far below its equilibrium level.

The sparking of crises in many other countries as investors decided to pull back from emerging markets in general represented the next step in this latter positive feedback process. And the very similar processions of ever-worsening developments that took place in individual economies from Indonesia to Argentina represented the next steps again. This fits with the typical pattern of positive feedback processes, with each step being greater in magnitude to that which went before, with key indicators showing an accelerating movement, and with the ultimate consequences seeming entirely disproportionate to their apparent causes.

Eventually, in each country, negative feedback did take over once again as currencies fell so low that investors could see they must be under-valued and capital flight abated. And, in the years subsequent to this, while the cycle of expansion and contraction did continue in the places affected, its amplitude was lessened as investors who had been burned in these markets were less prone to build up speculative bubbles to the same extent as before.

In any economy, however, this latter process cannot last for long; investors quickly forget past lessons, they come to believe that some new bubble is the result of real structural change – that 'this time is different' – and the whole disruptive process therefore repeats itself. The only things that have prevented another widespread emerging markets crisis in the years since 2002 have been some strengthening of economic management in such countries (after some of them were exposed to a misguided initial phase of austerity measures imposed by the International Monetary Fund), the fact that global finance boomed again from 2003, the fact that more-developed countries managed to have a financial crisis first in 2007-2009, and the fact that this new crisis has not, as yet, for various reasons, had disproportionate financial effects on less-developed countries (for countries that are already poor, the social effects obviously are disproportionate).

## The Global Credit Crisis and Recession, 2007-2009

On a more global level, the events of 2007-2009 resulted from a very similar set of feedback effects to those which affected emerging markets from the mid-1990s through to 2002. The US and, to a lesser extent, the UK, are central in this story, but other countries also experienced excesses in the years before the crisis, or played contributory roles, and essentially all countries suffered the eventual fallout.

## Root causes

The earliest roots of this calamity are to be found in the deregulatory zeal that gripped the US, the UK and some other nations from about 1980. This set free the speculative potential that is always present in a market economy and created what hedge-fund manager George Soros has called a "super-cycle" in financial markets that reached its peak in 2007, and then quickly reversed.

With variation across jurisdictions, financial deregulation entailed rescinding such things as interest rate controls, leverage controls, credit guidelines, restrictions on share dealing, restrictions on the buy-to-let mortgage market, divisions between types of financial institution and restraints on cross-border capital flows. Formal requirements for holding of capital buffers by banks were introduced instead, but these were weak, they could not take the place of all the controls that had been removed, and they did not apply to all financial businesses. Indeed, alongside these rule changes, a huge, minimally-regulated 'parallel financial system'* composed of enlarged investment banks, hedge funds and financial instruments fulfilling the same basic functions as banks was allowed to come into existence. And derivatives markets exploded in size as governments made clear that they had no real inclination to regulate these activities.

Another significant contributing factor leading up to the events of 2007-2009 was the accumulation of substantial foreign exchange reserves by China and other emerging market governments from the late 1990s. This resulted in their accumulated capital being poured into the laxly-regulated financial markets of the United States and loosened credit conditions there yet further[43].

As finance began to be deregulated from the early 1980s onwards, debt levels in the US and UK began to balloon as both the supply of, and demand for, credit blossomed, while the value invested in housing, shares and other assets

---

* This new realm of finance was also referred to as the 'shadow banking system', a sinister-sounding title that belies the fact that most of what went on was perfectly legal.

began to follow a similar trajectory (Figure 12, Figure 13). This expansion did experience setbacks along the way, such as the travails of certain parts of the US banking system in the 1980s (the savings and loans associations), and the stock market crashes of 1987, but it also showed a generally accelerating trend that, in a dynamical network system such as the economy, is the hallmark of ongoing positive feedback effects.

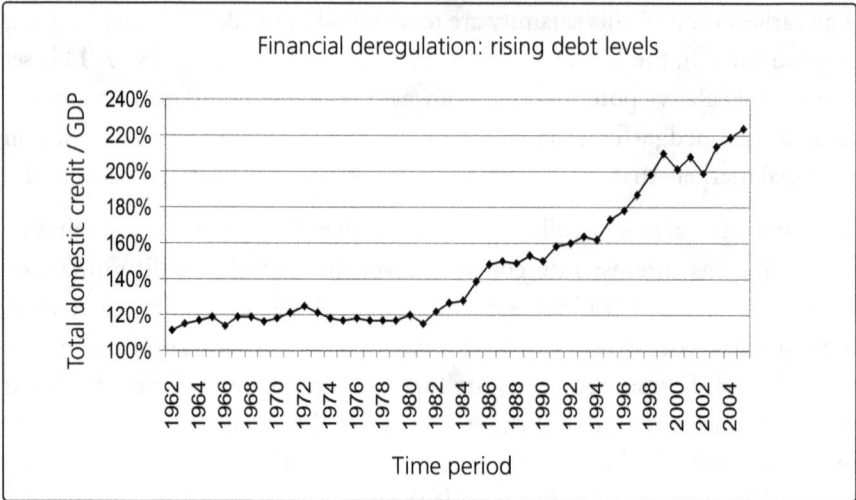

**Figure 12 – Annual levels of total domestic credit in the United States between 1962 and 2005 expressed as a ratio of GDP.** It is clear that something structural changed around 1980 and, given that progressively deregulating the existing financial system, while allowing a largely unregulated 'parallel' financial system to come into existence alongside it, increased both the supply and demand for credit, this is the most likely culprit by far. In later years, capital inflow from China also played a part. Foreign borrowing arising as a result of the persistent US trade deficit is excluded from the data. If we take only domestic credit to non-government borrowers, indebtedness comes out at 74% of GDP in 1962, 97% in 1980 and 195% in 2005. [Data from the World Bank.]

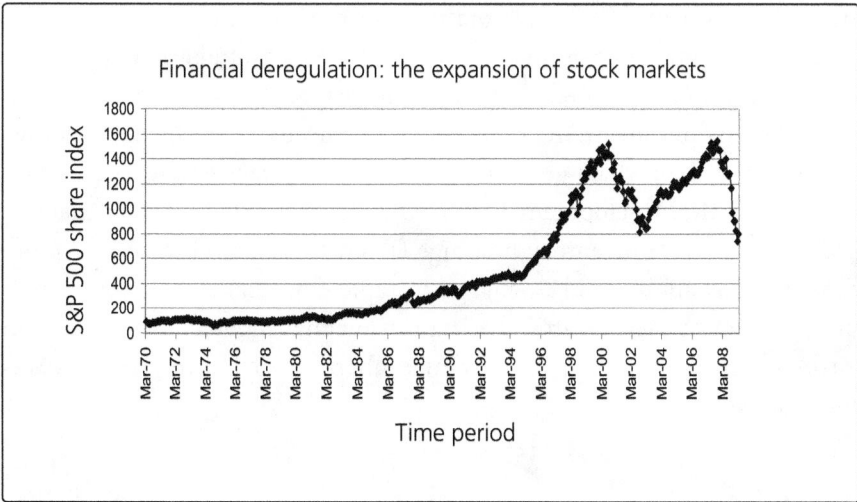

**Figure 13 – Daily values of the S&P500 Share Index in the US since 1970.**
It is clear that something structural changed in the 1980s, with the index rising from 100 to 350 between 1980 and 1990 – a much faster increase than its previous history, and more than twice as fast as nominal GDP (which rose 114% over the same period). However, it was in the 1990s, with the growth of the financial sector, and with the deregulation of various non-financial industries (especially telecommunications) that the trend really came into its own. [Data from Standard and Poor's.]

We also know from the behaviour of individual participants in the system – the micro-foundations that we must consider alongside macro outcomes – that positive feedback was underway. Hedge funds and other market participants traded on leverage and could borrow up to ever-higher multiples of their equity as their portfolios performed well over a number of years. The housing market attracted more and more people seeking to continually 'trade-up' as they observed the achievements of others. On TV, home-purchase shows proliferated. And, because of the consistent demand pressure resulting from these effects, economic output remained generally robust, people began to assume that structural change (deregulation and globalisation) had produced permanently better economic conditions, this made consumers more willing to borrow heavily in the expectation that the good times would continue, and it made banks more willing to lend freely for the same reason.

In the 1990s a number of factors gave further impetus to these trends. Financial deregulation continued. The entry of China, India and others into the world economy added huge scope for capacity growth that guarded against inflation and thereby pushed-back the day on which a negative feedback effect, in which growth impeded itself by causing inflation, would occur. And the development of information technology, which made it possible to reduce inventory holdings (fluctuations in which can amplify economic instability) and to engage in rapid financial transactions across multiple time zones, created the impression that previous constraints on business had been loosened and that exuberance at future prospects was therefore justified.

## The dot-com bust

Driven by these forces, in the late 1990s the share-price-to-earnings ratio of US-listed companies, especially IT companies, underwent a surge that was driven by what some observers at the time referred to as 'irrational exuberance'. This trend suddenly reversed in late 2000 as investors realised that their wild expectations were not being fulfilled and prices began to plummet. Overall, price-to-earnings ratios went from an average of 20:1 in 1995, to 44:1 in 2000 and back to 22:1 in 2003-2006 – one of the purest manifestations of bubble dynamics that recent history has produced. The fallout caused the US economy to tip into recession in early 2001.

Normally, after a bubble as great as this, an economy would experience a deep recession. But the early 2000s US recession was actually comparatively mild because a number of factors ensured that the underling speculative dynamics of the economy did not fully lose momentum. Specifically, because the mania of the late 1990s had focused mainly on IT shares, other asset classes were less affected and credit experienced only a mild downturn. Aggressive monetary loosening in response to the share bust, and in response to the terrorist attacks of 11 September 2001, further helped keep credit afloat. And capital had, at this point, started flowing in from China as a result of its undervalued currency and high consumer saving in what some would eventually dub 'a great wall of money' (the details of this process are discussed further in Chapter 9).

## The housing bubble

Instead of a deep recession, in the early-to-mid 2000s, housing and commodities became the final acts of the 'great bull market' that had prevailed since the 1980s. In the US, a housing bubble gained momentum as the effects of financial speculation and Chinese capital were compounded by interest rates that were probably kept too low for too long (as opposed to the sensible action of initially slashing them in response to a shock) and by federally-supported credit for poor people who should not have been given mortgages (reflecting government support for free-market 'solutions' to poverty). However, there should be no doubt that, as fundamental causes of the eventual crisis, everything else was of secondary importance compared to deregulation – the evidence of excesses building from 1980 as shown in Figures 12 and 13 shows this irrefutably*.

Nonetheless, there was a complex of forces, and, under all these forces, price-to-rent ratios in the US surged from about 110:1 in 2000 to about 165:1 in 2006, while the banking system began to engineer CDOs and other securitisation products that were built on mortgage loan repayments and which further compounded the entire process.

The surge in house prices in the absence of a similar surge in rents – especially when we consider the fall that came afterwards – represented a clear positive feedback effect whereby each rise in prices, and each homeowner seen to make a fortune, attracted yet more buyers into the market and drove prices ever-upwards. Likewise, the 'financial engineering' in CDOs and other securitisation products that accompanied this process represented a second, interlocking, positive feedback loop that amplified many of the effects of the first.

---

* Likewise, those who trace the crisis to 1971, when fixed exchange rates collapsed and the final link of the money supply to gold was broken, are misguided as there was no sign of rampant 'financialisation' of the economy in the 1970s. Some still argue that money was too loose in both the 1970s and in the period since 1980, with the only difference being that asset price inflation replaced consumer price inflation in the latter era. But evidence that the velocity of circulation of funds within the financial sector ballooned from the 1980s shows that it was deregulation, not the money supply, which was the problem. Put another way, speculation created an increased 'demand for money', tighter monetary policy would not have completely offset this, and it would have come at the cost of harming the real economy. All of the alternative theories (to deregulation being at the root of the crisis) that I refute here are essentially conservative Trojan horses for arguing either that the fact of government involvement in the economy caused the crisis, that regulation is unnecessary, or that money should be kept tight in a way that the wealthy see as preserving their advantage.

In this second loop, major banks bought pools of loans from local lenders, tranched these so that lower tranches absorbed all losses before higher tranches lost anything and sold the higher tranches on to investors who then seemed to gain a similar rate of return to the underlying mortgages, but at a much lower risk. This created huge demand for these products, gave traders whose bonus cycles were on a significantly shorter time-scale than the credit-asset cycle itself an incentive to turn a blind eye to any misgivings they might have, and gave local banks the incentive and funding (derived indirectly from final investors) to originate more loans and to extend these loans to ever-weaker borrowers. This stoked-up the property market even more and made the entire process seem even more attractive to all involved – a clear positive feedback loop.

The role of the US government in the housing market is worth clarifying. The federal mortgage agencies 'Fannie Mae' and 'Freddie Mac' acted as intermediaries in passing-on many of the mortgage pools that were sold by local lenders to larger banks – but, crucially, they did not devise the deadly CDO structure, and they did not foster the expectations of ever-rising-prices. Likewise, while the Community Reinvestment Act of 1977 and its various revisions required banks to be more lenient in the credit standards applied to certain demographics, at most 20% of the sub-prime lending that was carried out was under the provisions of the act. The role of these policies in the eventual crisis was therefore minor[44].

In the UK, speculative dynamics also gripped the housing market. Price-to-rent ratios inflated from 85:1 in 1995 to 165:1 in 2007, while mortgage and other consumer debt levels soared. The housing bubble played out over a longer time frame than in the US – possibly reflecting a national obsession with property and the belief that Britain's limited land area justified higher prices, together with the fact that America had fixated on IT shares before moving on to housing – and it was driven by many of the same factors.

State-supported 'sub-prime' mortgage lending and construction of complex securities from such mortgages were, however, not features of the landscape in the UK. This indicates that, since a dramatic housing bubble similar to that which occurred in the US inflated anyway even in the absence of these factors, such things are less fundamental in the volatility that arises in housing markets than the intrinsic volatility of asset prices and credit and the deregulation that can set this volatility free. Reaching this conclusion is an example of the kind of 'natural experiment' mentioned in Chapter 2: both the

US and UK (the test cases in our 'experiment') had housing bubbles, but only the US had state-sponsored sub-prime lending and complex securitisation based on it. Thus, such government 'distortion' of the mortgage market cannot be fundamental in causing housing bubbles and the busts that inevitably follow. This is in addition to the evidence above that such factors were not even very important in the US.

## Hitting limits

At the same time as all this was happening, from about 2003 onwards, global commodity prices began to surge as a result of demand from China and other emerging economies. This was a sign that the world economy was finally running up against the limits of capacity and it created inflationary pressures that caused central bankers in the west to gradually tighten monetary policy from late 2003. This dynamic accelerated in 2006 and, along with the realisation that house prices had gotten far out-of-line with fundamentals, it caused house prices to begin falling in the US. Eventually, as always, there had been a negative feedback effect whereby some consequences of the boom caused that boom to come to an end

## Banking unravels

The unwinding of property bubbles always causes pain for banks but, in this situation, the process of complex securitisation made things much worse. The calculations around which banks, and the credit rating agencies which supported them, had built CDOs and other securitisation products assumed that they were able to quantify default probabilities in the underlying mortgages with great accuracy and, even more unrealistically, that correlations between defaults would be low. These were both manifestations of the bubble-phase mentality that a systematic fall in house prices, which would be intrinsically unpredictable in its extent, was never going to happen. The consequence was that, when house prices in the US did begin to fall in 2006 – eventually getting down to about 110 times rent by mid-2009 – banks were left with greater losses than expected and, more critically, investors were left uncertain as to where in the banking system these losses had ended up.

As a consequence, the prices of CDOs collapsed in early 2007 and banks began to announce huge write-offs on the value of these instruments, with the expectation that more was to follow and that no one could know which major bank would declare losses next*. And, because finance was globalised, this included big European banks to much the same extent as banks headquartered in America, where the toxic CDOs had originated.

At this point, the interest rates at which banks could fund themselves in the money markets – a source of funds they had come to rely on in the confidence of the boom phase – began to rise (Figure 14), and bank share prices began to fall. Over the second half of 2007 and into 2008, each fall in bank share prices rattled money markets even more, made it harder for banks to raise funds, kept money market interest rates at a high level and therefore caused more stress for banks and more falls in share prices – a particularly vicious positive feedback loop that caused banks to burn through their reserves of liquidity and drove them inexorably towards collapse.

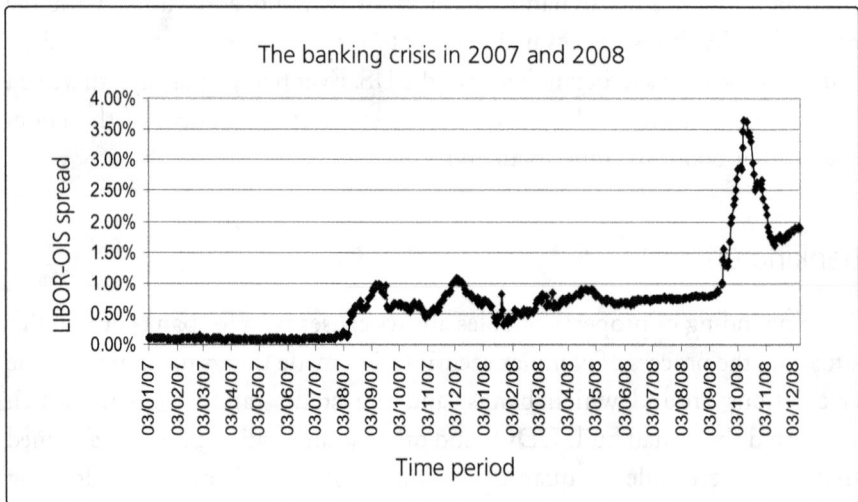

The banking crisis in 2007 and 2008

**Figure 14 – Daily values of the spread between interbank interest rates (LIBOR, the London Interbank Offer Rate, at 3-month maturity) and a benchmark interest rate not subject to bank counterparty risk (the OIS rate).** What the data show, in effect, is that banks and money market lenders did not have enough confidence in the continued existence of many banks to lend cheaply to them. [Data from the British Bankers Association.]

---

* Some people put part of the blame for the crisis on mark-to-market accounting – the obligation on banks under new accounting rules to continually update recorded asset values to reflect market prices. But this amounts to shooting the messenger and, in reality, had mark-to-market accounting not existed, it is possible that banks would have continued to speculate for longer and would subsequently have crashed even more spectacularly.

Beyond this, from late 2007, the withdrawal of credit lines to leveraged investors, together with a broader loss of confidence, caused share prices in general to begin collapsing. The FTSE 100 in London fell from a peak of 6700 in June 2007 to an eventual trough of 3500 in March 2009 – barely over half its original value. This caused losses to investors – including the proprietary trading divisions of major banks – and compounded the overall situation.

Under more normal circumstances, it would be possible for a 'universal bank' (the kind of bank which engages in both commercial-bank and investment-bank activities and which is likely to be funded by both money markets and conventional deposits) to shrink its money-market funding to the point where it was dependent on retail deposits only. But this is clearly not possible for investment banks that are financed entirely from the money markets, and even universal banks cannot successfully execute the manoeuvre in a crisis. Instead, the situation progresses faster than they can manage; and, eventually, because relying on money-market funding intrinsically entails raising new funds to pay-off old funds that are maturing, a bank default becomes increasingly likely. In essence, in 2007 and 2008, a money-market bank run was underway. And, because the public became aware that banks were somehow in difficulty, a number of small banks also experienced runs amongst retail depositors that could have spread to larger institutions.

## Big names fall

Looking at specific banks, the first explicit signs of financial distress came in July 2007 when US investment bank Bear Stearns warned that investors would get little of their money back from two hedge funds it managed. Then in September 2007 it emerged that UK mortgage bank Northern Rock – which had relied heavily on the interbank markets for funding – had been kept afloat only by emergency credit from the Bank of England, causing a run amongst retail depositors that was ended only when the state explicitly guaranteed the full amount of all deposits. In October 2007, Swiss bank UBS started off a string of announcements by large institutions of heavy losses on CDO positions. And, in December 2007 to March 2008, there was fear that large bond insurers would be driven into difficulty by liabilities arising from securitisation products they had covered and that panic-selling of many, otherwise unrelated, classes of bond would result.

In March 2008, the crisis reached a new intensity when the US government had to arrange the takeover of Bear Stearns by universal bank JP Morgan. And, over the summer of 2008 further government interventions were needed, culminating in the rescue of the state-sponsored mortgage agencies Fannie Mae and Freddie Mac in September 2008. But then, on 15 September 2008, the US government succumbed to worries that all of this would encourage reckless behaviour by banks in the future – so-called 'moral hazard' – and they allowed investment bank Lehman Brothers to go into bankruptcy so as to avoid this outcome.

This pitched the financial system into what, without intervention, would have been the final stages of collapse. Interbank interest rates soared to new highs and major banks were left in a position where they had only weeks, or even days, of liquidity left. Over September and October 2008 a range of major banks were rescued in one way or another: Merrill Lynch, Wachovia and Washington Mutual in the United States, Fortis in Europe, HBOS and RBS in the United Kingdom and many others. To avoid systemic disruption, the US insurance giant AIG also had to be rescued in face of the losses it was incurring on CDS contracts written during the boom years.

## Flight to safety

While this implosion was happening, investors who were pulling their funds out of at-risk banks sought safe havens in which to put their money. Some invested in gold or US treasury bonds – with the latter driving the dollar up even as America was at the epicentre of the financial crisis. Others invested in commodity futures, which had been rising strongly for years and which were thought to be capable of sustaining this pattern as demand from China – which some believed had 'decoupled' entirely from Western economies – was expected to keep driving the price of the underlying commodities upwards.

This latter move, as can sometimes happen, added a large measure of pure speculation to prices of physical commodities that had already been rising under the force of fundamentals. The prices of food, fuel and other materials surged. The oil price, for example, rose from about $80 a barrel in mid-2007 to $147 in mid-2008 (priced in March 2009 dollars to remove the effect of exchange-rate changes). Speculative pressures affecting commodities did fall away in late 2008, as investors realised just how weak the economy was, and prices fell, with oil dropping below $40 in January 2009 before returning to $80 in October 2009. But the process had caused hardship and unrest in poor countries and put pressure on the world economy at a very delicate moment.

## The 'Great Recession'

Indeed, due to loss of credit in former bubble economies and loss of trade for others, a global recession took hold in 2008 for the first time since the Second World War. The United States was the first to enter recession, quickly followed by the United Kingdom, Western Europe and Japan. China, India and other major emerging markets suffered reduced growth but, because of the sheer momentum of rapid development and the easier growth that can come with playing catch-up, they did not experience recessions. Overall, global output will have fallen by at least 2.5% as a result of the crisis[45] – a disaster in a world where populations are still rising and billions live in poverty*.

## The hangover

And this is not the end of the pain. The debt built up by governments around the world in order to support demand through the crisis will take years to pay off. With growth at 2% and inflation at 3%, a public debt of 110% of GDP takes nine years to get down to 40% if an amount equivalent to 5% of nominal GDP for each year is paid off through a mixture of tax increases and spending cuts. Accumulating public debt was necessary. If we consider the far deeper slump that would have occurred without it, the structural damage this would entail, the effect on inequality, the risk of serious political turmoil, the fact that public debt is unlikely to crowd out much private borrowing in the aftermath of the crisis (a topic we will return to in the next chapter), the fact that slightly-elevated inflation may erode the debt burden somewhat, and the fact that some of the borrowings were spent on infrastructure that should boost growth in the years to come – then it becomes clear that the costs of not spending the money would have been far greater than the costs of spending it. Nevertheless, this public debt, together

---

* For these reasons, the IMF considers any global growth rate below 3% to be a global recession.

with the effects of the recession on firms and workers, will put a drag on the economy for years to come.

Some investors also worry about the possibility of a dollar collapse in the years ahead. The dollar has, since the mid-1980s, been kept at a value above that which would balance US trade. This is as a result of the extra demand for dollars arising from its role as a reserve currency, especially from countries like China that have managed their currency against the dollar. This trend continued as investors used US Treasury bonds as a safe-haven during the crisis. Now, however, the dollar is sliding as investors become somewhat less risk-averse and as the effects of very loose US monetary policy are felt. This slide is helping the US by boosting its exports but, if investors become convinced that the prospects of the US are poor, or if foreign central banks begin to convert their funds out of dollars, it could turn into a capital flight and a collapse of the dollar – with devastating consequences for investors holding dollar assets, and thus similar devastation for the world economy.

Such an outcome, however, while not impossible, seems improbable. Even if the US fiscal position was slow to improve and some inflation resulted from the aggressive increases in the money supply that were enacted during the crisis, it is difficult to see investors losing faith in America to such an extent. Beyond this, most other developed nations are in no better shape than the US and are thus no more attractive to investors. And, in any case, there are few alternatives to dollar assets. The sovereign bonds issued in the eurozone are those of a range of separate countries – as opposed to those of the US, which are issued by a single powerful government – and the Chinese *renminbi* does not even have full convertibility for investment purposes.

## Anatomy of a crisis II

As regards our core theme of how feedback effects dominate the economy, just as self-reinforcing positive feedback was evident in the upwards phase of the 'super-cycle' lasting from the 1980s until early 2007, so too was it visible in the downward phase that has operated since then. Each financial shock damaged confidence and made life more difficult for other banks, leading to further shocks. Funding difficulties led to falls in bank share prices, leading to further funding difficulties. Reductions in house and share prices more generally led to falls in credit, leading to further falls in house and share prices. Reductions in credit also led to reduced economic activity overall, leading to further reductions in credit. Unemployment and loss of confidence led to reductions in aggregate demand, leading to further unemployment and loss of confidence. Disinflation (falls in the rate of inflation that may be short of outright deflation) led to reduced pressure to spend, leading to further disinflation. And, overall, there was the accelerating movement of major events and key indicators – with things becoming more dramatic over each passing month – that is a hallmark of positive feedback.

The only major positive feedback effect that has, thankfully, not yet been present to any great extent is that of capital withdrawals from small or backward economies leading to currency falls, and this leading to further capital withdrawals. Only Iceland, the Ukraine and a few others have thus far been affected by this to any significant degree.

Because of government action and the normal mechanisms that eventually cause the economy to reach a turning point, recovery is now beginning. But it is likely that this process will be slow, and there is a significant danger of a painful second dip if the economy is hit by unpleasant surprises along the way*. Such a dip might arise if increasing public debt pushed some already-weak government into default, or if a premature asset-price rally (such as has been underway from March 2009 to January 2010) were to break suddenly enough. It would be made more serious by the fact that policymakers have already committed all of their fiscal and monetary ammunition. The effects of such an event, however, might be somewhat counterbalanced by the simple fact that market participants have become used to adverse circumstances and might not react with as much shock and panic as in 2007-2008.

Either way, it is clear that the excessive instability of a deregulated economy has not made our lives easier. Ways in which we can construct an economy where there is less inherent cyclicality are the subject of the next chapter.

---

* This commentary was edited for the final time in January 2010, and it is likely that events will already have moved on somewhat when it is published a few months later.

# Part Three:
# Policy

# 6. Counter-Cyclical Policy

rrational exuberance, of the kind that was in evidence in the US and elsewhere during the 1990s and again in the early 2000s, can easily turn the normal cycle of expansion and contraction into a more dangerous process of bubble and collapse. This is not, however, the main differentiating factor between these two kinds of economic cycle. At a more basic level, it is government policy that makes the difference between relative economic stability and the violent instability that can threaten to tear society apart*. In essence, although the economy may be intrinsically cyclical over time, intelligent policy can dampen out the amplitude of this cycle, thereby reducing the chances that the downward part of the cycle will become deep enough to develop into a depression.

## Control of the Currency

The most fundamental tool of economic policy available to the authorities is monetary policy: controlling the amount of money that exists in a currency zone† by using the central bank to buy or sell financial assets[46].

### Expansionary monetary policy – methods and effects

A slight increase in the money supply, brought about by the central bank purchasing financial assets using newly issued currency, is amplified by the deposit expansion multiplier that operates in the banking system (see Chapter 3) and it leads to an increase in domestic demand as the money supply rises. Because this procedure entails the new money passing through the commercial banking system, it also manifests itself as a fall in market interest rates. In effect, the fact of holding more funds makes lenders more willing to lend so they cut their interest rates; lower interest rates make borrowers more

---

* This is no exaggeration; the economic upheavals of the 1920s and 1930s were, along with the political legacy of the First World War, amongst the main factors that brought Hitler to power in Germany. They were therefore partly responsible for plunging the world into a conflict that threatened to bring civilised values to an end.

† Such zones may correspond to one or several countries.

willing to borrow; and the combination of these two effects mediates the rise in money supply and aggregate demand. Not only does the deposit expansion multiplier play a part in this process, but the process itself may also strengthen the multiplier as banks gain in confidence and come to lend a greater proportion of their deposits – a positive feedback loop that runs until the proportion of deposits loaned out hits its legal limit.

Deposit interest rates also fall in these circumstances because, if rates on loans are falling, they must do so for banks to remain solvent.

Along with boosting aggregate demand in general, monetary expansion also has the consequence of pushing up the price of assets such as shares and housing – an effect that is mediated both by increased borrowing by investors, and by a search for yield that can no longer be obtained from deposits or bonds in an environment of low interest rates. For separate reasons, it also pushes up the price of sovereign and other bonds that are already trading in the secondary market, having been issued with fixed periodic payments some time ago. This effect occurs because a bond offering a given rate of payment becomes more attractive if deposits and newly-issued bonds are now offering less interest, and it continues until the bond rate, expressed as a ratio of the fixed periodic payment to the bond price, has fallen to approximate parity with the deposit rate, with variations occurring only as a result of different levels of risk. And, once this state of risk-adjusted parity is achieved, it then becomes part of the effect pushing investors into other asset classes where higher yields are achievable.

In apparent contradiction to some of this, when monetary expansion does take place, it might be argued that the lower rates of depositing resulting from lower interest rates should reduce the funds available to banks and should thereby drive interest rates back up again. However, since most income in a modern economy is deposited with commercial banks under all circumstances, and since the central bank actively administers liquidity on a day-to-day basis so as to maintain a given target rate of interest in the market, this clearly cannot happen. Likewise, the higher interest rates entailed in a monetary contraction have no tendency to reverse themselves as a consequence of people rushing to deposit.

## Exchange-rate effects

Beyond this, all else being equal, increasing the domestic money supply also causes its value to fall relative to other currencies. This is a logical consequence of the relative abundance of two currencies changing. It is mediated by investors withdrawing some funds from a jurisdiction in which they have less confidence, since its economy is slowing down, and in which they now earn less interest on bonds and deposits. Such a fall in the currency leads to increased demand for exports from the area in question – a phenomenon that, like the domestic effects of monetary loosening, also boosts aggregate demand and thereby supports the economy.

It should, however, be clarified that monetary policy actions intended to boost the amount of currency in domestic circulation differ in certain respects from actions intended specifically to push its value down relative to other currencies. Most fundamentally, actions intended to boost the domestic money supply involve purchases of financial assets denominated in domestic currency, while actions intended to push the currency down on the foreign exchange markets involve purchases of foreign currency or of assets denominated in such currency. The former places new funds primarily in the hands of domestic investors, while the latter places such funds primarily in the hands of foreigners and has an immediate effect on two currencies, not just one. These differences – together with the different signals sent to investors – lead to somewhat different outcomes. However, because of the ease with which funds can cross the boundaries between currency zones in the modern world, the effects of the two kinds of action tend to have a great deal of overlap, and, in the long run, are likely to be identical.

## Using monetary policy – when?

Expansionary monetary policy of either of these specific varieties is employed when an economy is clearly heading for a downturn – to pre-emptively employ it earlier might make the peak of the boom more dangerous by either fuelling inflation or by delaying the downturn. It serves to make the recession both shorter and shallower. Conversely, the opposite of these measures – contractionary monetary policy – is applied when a boom is beginning to over-heat. This has the effect of bringing the downturn forward, but it also ensures that there is less potential for an outright collapse arising from this event.

The moment when a boom is over-heating has, in recent years, been identified chiefly by means of monitoring increases in consumer inflation. But a more effective approach would be to tighten monetary policy either if inflation picks up, or if asset prices and debt levels are rising too far above trend levels. If only a single asset class is experiencing a bubble, a middle course might be to adjust specific controls on this asset class in an attempt to avoid the over-correction that might result from tightening monetary policy. This could, for example, involve increasing the margin requirements that stockbrokers must impose on those who are buying shares using borrowed funds, or other targeted measures. However, if the economy in general is undergoing a debt-fuelled speculative bubble in multiple asset classes, this approach is unlikely to be successful and broader monetary action is called for.

## Inverted controls?

In a slight complication to all this, it might be argued that, under certain circumstances, a loosening of monetary policy might hasten the fall of asset prices and credit, and that a tightening might do the reverse. If, for example, a country's banks were dependent on overseas funds to the extent that withdrawals following a monetary loosening would leave them unable to lend, a fall in asset prices might follow. Conversely, if such a country tightened its monetary policy, asset prices might rise. In practice, however, it is uncommon for countries to be in a position like this, and it would be best for policymakers to avoid being so dependent on fickle foreign capital. Likewise, the effects on investor confidence of knowing that the central bank felt the need to loosen monetary policy might work against the outcomes that such an action was intended to achieve. But this effect is not usually strong enough to counteract the more tangible profit-and-loss forces that are at work when interest rates change and it is, in any case, counterbalanced by the reassuring effect on confidence of seeing that action has been taken.

## Not just interest rates

Changes in monetary policy are normally thought of purely as changes in interest rates. This is because the changes in the ratio of the money supply to GDP that are implemented are normally small; they are normally reversed next time monetary policy moves in the opposite direction; and they are continually fine-tuned in order to maintain some target rate of interest in the market*. It is also because, whenever it makes such adjustments, the central bank often simultaneously changes the rate of interest that it will charge to commercial banks that borrow from it in order to maintain short-run liquidity. Along with the supply of funds in the system, this rate acts as a benchmark for commercial banks as to the rates of interest they themselves set. In a competitive banking sector they normally charge highly creditworthy borrowers a slightly higher rate than what they would pay to the central bank, and invariably offer depositors a slightly lower rate than that charged to the best borrowers. Thus, when the rate of interest charged by the central bank is lowered, commercial banks may themselves charge lower rates, lending may increase, the deposit expansion multiplier may strengthen, and the money supply may expand.

It is only when larger shifts in monetary policy are made that we stop talking of changes in the rate of interest and start talking instead of 'printing' or destroying money. These actions are normally taken by purchasing or selling assets that are more long-term than those which are usually transacted in the execution of monetary policy, and they naturally entail inducing very high or very low (0-1%) interest rates. In addition, because the psychological attractiveness of borrowing necessarily stops growing once the rate approaches zero, the action that is referred to as 'printing money' normally involves an increase in monetary injections far larger than would normally take place. This is necessary because all of the effect must come through the fact of banks feeling secure enough to increase lending volume (as opposed to cutting lending rates) after acquiring additional funds.

If some inflation continues into a recession where interest rates have been slashed – as may happen, for example, when capacity is lost – real interest rates may turn negative, since these are equal to the nominal interest rate minus the rate of inflation. However, this does not bring an additional stimulus effect, as commercial banks will generally set their loan rates so that they achieve positive real interest rates at the time of lending.

---

* This target is usually expressed in terms of the rate of interest that banks are charged on loans from one another – taken out for reasons of short-term liquidity – or from money market funds. Since banks must then charge higher rates on their loans to other counterparties, this interest rate is fundamental to the entire structure of interest rates in a currency zone. It is also more dynamic, and therefore a more up-to-date target, than the rate of interest banks pay to depositors, their other source of funding.

In addition to buying and selling financial assets, the central bank can also influence the money supply by changing the required reserve ratio – the minimum proportion of depositors' funds that commercial banks must hold in reserve with the central bank and not lend out – so as to alter the deposit expansion multiplier. If they reduce the reserve ratio, the multiplier may strengthen and the money supply may consequently expand. If they increase it, the opposite may happen. However, as a policy tool this can easily have a greater effect than intended; and as a means of expansionary policy, it runs the risk of making the banking system more fragile by rendering it more prone to bank runs. Both of these defects entail a significant risk of seriously damaging the economy and, for this reason, central banks rarely use changes to the required reserve ratio as a tool of monetary policy.

# Setting the Rules

A second tool of economic policy available to government is regulation. In relation to economic management as a whole, this includes regulation designed to protect workers, consumers, natural resources, the environment (upon which the entire economic edifice is dependent) and the political process from the more destructive consequences of the profit motive. But, in the context of economic stability, regulation mainly implies controls – imposed on banks and the holders of investment assets – that are designed to reduce the potential for extreme upswings in the credit-asset cycle and therefore to flatten out the economic cycle overall[47]. ·

## Deposit insurance

A simple example of such financial regulation is a requirement that banks buy into a state-sponsored insurance scheme designed to protect depositors' funds in the event of a bank failure. This has the effect of boosting confidence in the banking system and of making it less likely that bank runs will develop under conditions of financial stress.

## Segmenting the industry

Similarly, regulations prohibiting commercial banks from funding themselves through the money markets in the same way as investment banks; from engaging in some of the more risky functions of investment banks, or from backing hedge funds that engage in speculative investment, all can boost confidence in the financial system and make it more stable. Such restrictions reduce the chance that mishaps occurring in the investment banking industry will be transmitted throughout the rest of the financial system. Likewise, insurers should be segregated from both commercial and investment banks so as to mitigate the transmission of shocks. But, if investment banks are large enough, segregation does not remove the need for such institutions to be rescued by government in the face of a collapse: such a collapse would still reduce the amount of credit available to large corporations and might still cause a sudden collapse in the price of assets in which the institution was speculating.

## Leverage controls

Another example of responsible financial regulation is leverage controls that prevent borrowers from taking on debt equivalent to more than a certain multiple of the funds they themselves are putting into a venture (their 'equity' stake). Leverage is thought of in terms of the fundamental accounting equation, $A = L + E$, where A is total assets (the sum total of that which has been bought using debt and equity), L is liabilities and E is equity. In this framework, leverage is the ratio of A over E and a higher value reflects a greater proportion of assets funded by debt.

Limits on this leverage ratio should obviously be set at different levels for different borrowers: maybe somewhere around 3:1 for different kinds of corporate borrower, perhaps 5:1 for home mortgage borrowers, maybe 15:1 for banks (which naturally 'borrow' sums from depositors that far exceed their own assets), and unlimited for student loans and other specific cases where the total lending pool is naturally small and the borrowers have no assets. Controls such as these would keep debt levels from becoming excessive and would thereby help flatten out the economic cycle.

Leverage controls should also be applied to speculative investors such as hedge funds. By borrowing from banks, and by using the funds obtained from opening short positions* to fund long positions in entirely different asset

---

* The practice of borrowing an asset in order to sell it and making a profit by buying it back again later at a lower price.

classes, hedge funds can reach a position where their leverage ratio is more than 100:1. This enables such funds to have a disproportionate impact on the economy. In the case of less-developed countries experiencing economic difficulties, hedge funds can bet on large currency falls; and this can contribute to, or even cause, the capital flight scenarios that can affect such countries. And, in the case of a nascent asset-price bubble anywhere in the world, hedge funds can make reckless financial investments in the knowledge that traditional bankruptcy law (which is needed to protect and encourage genuine entrepreneurship) will allow them to walk away from their debts if it all goes wrong. This clearly contributes to the inflation of the bubble, and makes it likely that the subsequent contraction will be that much more painful. As a consequence, although all suitable forms of financial regulation should naturally be applied to hedge finds, it is leverage controls that are most relevant to them.

Leverage restrictions that are imposed on hedge funds should also be applied to another major class of leveraged investor that has arisen in recent decades: debt-financed private equity funds. Private equity operates according to the model of purchasing the complete stock of an exchange-listed company, delisting, restructuring and selling it onwards at an improved price. This can be a very useful function when it comes to reforming struggling firms, but, when it is done with excessive amounts of leverage, it can amount to a high-risk gamble on a firm that may not live up to expectations. The transaction may thus come back to adversely affect the banks involved. Beyond this, because the debt in question is usually loaded on to the balance sheet of the acquired firm, it allows private equity investors to repeat the process many times over and to adopt risky management strategies for acquired firms (in industries about which they may know little) in the knowledge that their equity losses will be acceptable if the firm collapses.

However, restrictions applied to private equity funds should not be applied to venture capital funds, similar organisations that specialise in taking an equity holding in start-up technology firms that might not have access to other sources of finance. These funds tend to be quite small relative to the size of the overall financial system, they do not make much use of debt finance anyway and their activities can bring huge benefits in terms of long-run economic growth – all of which are characteristics that argue against many restrictions being placed on their operations.

## Lending controls

Yet another example of prudent financial control is restrictions on who can borrow in the first place – restrictions that, like leverage controls, are necessary because banks cannot restrain themselves adequately during a rising credit bubble, partly because the incentives of individual bankers are not aligned with those of the bank itself. Such measures should prohibit the most egregious mis-lending, perhaps by imposing some legal liability on the loan officers involved, and should aim to ensure that almost all borrowing is in support of productive investment, or is at least used for the purchase of an asset that will act as a store of value. These principles are necessary on several counts. Restrained lending reduces the propensity for bubbles to form. The existence of assets that can be repossessed is good for bank stability. Productive investment increases future real output. And, if borrowers have control of such output (i.e. have an income), they will be less likely to default on their debts in a downturn. Special exceptions to the principle of only borrowing for investment should be made for things like working capital facilities, trade finance facilities and student loans: services that are needed to keep certain activities operating, where there might still be some collateral that can be claimed and where the pool of debt is naturally small*. But these should be the exceptions rather than the rule.

## Remuneration controls

A further way in which banks and investment firms might be regulated is to place controls on the remuneration and bonus systems that these firms employ in order to incentivise their staff, but which can instead encourage reckless lending and insufficient diligence in asset purchases. This might be done through regulations insisting that bonuses be paid on the basis of profitability, not volume; regulations insisting that payments be delayed for a number of years (allowing enough time for unprofitable transactions to manifest themselves); and regulations that make it mandatory for staff to forgo or repay bonuses when misconduct is subsequently detected.

---

* Including student loans on this list assumes that governments have opted for state-guaranteed loans as a means to fund higher education. However, from the point of view of national investment and social equality, it is likely that direct state funding of students and universities is a better option.

Regulations setting absolute caps on bonuses should, however, not be attempted. Such tight controls would just create an especially strong incentive for evasion.

## Capital and liquidity requirements

An additional example of banking regulation, and the only one listed here aside from deposit insurance that is currently practised systematically, is legislation requiring banks and other financial institutions to hold a certain amount of liquidity (cash, plus assets that can be reliably exchanged for cash) at all times and, under separate rules, to keep 'regulatory capital' (their own equity plus certain kinds of near-equity financing) above a certain proportion of their exposures. Historically, liquidity requirements simply involved being obliged to hold a certain proportion of depositors' funds as central bank reserves, but new rules are in the offing that will expand on this. In the case of regulatory capital, meanwhile, exposures are adjusted according to various risk metrics, a measure of 'risk-weighted assets' is thereby produced and a rule is imposed that the ratio of risk-weighted assets to regulatory capital must not exceed a certain level.

Rules such as these increase the chances that a bank will withstand a stress period, which typically takes the form of losses that are written-off against equity, leading to withdrawals of financing when the market feels that these losses will become deeper. However, because of the self-reinforcing nature of bank runs, and because the losses incurred are usually much deeper than any plausible capital or liquidity cushion, such measures may well fail once a crisis gets going. Their real function is that, by placing anchors on bank lending, they reduce the amplitude of credit bubbles and, because of this, and because they increase confidence in banks, they also reduce the amplitude of the credit busts to follow. They thereby make it less likely that a crisis will develop in the first place.

These rules should be maintained, but should be strengthened in terms of the amounts of capital and liquidity that must be held, while also being modified so that regulatory capital requirements are gradually increased in the expansionary phase of the economic cycle, and are reduced in the recessionary phase. This latter would exert a counter-cyclical influence on bank lending, and therefore on the wider economic cycle, but would have less potential for inadvertent destabilisation than using modulation of required reserve ratios as a primary tool of monetary policy, simply because it would not involve frequent up and down movements in the imposed target.

Complications arise in the space where requirements that banks hold regulatory capital interact with controls imposed on the leverage of banks (as opposed to the leverage of their borrowers, where there the case for regulation is clear-cut). These are closely-related things because the first considers the relation of total lending (the assets of a bank) to equity, while the latter considers the relation of a risk-adjusted measure of lending to regulatory capital, which will be similar in amount to equity. In essence, if a bank were to run into the limit on lending imposed by either the leverage restriction, or by available capital, long before it ran into the other limitation, then one of the controls would be redundant. Indeed, this could lead to a serious failure of regulation if a non-cyclical leverage control prevented counter-cyclical capital requirements from having any real effects, and likewise if non-cyclical capital requirements prevented a counter-cyclical leverage control from having any effects.

In principle, if a bank ran into the leverage restriction first, there might also be an incentive to direct a greater portion of permitted lending at high-risk, high-return activities. Similarly, if it ran into the capital limitation first, there might be an incentive to 'massage' risk metrics to reduce the level of risk-weighted assets and permit more total lending with a given amount of capital (massaging the leverage metric is more difficult because it is simpler, and therefore easier for external auditors to check). The problems with both approaches can also be mitigated in similar extent to one another. Restrictions on who can borrow in the first place, backed by legal sanctions on loan officers, can lessen the dangers of relying on a leverage control. And intrusive monitoring by regulators of risk systems and metrics can lessen the dangers of relying on capital requirements. Thus, neither capital requirements nor leverage controls are obviously superior to one another.

There are therefore two views that one can take. You can say that two lines of defence are better than one and that the best solution is to set the maximum ratios of assets over equity, and of risk-weighted assets over regulatory capital, so that they both tend to be hit at a similar level of lending for the average bank, or so that one tends to be a 'backstop' for the other. Alternatively, you can say that it is best for a regulator to focus on implementing one approach properly, and to not confuse itself with multiple tacks in the same area. I would tend to sympathise with the latter view and to say that, since the institutional structures already exist for the regulatory capital approach, we should stick with this method; but it is a matter for debate.

## Controls on traded instruments

Alongside regulations targeted mainly at commercial and investment banks, and at the issuance and uptake of credit, controls are also needed on the way in which financial assets and derivative instruments are traded. Most obviously, there should be central clearing houses for all traded instruments that absorb all losses if a counterparty defaults, ensure that all participants maintain a margin account to provide the clearing house with liquidity, support themselves by charging a small premium on all trades and publish information to make the market transparent. It should be a legal requirement that all market participants with exposures above a certain minimal size trade through such clearing houses. As well as ensuring that financial firms were protected against default by trading counterparties (something that is already partially achieved by regulatory capital requirements, which also cover this area), this would also have the effect of anchoring the size and complexity of financial markets.

In addition to this, there should be restrictions placed on the extent to which certain specific instruments can be traded. An example of this would be commodity futures, which can contribute to bubbles in the price of raw-material commodities when capacity limitations in this sector cause prices to begin rising. In this area, the role of futures contracts in destructive commodity price bubbles might cause some observers to question the desirability of allowing such contracts to exist at all. This, however, is a deeply misleading train of thought. Futures contracts play a vital role in permitting businesses to manage their cash flows and thereby allow them to produce and sell more efficiently. Likewise, an active market in futures is needed to enable firms to provisionally purchase commodities that they may not actually need, and to shift these onwards if they become superfluous. And, finally, the involvement of at least some speculators makes these markets more liquid and thereby serves the needs of real-economy businesses. If any of these factors were not in place, then real economic output would probably be lower.

However, it is possible for the volume of speculation to grow far beyond what is actually needed and, given that this is the case, there is a very strong argument for placing restrictions on the size of the speculative positions that may be taken in commodity futures. This might be done through a crude cap on the exposures that individual hedge funds and other speculators may build-up in this area or, more subtly, by having clearing houses impose different margin requirements or fees on different classes of market participant, and adjusting these requirements as market trends dictate. Beyond this, better financial regulation in general (such as limitations on the leverage of hedge funds) could reduce the propensity for speculation to occur. And facilitating investment in primary industries should lessen the capacity restrictions that usually serve to instigate a commodity price bubble in the first place.

Other areas where such controls might be needed include securitisation products, CDSs and any other product that might amplify risk or cause perverse behaviour. The details of how exactly this might be done require further analysis, but it is clear that the basic approach to trading regulation should be dynamic and that financial regulators should show a willingness to impose new controls on any 'innovative product' that financiers develop in an attempt to circumvent existing legislation.

## Smaller banks?

Further proposals that have occupied the minds of commentators of late, especially those of a free-market inclination, are the options of reducing the size of banks so that they can be permitted to fail without triggering a wider collapse, together with having a streamlined bankruptcy code for banks so that they can be unwound quickly. The real threat of failure that would then exist would supposedly cause bank shareholders to insist on more cautious behaviour and would cause those who finance banks to insist on higher risk premia in their interest payments, all of which would reduce the cyclicality of the system. It is, however, very questionable as to whether this would be the case. Bank shareholders have incentives that are more short-run than the interests of the wider economy would dictate, especially in the fast-trading world of today. The ability of shareholders to control individual bankers is anyway limited, and is further weakened by competition between banks for the 'top traders'. And depositors need somewhere to put their money, meaning that they are unlikely to be able to insist on higher risk premia from banks.

Credit bubbles would therefore still inflate if we relied on approaches such as these that aim to 'enhance the discipline of the market'. The failure of even a few small banks at the peak of the bubble would then be enough to trigger a collapse. And, in this situation, events would evolve more quickly than any bankruptcy code could control, with investors yanking their funds out long before the lawyers and accountants could tie-up the dealings of banks in an orderly manner. That this would be the case is firmly demonstrated by the banking crises that marked previous centuries – long before the banking behemoths of today came into existence and when banks were exposed to the 'discipline of the market'. Some reduction in the size of banks, provided it did not go so far as to erode economies of scale, would probably be desirable to reduce complexity and increase transparency, while a streamlined bankruptcy code for banks would certainly do no harm (provided that it still recognised the need for government backing to hold a bank together while it was being unwound). But these should just be small additions to our broader regulatory package.

## Summary

All of what is described here amounts to an extensive and reassuring set of regulations to keep finance under control. In summary, we have looked at ten major categories of financial regulation, almost all of which are essential:

1. Deposit insurance

2. The segregation of different types of financial institution

3. Leverage controls

4. Lending controls

5. Remuneration controls

6. Liquidity requirements

7. Counter-cyclical regulatory capital requirements

8. Clearing houses for all traded securities and derivatives

9.   Controls on the trading of commodity futures and perhaps other instruments

10.   Possibly a reduction in the size of banks, combined with a streamlined bankruptcy code for banks

All of these would limit the ability of the financial sector to push the inflation of credit bubbles without choking off the supply of credit to productive firms (as is discussed further in Chapter 9). They are thus supportive of both growth and stability.

## The Public Purse

A third tool of economic management is fiscal policy: the spending and taxation activities of national governments[48]. Under normal circumstances, fiscal policy is used to stabilise the economy by planning taxes in relative terms (as a percentage of income), by planning spending in absolute terms (a specific amount of money) with additional contingent liabilities (social security payments), and by setting the combination of the two at such a level that it produces budgetary balance on average but with oscillation from deficit in recessions to surplus in booms*. The deficits that arise in this process are funded by issuing sovereign bonds of various maturities and the surpluses are used to pay these debts off. All of this has the effect of ensuring that the most creditworthy borrower in the system – the government – borrows and spends in a recession when no one else will, and pays its debts down at a time when everyone else is building theirs up. This flattens-out overall borrowing and spending and reduces the amplitude of the credit, asset and economic cycles†– an effect that is known as the 'automatic stabiliser' effect of fiscal policy.

---

* To be precise, deficits and surpluses should be managed so as to cancel each other out only when total debt is expressed as a percentage of nominal GDP. And, because nominal GDP grows, due to both inflation and real growth, this allows governments to be slightly profligate and stimulatory in absolute terms without digging themselves into a fiscal hole or inducing inflation.

† While it is clear that supporting demand in a recession is stabilising, it could be argued that repaying government debt afterwards gives creditors funds to re-lend and could thus push-up asset prices. But the restraining effect on revenues, wages and consumption of the state taking more in taxation than it spends on payments to its staff and purchases from real-economy businesses, restrains business confidence and market activity and thereby swamps this effect.

In terms of debt levels, private debt peaks at the end of the boom and falls through the recession and the early stages of the expansion to follow. Managed properly, government debt peaks just after the end of the recession and then falls through the duration of the expansion to follow. The combination of these two patterns should therefore allow overall debt levels to remain roughly constant as a percentage of GDP.

Policy of this kind also fits neatly with the government's duty to provide unemployment cover and to invest in things like health, education, infrastructure and scientific research – activities that the private sector has no incentive to fund adequately – so as to provide social protection, support economic growth and counterbalance the excessive, unnecessary and destructive inequality that can build up in an overly-free market. Such social investment and social insurance typically requires spending and taxation of 40-50% of GDP[49]; a level that is also sufficient to act as a stabilising anchor on the economy, and which has little or no detrimental effect on overall productivity.

## Private sector crowded out?

Government taxation and spending do obviously 'crowd out' a roughly equal amount of private sector consumption and investment but, because the composition of private sector investment would be more short-run in orientation, it is actually better for long-run growth that some of the spending is done by government. Likewise, even if 40% or more of all income is taken as taxation, the profit motive remains more than strong enough that little or no weakening of the incentive to work tends to follow. Indeed, empirical evidence shows that government spending at this level has no adverse effect on growth (see Chapter 10 for further discussion) and that such spending, if targeted appropriately, can boost trend rates of GDP growth*.

---

* Classical economists like to speak of the 'deadweight effect' of taxation – the idea that, because of disincentive effects, overall output will still be lower even if the proceeds of tax are reinvested. This is a result of simplistic extrapolation from micro- to macro- economics (i.e. assuming that the disincentive effects of higher taxes targeted at a single market also apply to the economy overall) and it completely ignores the very high long-term rates of return to society that can be achieved through public investment.

## Responding to extreme downturns

In addition to automatic fiscal policy of the kind described here, when there are signs that an extreme downturn is beginning, the government may also engage in discretionary fiscal policy; taking on extra spending above that which was planned anyway, funding this through borrowing and thereby keeping up the level of aggregate demand. In effect, deflationary conditions are avoided by borrowing money from those who are unwilling to spend, and spending it for them (something that is possible because of the creditworthiness of the government). Of course, when sufficiently strong growth resumes, taxes will have to be temporarily raised, or spending cut compared to pre-recession levels, in order to pay down the debt. However, the contractionary effects of this can be partially offset in advance by ensuring that the majority of deficit spending during the downturn is on growth-promoting investment in infrastructure, skills and scientific research.

## Government debt

In general, government debt levels should be kept at an average of about 25-30% of GDP, with variations of 10-15% on either side of this over a normal economic cycle. This level is sufficient to maintain an active sovereign bond market (which is more convenient than other asset classes for the execution of monetary policy, and also facilitates future borrowing) but still leaves room for expansion if faced with an emergency situation. And, if a depression does threaten, the debt levels of developed-country governments should be expanded to a peak of 100% of GDP, or more. This level is sufficient to give an extensive boost to the economy, but a developed-country government can still sustain it without risking sovereign default and the financial chaos that this inevitably entails.

This latter is true because such countries have the tax base to absorb interest payments on the debt and because sovereign bond investors, who provide the borrowings, recognise the structural soundness of such countries. It is also proven by the successful management of high debt by countries such as the US and UK in the late 1940s, and by Japan in recent decades. This does not mean that a country will definitely avoid a calamitous positive feedback effect where, if bonds are short-maturity, the fear of investors pushes up the interest burden of the sovereign as bonds are rolled-over, this causes more fear, and this pushes the interest burden up further. But the evidence of history suggests that this usually does not happen, especially when bonds are longer-maturity, or when many countries are in distress at the same time – meaning that bond investors have nowhere else to go. And the risk is definitely less than allowing a depression to develop unopposed.

Like taxation, government borrowing obviously does take up lending capacity that could otherwise be used by the private sector, and can thereby also crowd-out a certain amount of private investment. The primary mechanism through which this takes place is that heavy government borrowing can push up market interest rates beyond what many private borrowers are willing or able to pay. However, in the kind of recessionary conditions where the state is increasing its debt levels, it is unlikely that the private sector has the confidence to take up any of the borrowing capacity that ends up being used by the government. Indeed, even well after a crisis, non-state actors are likely to be focused on paying-down debt. Beyond this, in a recession, monetary policy is typically also being loosened and this, combined with the unwillingness of the private sector to borrow, ensures that surges in public debt under such circumstances usually have much less of an effect on market interest rates than might be expected*.

## Saving the Banks

Beyond general economic stimulus, a further aspect of discretionary fiscal policy that may be necessary under sufficiently adverse circumstances is financial sector intervention, where governments faced with a large-scale banking crisis guarantee the funds of all depositors† and rescue distressed financial institutions that are deemed 'too big to fail' (as are even modest-sized banks). These policies are only relevant when bank runs and an extreme downturn threaten but, in this scenario, they are vital to prevent a self-reinforcing collapse from taking place[50]. Recapitalising banks using

---

* Monetary policy specifically targets short-term interest rates but the effect of a monetary expansion is felt at all maturities along the yield curve because lower short-term interest rates inevitably drive some investors into longer-maturity bonds.

† This is in addition to deposit insurance schemes that commercial banks are required to pay into throughout the economic cycle, but which cannot cope with a generalised bank run.

government funds staves off the prospect of a wave of withdrawals by depositors and money-market investors, and enables society to avoid the situation where banks cut off lending entirely.

The effect of such rescue measures on the willingness of bond investors to fund the government can be reduced by structuring the rescue packages as loans that will eventually be repaid, or simply by taking banks into temporary public ownership. Either of these measures gives the government a claim over the future revenue of the bank and therefore mitigates the effect of a rescue on the forward-looking fiscal position of the state*. Nevertheless, the maximum debt capacity of a government that has engaged in extensive bank rescues may be reduced by perhaps 10-30% of GDP.

The need to rescue specific banks in order to protect the wider economy raises the question of whether or not governments should also directly support other systemically important organisations, such as large manufacturing firms, if they are on the verge of failure in the midst of an economic crisis. The answer to this must be that, if the failure of such an organisation would genuinely have as much impact as that of a major bank, then it must be rescued. However, in a market economy, directly supporting a large number of such firms might be beyond the financial and administrative capabilities of any government. Further, it may just mean propping-up organisations that were already out-of-favour with the consumer. It should, in any case, rarely be necessary, even in a serious economic crisis.

The reason for this latter point is that banks, because they represent the financial plumbing of the economy, are financially interconnected with other organisations to an extent that is far greater than for any other firm. Thus, other firms can rarely be of the same systemic importance as banks. And, because of the fractional reserve nature of banking, banks are also much more fragile and prone to panic-driven collapse than other kinds of organisation. As a consequence, it is usually best if governments faced with an economic crisis rescue individual workers through unemployment insurance, and rescue the wider economy through fiscal and monetary stimulus and bank rescues,

---

* Indeed, much of the money spent can legitimately be excluded from the net debt position of the state because it will be repaid.

but let individual industrial and retail firms go under if they are facing difficulties.

## Prevention is Better Than Cure

Although governments faced with extreme downturns should intervene heavily, it is better to avoid such situations in the first place. The key message of this chapter is that a set of economic policies involving discretionary monetary policy, sensible regulation of the financial sector, and automatic fiscal policy designed to flatten-out the fluctuations of the economic cycle, has the potential to exert a strong stabilising effect on the economy and to reduce the risk of a severe contraction to low levels unless it is induced by an exogenous shock. That this is the case is demonstrated by the stability experienced by the world as a whole in the 1950s and 1960s when policies similar to these were in force (Figure 15), and by the comparatively greater financial stability demonstrated by countries such as Canada, Australia and Brazil, which have maintained some of these policies in more recent times.

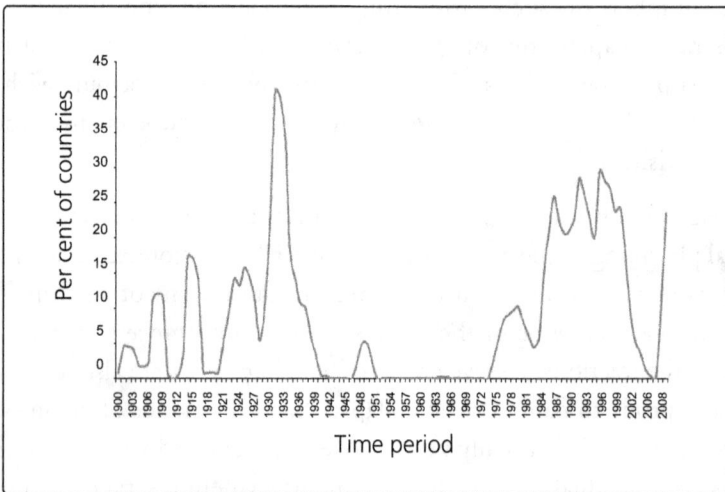

**Figure 15 – Banking crises over the past century.** The data shows the proportion of countries experiencing a banking crisis in each year from 1900 to 2009, weighted by proportion of world income. Clearly, when it came to financial stability, something was very right in the years 1951-1973. Most likely, this was the combination of tight financial regulation together with fiscal and monetary policies that, by stabilising the economy overall, indirectly stabilised the financial sector. [Reproduced with permission from Reinhart, Carmen M. and Kenneth S. Rogoff (2009) *This Time is Different: Eight Centuries of Financial Folly*, (Princeton University Press).]

However, there are individuals – usually those of a radical socialist inclination – who would expect too much from such measures, and would think that it is possible for the state to ensure strong growth with full employment at all times. It is therefore very important to be fully cognisant of the limitations of macroeconomic management. These limitations are the subject of the next chapter.

# 7. The Limitations of Counter-Cyclical Policy

**N**o tool or methodology is perfect. This fact is widely understood in most walks of life but it seems to be easily forgotten when it comes to economic policy, where the issues are often intangible and where the tendency for ideological excess is common. It is therefore essential that we review the major limitations that affect the counter-cyclical policies advocated in the preceding chapter. And, as with the policies themselves and the underlying issues they address, these limitations can often best be understood in terms of the concept of feedback and the complications it can entail.

## Delayed Effects

The single greatest weakness of both monetary policy and of discretionary fiscal policy is that they each entail time lags before policy decisions take effect. In the case of monetary policy, central bankers must decide that action is needed and new funds must be injected into the system, deposited with commercial banks, loaned out and used to fund ventures in the real physical economy before they take effect. Likewise, in the case of discretionary fiscal policy, politicians must decide that action is needed and spending must be planned and implemented before it takes effect. From the moment that the need for action is recognised, monetary policy generally takes effect with a time lag of 6-12 months and discretionary fiscal policy with a longer delay[51].

Nevertheless, with careful monitoring of the economy, it is possible to make fairly reliable directional forecasts for the next six months and approximate forecasts for the next 18 months; a state of affairs that enables central bankers to see fluctuations coming, and to respond to them in advance through monetary policy. Likewise, automatic fiscal policy, because it is automatic, intrinsically overcomes time-lag problems. Discretionary fiscal policy, however, is more problematic. Because it involves longer time delays and because, in a normal business cycle, the economy is likely to be recovering 18-24 months after it becomes clear that a recession is imminent, discretionary fiscal policy runs the risk that the effects of increased government spending will be felt when the economy is actually in the early stages of an expansion, and that it will therefore increase the amplitude of the economic cycle*. As a consequence, fiscal policy should normally be operated in automatic mode only (albeit with strong stabilisers built-in) and discretionary fiscal policy should be attempted only when it is clear that the economy is entering a slump sufficiently deep that there is little chance that it will be recovering on its own by the time policy decisions take effect.

Another way in which the problem of time lags inherent in counter-cyclical policy can be mitigated is policy gradualism. This is of little use in relation to fiscal policy – where a series of frequent small changes in unpredictable directions would cast government programmes into chaos. But it is ideal for monetary policy, where the interest-rate target can be changed by increments of a quarter of a per cent at monthly intervals, as appropriate. This approach ensures that policy is moved in the appropriate direction, as suggested by measurements of the economy, that it can be reversed if these measurements prove to be misleading and that there are no sudden movements that cause central bank action to go too far and to actually be destabilising. It is thus only if an extreme upheaval such as deflation or severe inflation is threatening that more sudden movements are called for.

## Liquidity Traps

In addition to the time delays that affect monetary policy, this tool of economic management has the further drawback that it may be of limited effectiveness in the face of a very serious downturn. Under these circumstances, it is likely that debt levels are very high, that confidence is very low, that banks are keen to accumulate capital instead of lending and that they will only lend at higher rates of interest than normal (i.e. the gap between prime lending rates and the interbank rate targeted by the central bank will be wider than normal). This situation is known as a *liquidity trap* and it causes much of the new funds that are issued as part of a monetary expansion to languish in the banking system instead of increasing demand in the economy – an effect that reduces the potency of monetary policy in stimulating the economy[52].

---

* This makes nonsense of the claim once made by over-enthusiastic Keynesians that they could "fine-tune" the economy through fiscal measures.

One possible response in a situation such as this is for the central bank to sidestep the banking system altogether and to lend newly-created funds directly to non-financial organisations. The Federal Reserve in the United States recently did this on a large scale, by purchasing commercial paper – short-term bonds issued by corporations – and other measures. These funds, when they are inevitably deposited with commercial banks, do not go through nearly as much of a multiplier effect as they normally would, and much larger injections are therefore needed to have the same effect on the economy. But, provided this is understood, and provided that the extra liquidity is gradually withdrawn as soon as the conventional banking sector begins to recover, this represents an attractive way to circumvent the problem of the liquidity trap. In a situation such as this, Milton Friedman described the correct policy as being akin to "dropping money from helicopters" and in this, as in some of his other technical work, the arch-conservative was right.

A slightly different policy in the face of a liquidity trap would be to alter the target that the open-market operations of the central bank seek to control. Targeting prime lending rates directly, for example, would in principle weaken the liquidity-trap effect that involves a wide gap opening up between interbank rates and prime rates. As in conventional monetary policy, this would still entail injecting liquidity into the banking system, as opposed to into non-financial organisations. However, it would involve doing so with enough aggression to ensure that the funding available to such non-financial organisations was affected. It would thus be an alternative means to achieve the same objective as having the central bank lend directly to non-financial firms.

A more radical variant of the latter policy would be to switch both the target used in setting monetary policy and the method used to pursue this target. This could involve, for example, directly targeting asset market indices like the FTSE 350 or the S&P 500, while using purchases of share-index futures (instead of government bonds) to achieve this goal (as in the case of commodities, movements in the futures price has a direct effect on demand for the underlying asset). Indices such as these would be a more difficult target to control than interbank rates because of all the additional speculative forces affecting stock markets, and targeting them might involve flooding the economy with liquidity; but, as with lending directly to non-financial firms or targeting prime rates directly, this approach would at least provide some measurable benchmark to guide the activity of 'printing money'. And, by targeting a highly observed benchmark index, it might also have desirable effects on business confidence.

Needless to say, strategies such as these would be very experimental and probably highly dangerous; meaning that they should only be attempted in desperate situations, where the risks of sticking to conventional policies are even greater. They should also be gradually reversed as soon as the conventional banking sector begins to resume its role of supplying credit. And, as we have already noted, in a well-managed economy, it should never be necessary to have to consider such extreme measures in the first place.

## Enforcing the Rules

As with fiscal and monetary policy, the other major tool of economic management, regulation, also faces limitations. The chief weakness of regulation is that it inevitably pits the administrators of the rules and guidelines it entails against financiers who are better funded, more numerous and possibly better educated. The regulators do have the backing of law and of the state's monopoly on coercion, but there will always be a tendency for 'innovative' financiers to find ways to circumvent their oversight.

This tendency can, however, be counteracted in a number of ways: by making the rules governing finance strong enough, by enforcing tough penalties for financial crime, by giving regulators extensive discretionary powers in certain areas (probably the most crucial element here) and by paying regulators more than other civil servants, so that the attractiveness of their job is not entirely out-of-line with that of private-sector finance. These measures will never entirely eliminate the potential for financiers to behave recklessly, and for credit-asset bubbles to inflate. But they are clearly better than the absence of any prudent regulation at all – which is the answer of free-market thinkers to the limitations of regulation.

In addition to this, national governments, or ideally supranational bodies such as the EU, should ensure the independence of financial regulators; giving them a clear and strong mandate to keep finance under control and then stepping back to avoid direct influence over the process, which can be distorted by politics. Governments should also avoid sending messages that their regulator will be in any way 'light touch'. And they should be very clear that any attempt by financiers to influence the approach of the regulator, so as to ensure that it is 'light touch', will be viewed most harshly. In many ways, signalling the resolve of the state to keep finance in check has itself a strong effect on financiers' behaviour.

## Moral Hazard

Alongside the limitations of financial regulation and of general monetary and fiscal policy, there is also a danger inherent in the policy of being ready to rescue banks that get into difficulty: the danger that the expectation of being bailed out if they encounter problems will lead banks to behave recklessly during the boom phase of the economic cycle, and that it will thereby actually contribute to the formation of speculative bubbles. This danger is known by the somewhat puritanical term of *moral hazard*, and it was a major preoccupation of conservatives as the financial system began to quickly unravel in the autumn of 2008, a preoccupation that probably caused the US and UK governments to hesitate in intervening to stabilise key institutions.

Such preoccupations compound the fact that, from a political point of view, rescuing banks that have most likely been the principal agents of economic disruption in the first place can be problematic. It may be true that, as one government official in the United Kingdom recently commented, it is not so much a case of saving the banks, as "saving the economy from the banks". But, in terms of practical action, either objective amounts to much the same thing, and we can therefore face the unpalatable necessity of having to insulate reckless financiers from the full consequences of their actions.

This does not, however, change the fact that the alternative to rescuing the banks is much, much worse and potentially involves a complete failure of the lending and payments systems, as a domino effect of successive bank failures tears the financial system apart and thereby causes widespread economic and social disruption.

As a solution to these problems, simply promising to punish bank bosses who have engaged in speculative excess, while rescuing the organisations they were responsible for, does not necessarily represent a desirable strategy. Such a stance might just lead executives to try and conceal the fact that their organisations are in trouble until it is too late to take effective action, and it might therefore prove to be highly counter-productive. The only way forward may be to severely punish those individuals who have breached actual financial regulation but, aside from removing them from their positions, to allow those who have simply been reckless to get away relatively unscathed. This may be distasteful, but it is clearly a lesser evil than anything which increases the risk of bank failures. And we can hope that the shame of failure will act as some kind of deterrent to those who might otherwise be reckless leaders of finance.

Such things, however, need never be a dilemma in the first place. If banks are regulated carefully enough during the good times, then the chances that they will ever need to be rescued by the state during the bad times can be minimised. It is, for example, very difficult to fund speculative investments from a position where borrower leverage is controlled, where banks are prohibited from certain questionable lending, where regulatory capital requirements are tight, and where other questionable aspects of finance are kept under tight scrutiny. In short, recognising that banks can never quite be trusted to behave 'morally' in the first place, and regulating them accordingly, is the solution to the problem of 'moral hazard'.

## A Policy Philosophy

As a general philosophy, economic management should operate on the principle of *leaning against* undesirable trends and *leaning with* desirable trends. In other words, policy should operate in terms of setting general directions and should usually avoid setting exact targets for what the economy should look like, or for what it should be composed of.

Financial regulation, for example, should be structured so as reduce the tendency for speculative bubbles to form; automatic fiscal policy should be used to keep spending and debt levels roughly constant over the economic cycle; and discretionary monetary policy should be used to counteract consumer and asset price inflation. At the same time, as we shall discuss in Chapter 10, public spending should be organised so as to boost growth, give the disadvantaged a base from which to compete and generally nudge the economy in desirable directions. An example of this latter might include targeted support for nascent technology industries, provided that the acceptability of such support is agreed across countries and does not run the risk of triggering more generalised protectionist measures in response. It might also include measures designed to suppress clearly undesirable industries such as tobacco manufacture.

But, since the state has no way of knowing everything that people need and want, or of micro-managing the entire economy, policies such as these should not extend into any attempt to plan-out the detailed composition of economic output.

Any of the policies recommended in this book might entail intermediate targets – such as a target level of interest rates or specific limits on borrower leverage – but final targets should be avoided as much as possible. This includes avoiding controls on prices, volumes and product characteristics for the great majority of goods and services. Such controls create a powerful incentive for evasion and, if they are implemented on a wide scale, they quickly become impossible to enforce effectively. This leads to wasted effort on the part of government and undermines respect for the rule of law. And, in any case, since it is usually impossible to know the appropriate way in which such controls should be set – that is, to know what prices, volumes or characteristics should be required – all that such controls usually achieve is to distort economic activity for little real gain.

## Some exceptions

However, as is usual in economic policy, there are some important exceptions to the principle of avoiding prescriptive final targets. Most basically, since it is managed by the government, the public sector must have a greater number of centrally-defined targets than the rest of the economy, although, even here, managers on the ground should be given as much discretion as possible.

Likewise, stringent environmental policies are needed to keep pollution under control and these must often take the form of defined specifications that must be met by different pieces of machinery. An alternative to such controls may be found in pollution taxes, or in markets where declining amounts of pollution permits can be traded. But, in most cases, prescriptive targets are enforceable in this area and can produce more reliable results than other mechanisms*[53].

In addition to this, it is clear that measures to protect workers and consumers must generally take the form of prescribed standards in relation to things such as product quality, work conditions and the length of the working week. Such measures have been an increasing part of every progressive society for more than a hundred years, with only the most aggressive free-market conservatives now doubting their necessity. And, finally, there is empirical evidence to suggest that minimum wage laws can be enforceable and that, in some cases at least, they can lead to economic and social improvement[54].

However, aside from these particular cases, prescriptive targets for the prices, volumes and product characteristics of goods and services should be avoided, for all of the reasons that have already been specified. Government should seek to manage the overall direction and dynamics of the economy, but, outside of the public sector, should not seek to control the system on a micro level or to manage more than a few key details of its composition.

## A Stabilisation Strategy

Within the remit of the above philosophy, there is an obvious way to integrate the stabilisation policies discussed in this and the previous chapter, at least for more-developed countries. Over the course of a normal business cycle, regulation, automatic fiscal policy and discretionary monetary policy (the latter accompanied by clear guidelines to allow market participants some idea of what to expect) should be used to maintain stability. And, in the face of a severe downturn, monetary and fiscal policy that is discretionary in both cases should be used to deliver a strong stimulus alongside rescue measures designed to support weakened banks. An aggressive combination of expansionary monetary and fiscal policy is possible under these circumstances, because there is no chance that the economy will recover without policy action – meaning that there is no risk of boosting the economy

---

* A major instance where there is a case for both direct final targets and either a pollution tax or a system of tradable permits is that of the carbon dioxide emissions responsible for global warming. Since fossil fuels are currently so fundamental to our economy, reducing emissions entirely through technical standards might have massive distortionary effects and should therefore only be part of our response, alongside carbon taxes or tradable carbon permits and public investment in new energy technologies.

in an upturn – and is necessary because the effectiveness of monetary policy alone is limited under such extreme circumstances.

Despite the limitations on its effectiveness when a severe downturn is threatening, a substantial monetary boost (probably involving at least some unconventional measures) should still be attempted alongside any discretionary fiscal stimulus that is undertaken. Any effect it produces will be welcome, the two processes may boost each other's effectiveness and there is little risk of triggering runaway inflation in a situation where the propensity to spend is at a deep low.

In addition, when recovery does take place, some of the additional funds in the system can be withdrawn and those that remain may cause a moderate one-off increase in average price levels that actually helps the economy by eroding some of the real value of the accumulated debt stock, making its repayment easier and enabling consumption demand to pick-up faster. Such an increase in price levels would also erode the real value of wages and would therefore provide an impetus for increasing recruitment and reducing unemployment. Indeed, even as a recovery gathers pace, the adverse outcome obsessed upon by conservatives, whereby a one-off increase in price levels leads to runaway inflation, can still be avoided provided that the central bank makes clear that it would fight any such development by further tightening policy.

On the fiscal side, it is also clear that, if a depression threatens, strong stimulus is the best option for maximising GDP and overall well-being going forward. With fiscal stimulus, a deep slump with a great deal of lost GDP and soaring unemployment is avoided. The costs of inequality arising from unemployment are mitigated. The risk of disruptive political unrest is reduced. Structural damage that would impede growth for years is avoided. Some of the stimulus can be spent in infrastructure so as to give growth a boost. Government debt relative to GDP may actually turn out lower than without stimulus. And there will be little crowding-out of private borrowing because, through the crisis and after, the private sector will be deleveraging. All of these effects far outweigh the drag that will arise from paying-down high levels of public debt and mean that the trajectory of output and welfare will be far, far better than would be the case without stimulus.

As alternatives to the policy of using both fiscal and monetary tools to deliver a strong stimulus in the face of a deep recession, other combinations of the two are possible, but are less advisable. One possibility is seigniorage; having the central bank issue new currency to the government that is then spent as part of a fiscal stimulus. Or, on the opposite extreme, the central bank may practise sterilisation; reducing the money supply to offset the perceived inflationary effects of deficit spending.

The former may be justified to give an especially strong stimulus from a position of sufficiently extreme economic weakness (at least as bad as in United States in 1933) but, if governments do resort to this, they should make very clear that it will not become an ongoing policy; otherwise people might lose confidence in the value of money and an inflationary spiral might set in despite the weakened state of the economy*. The latter option, conversely, just makes fiscal stimulus less effective, casts aside the potential benefits of a one-off increase in price levels as the economy recovers and makes the future debt repayments of the government more burdensome. It should never be employed.

The limitations on counter-cyclical and other economic policy mentioned in this chapter have, whether they have been understood or not, applied throughout all of the time since modern economic institutions were established. However, in an age of economic globalisation – which does have the potential to bring huge benefits in terms of increased trade flows, cross-border investment and increased global output – further considerations for effective economic policy have arisen. These are the subject of Chapter 8.

---

* This is a real possibility since people can be more suspicious of policies that involve giving 'free money' to the government than of other unconventional monetary policies giving such money to the private sector. This is especially true in economically conservative cultures, such as that of the United States.

# 8. Counter-Cyclical Policy in a Globalised World

The phenomenon of globalisation is perhaps one of the most controversial, and misunderstood, developments of recent times. At its most basic level, globalisation is nothing more than an increased interconnectedness, convergence and homogenisation of the world in terms of science, technology, economics, politics and culture, which is the inevitable result of developments in transport and communications. This process entails greater interdependence and mutual understanding, with the enormous benefit that this creates a huge disincentive to war, and it lifts the maximum economic output that can be achieved with a given level of technology by enabling a greater division of labour across the globe (a topic we will cover in more detail when we discuss the dangers of trade protectionism in Chapter 9).

However, globalisation should not be thought of as being purely some blind force of nature, beyond human control. Instead, the rate at which it can progress, and the exact form it takes, is determined by the extent to which governments are willing to remove barriers to international movement, communication and commerce, and by the structures they are willing to put in place in order to facilitate these things. As just one simple example of this, globalisation proceeds a lot faster, and a lot more smoothly, if reliable and transparent cross-border payments systems are in place.

At the same time as not being purely an inexorable force of nature, neither is globalisation a pure and undiluted blessing. As well as huge benefits, it also brings inevitable problems, such as the greater rate at which new infectious diseases can spread and the fragility inherent in very long supply chains that have been whittled down to a bare minimum capacity by market forces. Globalisation also makes it more difficult for societies, through their elected representatives, to manage their economies in desirable ways. This is a problem that is, perhaps unsurprisingly, most severe for poorer countries that carry less weight in the financial world[55].

# The Agonies of the Poor

Poorer countries can face painful dilemmas when managing their economies in the face of a crisis[56]. If they lower interest rates, this makes bonds and deposits in their jurisdiction even less attractive to foreign investors and adds to the currency depreciation that threatens to trigger outright capital flight and sovereign default. As we have already seen, this is a scenario that does not usually affect more-developed countries in a similar position. Advanced countries are generally less dependent on net external investment, are perceived as being stronger, borrowers within them can borrow in their own currency and there is, in any case, no rank of more attractive countries for investors to flee to. In this case, a currency fall usually just leads to a restoration of competitiveness and therefore promotes subsequent economic growth. But, for less-developed countries, any movement in this direction can be the harbinger of disaster.

If an emerging market is facing a mild recession and more-developed countries are also cutting interest rates, then the less-developed country in question may also have some scope to cut them so long as the comparative level of attractiveness to investors remains the same. However, if an emerging market is facing a serious crisis, it may have no option but to increase rates sharply. This will clearly cause a severe reduction in domestic demand but this may be a lesser evil than the consequences that would follow from a capital flight scenario. In other words, while more-developed countries in a recession should use monetary policy to support domestic demand and should let their currency fall, less-developed countries may have no choice but to do the opposite and support their currency while letting domestic demand fall.

Less-developed countries also face difficulties in using fiscal policy to stabilise their economies. They can practise automatic fiscal policy in a similar way to more-developed countries, but they may have to limit even cyclical deficits – by cutting some spending or raising taxes in a recession – if there is a danger that the existence of such deficits might act as a panic signal to investors. And, even if developing countries can safely run cyclical deficits in a recession, their scope for resorting to discretionary fiscal policy may be very limited. This is because their cost of borrowing tends to rise rapidly as bond investors become wary of them under conditions of economic distress – especially if they are competing with more creditworthy governments for credit – and also because investor panic can set in at a much lower ratio of public debt to GDP than would be the case for more-developed countries.

All of these limitations, however, seem to be more stringent at some times than at others. For example, recent events have shown that even a severe global recession may not automatically lead to external crises in less-developed countries. If the domestic finances of such countries were basically sound to begin with; if the downturn has originated in more-developed countries and if there is not an idea that emerging-market economies will be affected more than others – all of which have been the case in 2007-2009 – then there may not be an investor flight from the periphery of the global economy. The governments of less-developed countries may therefore have more scope to support their domestic economies. However, there are also cases – such as in the emerging market crises of 1997-2002 – where investors do take flight from developing countries and where the room to manoeuvre of those governments affected is therefore severely limited.

Beyond this variation, even in a situation where foreign investor panic does threaten, there is also a possibility that taking such punitive measures as tightening monetary and fiscal policy in the face of a recession might themselves trigger financial panic and withdrawal from a less-developed country – to just the same extent as would loosening them. If this is indeed the case, then the country in question may be as well to loosen monetary and fiscal policy, or at least to leave them constant, in order to support domestic demand and thereby mitigate some of the effects of the crisis. However, it is usually impossible to know in advance what investor sentiment will be, and these alternative possible outcomes just serve to demonstrate that there may be no good monetary and fiscal policy responses available to less-developed countries faced with an economic crisis in a globalised world.

## Possible answers

A possible way to avoid the situation in which less-developed countries face such agonising choices is for more-developed countries to manage their own economies better. If, for example, the leverage of hedge funds based in London and New York was regulated, there would be less scope for them to contribute to currency crises in more backward places.

Another possibility is for less-developed countries to maintain controls on the movement of capital across their borders. A quite aggressive way of doing so is for developing countries to reject foreign borrowing and inward investment in financial markets altogether, instead relying exclusively on foreign direct investment (FDI) in physical assets that cannot be quickly withdrawn. FDI enables structurally weaker countries to benefit from the growth-promoting effects of foreign investment without facing the risk of sudden capital flight and economic disintegration, and an FDI-only policy is therefore justified in certain cases.

However, caution should be taken with such policies. For starters, while it might seem attractive to discriminate harshly against short-run speculative capital flows while permitting long-run commitments, having continuous access to a pool of capital, even if it is continually rolled-over between different investors on a short-run basis, can be beneficial. At the same time, in the process of actually transferring funds, it can be difficult to distinguish between trade flows and short-run capital flows and the consequence of introducing capital controls can either be that trade is hurt, or that some investors disguise short-run capital flows as trade flows. As regards the latter, if capital controls are too tight in a jurisdiction that is legally and institutionally weak, they may simply lead to widespread corruption amongst those officials charged with administering them.

Meanwhile, a policy of having milder controls in normal times and tightening them in the face of a crisis can be just as dangerous. While such tightening might have the beneficial effect of earning the country in question time to restore confidence in its financial position, giving any hint that the government is even considering such a move could just as easily have the effect of feeding the crisis by convincing investors that they have to get out quickly before the tightening takes place.

One way for poorer countries to implement sensible capital controls is to impose variable time delays on withdrawals of different sizes, with the aim both of discouraging speculative inflows and of damping the momentum of outflows, and then making it very clear – possibly by enacting self-restrictive legislation – that such controls will not be tightened further in the face of a crisis. If such a policy were combined with global controls on the leverage of hedge funds and other speculative investors, then it should be possible for less-developed countries to benefit from international financial flows while mitigating the risk of capital flight and consequent social disaster.

Another way that such controls might be instituted is by means of the so-called 'Tobin tax', named for the Nobel Laureate economist James Tobin who proposed it in the 1970s. This would involve imposing a very small tax on cross-border or currency exchange transactions, perhaps at a rate as low as 0.1%, so as to discourage very short-term capital flows without adversely affecting trade or longer-term capital flows (both of which generally yield returns to direct participants far in excess of the 0.1% range). As with a policy of variable time delays, this would be unlikely to entirely eliminate the dynamic of speculative inflows followed by outflows (which can play out over years and generate large returns for some short-term participants along the way, weakening the effect of controls) but it should at least mitigate it, by filtering out the most short-term participants, without harming investment or trade.

Given the existence of the time-delay and Tobin tax alternatives, an aggressive policy of restricting inward investment to FDI should be pursued only if the hazards of speculative in- and out-flows are thought to be especially great, and if the legal framework is thought to be strong enough to make it work without inducing corruption.

As a less advisable alternative to all these policies, in order to reduce the potential for foreign investment to stimulate asset-price bubbles in the domestic economy, the central banks of less-developed countries have sometimes also resorted to the kind of sterilisation policies mentioned in Chapter 7, albeit for a different purpose: to reduce the domestic money supply so as to offset the extra demand driven by a foreign-currency inflow. However, in the absence of stringent controls on cross-border capital flows, this tends to be self-defeating as it entails a rise in domestic interest rates that simply attracts further foreign investors.

A final line of defence for low- and middle-income countries is for international bodies such as the International Monetary Fund (IMF) or European Union to grant them loans that are lower-cost, compared to the market, in times of crisis. This allows them to avoid sovereign default and to engage in fiscal stimulus, while also restoring investor confidence and reducing the risk of capital flight.

In years past, the IMF mandated that less-developed countries receiving its help increase their interest rates, and it also forbade that its loans be used for fiscal stimulus over and above essential core expenditures. In addition to these measures, the IMF often forbade that capital flows be restricted in any way, during the crisis or afterwards, and it even imposed structural 'reforms' that entailed deep cuts to taxation and government spending in the long run, reducing the automatic stabiliser effects of fiscal policy on the economy. Some elements of this policy package – such as increased interest rates – may, unfortunately, have been necessary in certain cases, but the package as a whole was senseless and based on nothing more than free-market ideology. This approach has been moderated to a great extent in more recent years, but the change needs to be formalised if the IMF is to be a more effective backstop for less-developed countries facing difficult circumstances.

## Problems of Rich and Poor

Even for comparatively advanced countries, economic globalisation can make management of the economy more challenging[57]. In one possible scenario, new currency issued and money spent through fiscal stimulus can both leak out of the country. Alternatively, flight of investors to a given jurisdiction that, in the midst of a global recession, is seen as the least dangerous place to put their wealth*, can push up the currency valuation of that jurisdiction – thereby reducing its exports and making it harder to recover from a downturn.

At the same time, for all major developed and emerging economies, employing aggressively expansionist monetary policy in the face of a crisis can weaken the currency to the point where it is seen abroad as an anti-competitive measure designed to give exporters an unfair advantage. This runs the risk that misguided politicians in other countries will use it as an excuse to respond with non-monetary trade barriers, that protectionism will rise, and that international trade will fall. In the extreme case, this might not only reverse the gains from globalisation but might cause even greater damage, at least for a transient period, by disrupting business structures that have become dependent on international exchange.

---

* Switzerland, with its bank-friendly laws, is an obvious example.

As a final problem, maintaining stringent regulation in some jurisdictions can simply have the effect of driving some mobile employment away, and of driving financial services firms to other locations from which they can still destabilise the world economy with their pro-cyclical activities. In particular, it might be attractive for some emerging-market jurisdictions to defect from international norms of regulation by setting themselves up as low-tax, light-regulation havens designed to attract hedge funds and other speculative investors.

## The need for cooperation

In principle at least, the solution to all these problems is simple. The governments of major economies should coordinate their monetary, fiscal and regulatory policies in order to manage the economy on a planet-wide basis. If they all followed well-aligned fiscal and monetary policies, then the effects of cross-border leakage of stimulus packages and of unintended trade disruption should be minimised. And, if regulatory standards were aligned, then there would be no substantial havens for financial services firms to flock to in order to avoid oversight. A handful of small jurisdictions opting-out from such arrangements should, if they lacked large indigenous banks to provide leverage, or if they were unattractive homes for traders, not be a serious problem. And if one of these locations did grow economically big enough to become a problem, it could be pressured to conform.

In terms of actually achieving coordination such as this, on the monetary and fiscal side, things are actually quite easy. Since a significant downturn creates a powerful incentive to support aggregate demand and since, in a globalised economy, a significant downturn is likely to affect many countries at the same time, all countries should tend to move together. In terms of regulation, however, things are more difficult; there is a clear incentive for individual countries to defect from any international accord by having lighter regulation and thereby benefiting from the revenues they can skim-off by hosting financial services firms. But, here too, there are two significant forces pushing countries towards international coordination: the painful effects to all of the crashes that result from too much financial freedom; and the fear that, if finance is not controlled internationally, trade partners will resort to protectionism in order to insulate themselves from upheavals in the global economy. Thus, some international standards of regulation should be achievable*.

In addition to the other problems mentioned in this section, it has also been argued that, if several countries are simultaneously issuing bonds to finance stimulus packages, they may end up competing with one another, thereby driving-up their collective borrowing costs. This might be true if the bond issuances in question took place on the exact same day but, since there is great appetite for the bonds of creditworthy sovereigns in a downturn, and since capital markets are deeper today than they have ever been, developed-country governments should still be able to borrow up to their debt capacity, and at a reasonable cost, during a severe downturn.

## Currency Exchange: Help and Hindrance

Currency exchange obviously plays a central role in international economic events; both in the normal functioning of the global economy, and in the serious disruptions that can sometimes occur instead. Indeed, such exchange is by far the most complex and intellectually challenging aspect of a country's international economic relations. Thus, in order to better understand these relations, we must look at the forces that determine exchange rates between different currencies, and at how these forces relate the question of how globalisation can complicate economic outcomes[58].

### The law of one price

The price of one currency in terms of another is influenced by supply and demand, in the same way as any other price. If people start to demand more

---

* Indeed, some kinds of international regulation are already in place, such as the Basel I and Basel II accords in banking that were agreed in 1988 and 2004, respectively. The latter, which became law in many countries from 2007 – too late to have any effect in preventing the current crisis – imposes regulatory capital requirements; together with supervisory review processes and market disclosure arrangements to support these requirements.

of a given currency compared to other currencies, its relative price will rise and, if they start to demand less, its price will fall. Similarly, if the supply of a currency reaching the market rises, its relative price should fall and, if the supply falls, its price should rise. These phenomena give us an insight into the situations where exchange rates should move, and the situations where they should not. For example, if nominal price levels in a country rise (as a result of an increase in the money supply or in the velocity of circulation) then foreigners will be willing to pay less than before for a unit of the affected currency, because its buying power is now less. At the same time, and for the same reasons, domestic residents will also become willing to accept less for a unit of their currency; giving us a simultaneous change in both supply and demand that together cause the relative value of the currency to fall. Conversely, if price levels in a given currency fall, then the foreign-exchange value of the currency should, all else being equal, tend to rise.

In fact, these forces tend to produce an outcome where, excluding the effects of transaction costs, the real price of a given item should remain roughly the same regardless of what currency it is priced in. For instance, if an item costs £100 and converting pounds to euro yields 140, then that exact same item, once we adjust for transaction and shipping costs, should tend to cost about €140. If it and other items tended to cost more when priced in euro, then people would want to purchase in pounds instead. They would become more interested in holding pounds than in holding euro and the relative value of the euro would fall until real prices equalised. Conversely, if items tended to have a lower real price when priced in euro, people would rush to buy euro so that they could shop in that currency, and the euro would rise until real prices again equalised. And, if general price levels in sterling changed so that the item in question now cost £110 pounds, but general price levels in euro remained constant, the relative value of the pound should fall by a factor of 110/100, shifting the exchange rate from 1.4 to 1.273.

Obviously, because production costs differ, similar but non-identical items can cost different amounts in different places – a Turkish beer in Turkey is likely to have a lower real price than a similar English beer in England. But the exact same item, allowing for transaction and shipping costs, should tend to have a roughly constant real price regardless of what currency it is priced in. In addition, while some specific goods may in the short run go against the general trend for real prices to be equal across currencies, this situation tends to be reversed by changes in the price of the item itself. For example, while real prices for identical items in general may, when we allow for production and shipping costs, tend to be the same in pounds or in euro, a particular category of items – cars say – may on some occasions still turn out to be temporarily cheaper when priced in euro. However, in this situation, more buyers would purchase their cars in euro and fewer would do so in sterling, causing the euro price of a car to rise and the sterling price to fall, until real prices were again roughly equivalent.

This tendency towards real price equalisation tends to produce one real price for any item that is traded in a global market, a phenomenon that is referred to as the *law of one price*. For instance, while the absence of shipping costs may cause a shoe made in China to be significantly cheaper in China than elsewhere, its real price should – unless there are additional costs imposed by country-specific trade barriers – be roughly the same for a wholesale importer in London, Paris or New York. If it were cheaper by a sufficient margin (a margin greater than the difference in shipping costs between different locations) in any one of these places, then businesses would purchase in that location instead of their home country and would simply trans-ship to their home market. This process would push wholesale prices down in that home market (by increasing supply), while pushing them up in the foreign market (by increasing demand), until a rough parity was once again achieved.

## Currency trends

Real price equalisation also produces secular trends in relative currency values. For example, if one country consistently expands its money supply at a faster rate than another, then nominal prices in that country are likely to rise faster and the relative value of its currency is likely to have a tendency to fall. Another way of looking at this is that, if the stock of one currency consistently rises compared to the stock of another, then the relative value of the more rapidly expanding currency must have a tendency to fall.

Alternatively, if the productivity of one country tends to rise faster than that of another – meaning that the volume of output it can produce from a given amount of inputs in the form of labour and other resources tends to rise faster – then its currency will also have a tendency to rise. This happens because, as the cost of each unit of output in terms of physical inputs falls, the producers of this output become able to sell at lower prices while still making a profit. This phenomenon enables them to undercut foreign rivals and therefore, by claiming a much greater share of the global market, to experience an increase in sales volume that, in percentage terms, is greater than the fall in price which caused it. This causes an increase in total revenue that attracts more buyers to the national currency of their home country, and away from the currencies of rivals, causing their currency to rise.

Another phenomenon that can also cause trends in relative currency valuations is changes in the terms of trade faced by a country – changes in the ratio of the real price of its average export to that of its average import. Shifts in this ratio can come about, for example, when demand for a country's exports has shifted on the world market, or when demand for the goods it imports has shifted, either within its own borders or elsewhere. And, like a rise in productivity, an improvement in the terms of trade causes the currency to rise, since foreigners have started demanding more of the domestic currency compared to the amount of foreign currency that domestic residents are demanding. Conversely, a deterioration in the terms of trade causes the currency to fall.

A currency movement arising from improvement or disimprovement in comparative productivity or in the demand for exports leaves domestic residents with either more or less import-purchasing power than before. If they end up with less such purchasing power, they must buy less and overall trade values will be kept in rough balance. Conversely, if they end up with more such power, they will tend to use it and trade will again be kept in rough balance. The following boxes give simplistic examples (with no capital flows and only two goods exchanged between currency zones) that isolate these, sometimes slippery, ideas.

## A (simplified) change in comparative productivity

Imagine that there is one item, A, exported by China to the US, and one item, B, imported by China from the US.

Initially, China exports 100m of A to the US at a price of RMB10, it imports 100m of B from the US at a price of USD10, and RMB1 = USD1.

Exports = RMB1000m = USD1000m

Imports = RMB1000m = USD1000m

Trade is in balance

Then, technical improvement in China makes it possible to sell at a price of RMB8.

This causes China's market share of this good to increase by a greater percentage than the fall in price because it attracts buyers away from other exporters.

If volume exported to the US increases to, say, 150m, then exports to the US must now be RMB1200m.

There is thus a Chinese trade surplus that entails excess demand for RMB over USD.

This excess demand for RMB persists, and the RMB rises, until China is purchasing an extra RMB200m of B from the US.

This will not be achieved through a rise in the dollar that makes B more expensive, simply because the excess demand is for RMB.

It may, however, be achieved through some combination of a fall in the dollar and increased Chinese imports of B.

For example, if the dollar fell to RMB0.75 and China imported 160m of B, then the system would come back into balance (1200m/[0.75 x 10] = 160m).

## A (simplified) change in the terms of trade

Imagine that there is one item, X, exported by the UK to the eurozone, and one item, Y, imported by the UK from the eurozone.

Initially, the UK exports 100m of X to the eurozone at a price of £10, it imports 100m of Y from the eurozone at a price of €10, and £1 = €1.

> Exports  =  £1000m = €1000m
>
> Imports  =  £1000m = €1000m
>
> Trade is in balance

Then, because of an increase in some practical need, demand for X in both the UK and eurozone increases, the price rises to £11, and the volume exported to the eurozone increases to 120m.

Total UK exports to the eurozone rise to £1320m.

There is thus a UK trade surplus that entails excess demand for sterling over euro.

This excess demand for sterling persists, and sterling rises, until the UK is purchasing an extra £320m of Y from the eurozone.

This will not be achieved through a rise in the euro that makes Y more expensive, simply because the excess demand is for sterling.

It may, however, be achieved through some combination of a fall in the euro and increased UK imports of Y.

For example, if the euro fell to £0.8 and the UK imported 165m of Y, then the system would come back into balance (1320m/[0.8 x 10] = 165m).

Note that the terms of trade for the UK initially improved from 1 to 1.1 and then improved further to 1.375.

An important distinction between trends in currency valuations brought about by consistently different monetary policies on the one hand, and by divergence in productivities or in the terms of trade on the other, is that the former represents a trend in nominal exchange rates whereas the latter represent trends in both real and nominal exchange rates. Put simply, changes in nominal exchange rates have not been corrected, when we look at them in our analysis, for relative changes in price levels, whereas real exchange rates have been so corrected. Thus, if changes in nominal exchange rates are not accompanied by changes in real exchange rates, they have no consequences for import-buying power in the long run. For example, if the relative value of a currency has halved but this has happened purely because its supply has doubled and nominal price and wage levels in the home market have therefore also doubled, then the import-buying power of the average income in that currency has remained unchanged.

Changes in real exchange rates, by contrast, do reflect real changes in import-buying power. For example, if the value of a currency halves and this is entirely due to a decline in productivity compared to competitor countries, then the real import-buying power of an average income in that currency has halved, compared to other countries. In effect, countries that become more productive, or which produce something of which the world wants more, are rewarded with a higher real exchange rate and a greater buying power on the international markets.

Taken together, all of the forces outlined here produce a 'correct' long-run valuation for a currency. And negative feedback processes relating to trade keep the currency near this value. If, for example, a currency moves above its correct valuation for whatever reason, the real price of imports will fall and that of exports will rise. This situation causes domestic citizens to purchase more foreign goods and foreign currency, while foreigners purchase less domestic goods and domestic currency – a process that continues until the currency falls back to its trend value.

Equivalently, if we see it as trade that is out of balance, negative feedback effects relating to currency tend to bring it roughly back into line. If, for example, a country starts running a trade deficit – importing a greater value of goods than it exports – it will need to purchase more foreign currency than before; an effect that causes the domestic currency to fall and which therefore reduces imports, increases exports and brings trade back into balance. And, if it is a trade surplus that exists, the domestic currency will tend to rise, imports will also tend to rise, exports will tend to fall and trade will again be brought back into balance.

## Complications

Everything I have said thus far in this section is what happens in the long run, when enough time has passed for all variables in the system to fully adjust to changed circumstances, and in the very long run, when enough time has passed for the position of long-run equilibrium itself to change. In the long run, the system is dominated by negative feedback effects that bring currency valuations back to trend levels, or, equivalently, bring trade back to balance whenever it strays. Conversely, in the very long run, the system is influenced by positive feedback, which occurs when gains in productivity or the terms of trade give a country the wherewithal to import comparatively more capital goods than countries which have been less successful, therefore enabling it to increase its productivity and extend its advantage over these competitors.

This latter process, fortunately, does not give leading countries a tendency to pull ever further ahead of other nations, as there is simply nowhere yet-more-advanced from which they can import capital goods. And, while it may give the most advanced countries an overall advantage in accessing raw materials, accessing new technology probably represents a far more powerful force. Positive feedback in this area therefore probably represents a desirable net benefit to middle-income countries, enabling them to close the gap with advanced countries more rapidly – although it also implies that low-income countries, where such feedback has not yet taken hold to the same extent, get left further and further behind.

Dynamics such as these occurring in the long run and in the very long run are extremely important. But, in spite of this, we should also remember Keynes' dictum that sometimes "the long run is a misleading guide to current affairs"; an idea that is as applicable to the currency markets as any other aspect of the economy. Indeed, bearing this in mind, we should reject the near-exclusive focus of classical economists on long-run equilibrium. Instead, if we truly want to understand the world in which we live, we should place an equal emphasis on understanding the short run. After all, in macroeconomics, the short run can last for a number of years.

## Short-run volatility

In foreign exchange, the short-run is dominated by positive feedback effects that drive currency valuations away from their long-run equilibria. As with other markets, it is only when currencies move far enough from their long-run equilibrium that negative feedback effects take over and cause the system to change direction. But this merely enables positive feedback to take over again (albeit operating in the opposite direction to before) and it therefore causes the currency to power past its trend value once more, until it reaches another extremum on the far side and turns back again. The net effect of all this is to cause currency valuations to yo-yo around their long-run equilibrium positions[59], implying that we should think of these positions as anchor levels that the system never moves too far away from, but which it never quite settles at either (Figure 16). If, for example, one pound is worth 1.4 euro in the long run, the daily exchange rate may fluctuate between 1.2 and 1.6 over time – neither exploding towards infinity nor collapsing towards zero, but never quite flattening-out at 1.4 either.

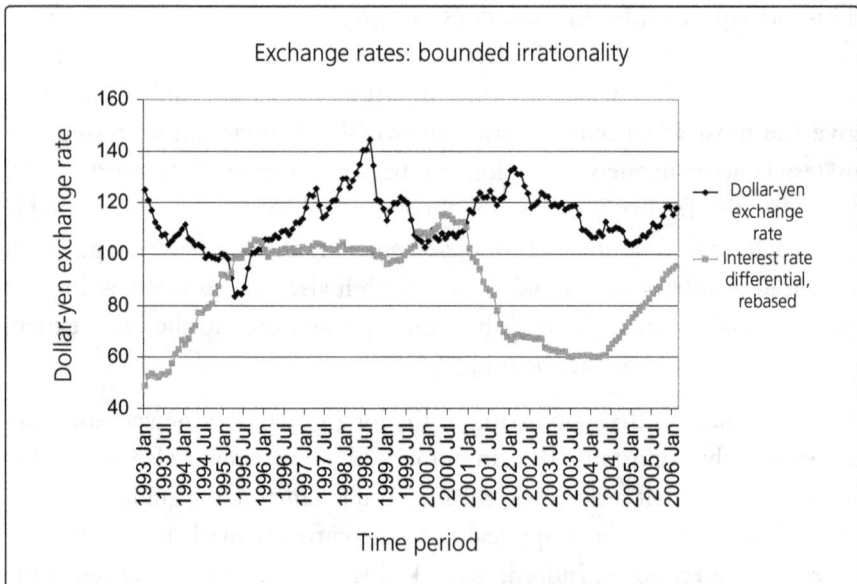

**Figure 16 – The number of Japanese Yen that could be purchased with a US Dollar over a thirteen-year period (black series).** Given that these are both advanced, diversified economies, comparative changes in productivity or the terms of trade cannot explain volatility to this extent. Neither can changing trade imbalances; the United States consistently ran current account deficits over this period while Japan ran surpluses. Likewise, neither can monetary conditions; the grey series shows the monetary attractiveness of the United States compared to Japan at the same time points as the exchange rate data – and it is difficult to see much co-movement in the two series. We can only conclude that foreign-exchange markets are driven largely by internal dynamics of their own. However, given that the maximum exchange rate here is 173% of the minimum, it is clear that the rate does not completely untether from the comparative buying power of the currencies either and that there is something resembling a long-run equilibrium in the system. [Data from the IMF.]

One specific kind of positive feedback that affects currency valuations arises from the familiar activity of trend-following, which traders engage in because performing calculations based on real economic prospects is too difficult and because they anyway expect that everyone else will also just follow the trend. Thus, the sight of a rising currency trend creates yet more attraction for investors; the sight of a falling trend creates yet more revulsion and extrema occur when the currency has moved far enough above or below trend that people (investors and shoppers) realise it is out-of-line with fundamentals and act accordingly. The net effect is to give rise to exchange rates that, as with many other economic variables, plot as undulating waves over time.

Another process contributing to such outcomes relates to the phenomenon of investment flows chasing trade flows. If the productivity of a given country is increasing strongly, or its exports are continually becoming more valued, then foreign investors will want 'in on the action', and will invest heavily in the country in question. This creates a net inflow of financial capital and, as a consequence, creates another upward pressure on the currency. Indeed, since international investment flows nowadays dwarf trade flows, this effect can be quite potent. The overall outcome may be to boost the exchange rate of a country undergoing an export boom above what trade alone would dictate, and to cause it to fall back again when the period of comparatively faster productivity growth (or of improving terms of trade) comes to an end. This process is limited by the fact that the attractiveness of the country in question may be undermined if the currency appreciates to the point where its export advantage is eliminated. But, if investors have sufficiently optimistic impressions of the country's future, even this may not be a rigid limitation.

In a similar fashion, and as we have already mentioned in Chapter 3, a domestic bubble in some asset classes may also extend into a currency bubble as foreign investors rush to participate. However, unlike an export boom, none of the currency appreciation that occurs in this situation is sustainable in the long run. A greater fall will therefore take place when the process comes to an end, possibly leading to a large over-correction that compounds the effects of the bubble bursting domestically.

A further kind of positive feedback affecting currencies, as we have already seen in earlier chapters, relates to panic-driven outflows of capital, triggered by some kind of crisis in the domestic economy. This can lead to a collapse in the currency far below its long-run equilibrium and it can therefore have the most disruptive effects of all on a nation's economy. For poor countries, of all the complications that can arise from economic globalisation, this is undoubtedly the most significant.

A final kind of short-run positive feedback effect that affects currencies relates to the so-called 'carry trade'. In this, investors borrow in a currency where interest rates are low, exchange into other currencies, invest in some asset class that earns a higher return and eventually repay their debts, keeping the difference between the two rates of return and also gaining from probable depreciation of the source currency (if its interest rates were low, chances are it was falling). This manoeuvre, so long as its use is expanding, also drives the low-interest currency down further and therefore makes the trick yet-more-attractive to investors. Thus, a positive feedback loop has been established that drives the currency steadily downwards. However, as soon as the process falters, for whatever reason, the repayments on previous carry may end up being greater than new carry trades and this creates an upward pressure on the source currency. New carry trades thus become less attractive and the currency consequently rises further, until it eventually gets back to its pre-carry level. And, as with the other phenomena listed here, unpredictable volatility in exchange rates is the overall result.

## Temporal disjoin

A consequence of all these short-run fluctuations in exchange rates is that the law of one price mentioned earlier only ever holds approximately. If an item costs £100 in England and costs €140 on the other side of the English Channel, and if the exchange rate is continually fluctuating between 1.2 and 1.6, then the item will sometimes be comparatively over-priced in the eurozone, sometimes comparatively over-priced in the sterling zone and obeying the law of one price only when averaged over time. In essence, long-run negative feedback effects prevent the law from being broken entirely, but short-run positive feedback effects ensure that it is never obeyed precisely either. In this process, movements in the price of individual items (as opposed to movements in exchange rates) are even less effective at ensuring that the law of one price is obeyed. This is because, as is well known, real-economy prices are 'sticky' and slow to change in the short run.

Similarly, disjoins between the long and short run also explain why, when a country is entering recession, a loosening of monetary policy boosts exports and thereby supports the economy. In essence, when monetary policy is loosened, the fall in market interest rates that occurs as a result causes some foreign investors to withdraw immediately, and thereby causes the currency to fall immediately. However, because consumer prices are sticky and because spending slows as the economy goes through a recession, any rise in domestic price levels that also occurs as a result of looser monetary policy does not materialise until the recession is over. A rise in the price of domestic goods, that would counterbalance the export-boosting effect of currency weakening, is therefore delayed. Thus, there is a period of time where domestic exports have a lower real price than those of other countries that are not experiencing similar circumstances, and they therefore gain a larger market abroad.

## Policy challenges

However, despite this beneficial phenomenon, the existence of irrational fluctuations in currency valuations makes the task of setting economic policy even more complicated than it would otherwise have been. And, in a world where it is routine for the sum of exports plus imports (a measure of the 'openness' of an economy) to be equivalent to 50% or more of GDP, the occurrence of such irrational fluctuations can make it particularly hard to identify the correct policies to pursue. In particular, countries face a *trilemma* where they can have two of the three desirables of being able to use monetary policy to manage domestic demand, being able to use it to maintain currency stability, and being generally open to international capital flows; but can never have all three[60].

In essence, if a country opts for using monetary policy to manage domestic demand, and also opts for openness to capital flows (the most common choice in recent decades), it cannot also stabilise short-run currency fluctuations because monetary policy is otherwise engaged, and because it cannot be used to control two targets (interest rates and exchange rates) in what is essentially a single pool of funds (currency inside and outside the country). If it tried to control both targets, perhaps increasing the supply of its currency in existence inside the country, while reducing it outside, then capital would simply flow from one location to the other, and both targets would be missed. Alternatively, if a country opts for openness to capital flows and for stabilising short-run currency fluctuations, then it cannot also use monetary policy to manage domestic demand. And, if it opts for using monetary policy to stabilise domestic demand while also avoiding short-run currency fluctuations, then it must place severe limitations on capital flows (essentially limiting itself to FDI only).

It was thought by Keynesians in the 1950s and 1960s that using discretionary fiscal policy to manage domestic demand, if combined with moderate capital controls and use of monetary policy to control the exchange rate, represented a way out of the trilemma described here. But this ignored the fact that discretionary fiscal policy simply lacks the agility to modulate demand outside of a serious economic downturn.

On a more positive note, however, open trade is broadly compatible with any of the three options outlined here. (Although there might, as we have seen, be some complications arising from the fact that funds transfers for trade and for short-run investment can look similar.) In essence, changes in trading performance (comparative productivity and the terms of trade) are not a source of irrational currency fluctuations in the same way as changes in investment flows, since these changes are generally more gradual and thus relate to long-run currency valuations.

## Some solutions

For more-developed countries, as we have seen, the dangers of irrational currency fluctuations are not usually too serious, and falls in the currency following a dip in business prospects and a cut in interest rates are usually beneficial because they support aggregate demand. At the same time, the ability to use monetary policy to manage the domestic economy brings great benefits, while international capital flows can probably still bring some productivity gains to places that are already economically advanced. And, beyond this, as we shall see in Chapter 9, the system of *fixed but adjustable pegs* that is the best option for resisting short-run but not long-run trends in exchange rates features devaluations that, if combined with capital openness, can become progressively more dangerous as economies develop and capital markets enlarge. Thus, for such countries, it seems best to sacrifice short-run currency stability and to opt for use of monetary policy to control domestic demand, along with being generally open to international capital flows.

However, making this choice does not mean that the economy must be entirely without capital controls. Indeed, establishing some mild controls of this nature – such as the time delays or Tobin taxes mentioned earlier in this chapter – would probably be beneficial. These would add to the reduction in speculative cross-border flows that would result from financial regulation bringing finance to heel more generally. Such measures would not eliminate short-run fluctuations in the currency entirely but they should provide a means to moderate such fluctuations without significantly affecting beneficial cross-border investment. A Tobin tax could also, as some have suggested, provide a fund that could be used to finance bank rescues or economic development in less-advanced countries.

For less-developed countries, as usual, the picture is more complex. Openness to foreign capital brings much greater benefits to these locations than it does to rich countries, because they need investment to access foreign technologies; but it also brings a much greater risk of capital flight and consequent economic collapse. And, while stabilisation of domestic demand is likely to still bring more benefits than stabilisation of the currency under most circumstances, under circumstances where an external crisis is threatening, the opposite may well be true.

As a consequence, less-developed countries should probably pursue much the same policy mix as advanced countries but with an unfortunate need, under circumstances where an external crisis may be imminent, to switch from using monetary policy in support of domestic demand to using it in defence of the currency. In addition, such countries seem to need more substantial time delays or Tobin-style taxes on capital movements across their borders, even while being generally open to such flows. And, in cases where a developing country feels that it is especially vulnerable to the effects of in-

and out-flows of 'hot' speculative money, rejecting all foreign investment except for FDI and opting instead for a policy mix of managing both domestic demand and the exchange rate may be advisable.

## Supporting international trade

Beyond the danger that any kind of economic volatility will lead to more extreme fluctuations, an additional argument that is sometimes made in favour of avoiding short-run currency fluctuations is that removing uncertainty in this area removes a major deterrent to international trade. This may well have been true in the 19th century when there were fewer financial instruments available to hedge exchange-rate risk, and when the risk profile of international trade was higher in general, but it is not true today. Today, import and export businesses can lock-in an exchange rate on their planned shipments a few months in advance and, with rapid global transportation, this is longer than almost any physical exchange takes to complete. Businesses are thus at little risk of loss and, since banks providing such facilities should have many customers with exposures in both directions across any pair of currencies they are dealing in, these banks should also be at little risk since their wins and losses should cancel out. As a consequence, seeking to provide a stable environment for international trade is no longer a real reason to seek short-run currency stability.

There may be some exceptions to this general principle in the case of frontier markets where the general risk profile to trade is high and where domestic credit is not a major component of the economy, meaning that interest rates have little potency anyway in managing domestic demand, and that it might actually be better to focus on stabilising the currency. However, we can expect such cases to be rare and the economies in question to be small.

This brings us to the end of our discussion of the special challenges that countries face in stabilising their economies in a globalised world. The next chapter, rather than focusing on the challenges of achieving good policy outcomes, looks at the ways in which governments can sometimes make a poor job of executing counter-cyclical policy.

# 9. Harmful Effects of Counter-Cyclical Policy

From everything we have discussed thus far, it should be clear that an economy without any central management would likely be highly unstable. But, precisely because of the importance of good policy in maintaining stability, bad economic management can be nearly as dangerous as the absence of any meaningful control at all. The purpose of this chapter is to discuss the ways in which the managerial responsibilities of government can be executed poorly, and to review the consequences that can follow from this. After all, part of good management entails anticipating and avoiding potential errors.

## Drowning in Red Tape

The idea that regulation always places an onerous and unnecessary burden on free enterprise, and the parallel idea that such rules almost always produce perverse and unanticipated outcomes, is a favourite bug-bear of political conservatives. When discussing such matters, conservatives like to depict even moderately-regulated economies as drowning in red tape and as being 'sclerotic' compared to those which have set free the dynamic power of unrestricted capitalism. To most neutral observers, it is clear that this outlook is based largely on ideology and, in some cases, on barely-concealed self-interest. But this does not mean that it is always incorrect. Indeed, it is clear that there must come a point where regulations are so numerous, complex, restrictive or poorly-designed that they are doing more harm than good in the economy.

In this section, we will focus specifically on ways in which regulation designed to stabilise the economy can end up having adverse effects.

For example, if requirements on banks to hold regulatory capital are based on point-in-time measures of risk (as opposed to through-the-cycle measures), the result can be that banks are pushed to lend more in the good times and less in the bad as their risk metrics change. This is clearly a pro-cyclical outcome that increases the amplitude of the economic cycle and it is therefore a major example of how attempts at economic management can sometimes be counter-productive.

Similarly, excessive financial regulation can put a dampener on the rate of economic growth. For example, if leverage and lending controls on business banking are very tight, they may lead to a dearth of credit in the economy and consequently to slower rates of real investment and economic growth. An outcome such as this might also drive firms to rely more on equity investment, unless there were highly restrictive controls here too, and this might leave businesses hostage to the fickle demands of stock market investors even more than they are already – a situation that would hardly be conducive to good long-term business development.

In avoiding such outcomes, the critical point is to remember what the financial industry is for in the first place. Commercial banks should give people safe storage of their deposits, should maintain payments systems, should finance business investment, should provide backing for certain specialist transactions that need it – such as trade finance – and should provide home mortgages at reasonable degrees of leverage. Financial-market institutions, meanwhile, should facilitate the issuance of new shares and bonds, should provide a liquid market for people to buy-into and dispose of these instruments, and should trade futures and other instruments needed by real businesses to manage risk.

None of these, however, require the kind of hyper-active financial sector we have seen in recent years. Indeed, in those historical time periods when finance was more sedate (there were also periods when it was quite wild) it served its role just as well, and economic growth did not suffer for want of unbridled speculation – indeed, it probably benefited because real businesses could have confidence in a stable future.

To give some examples, corporate leverage ratios of less than 3:1 have always been sufficient to fund business expansion; especially considering that much of that investment comes from retained earnings. Mortgage leverage ratios of 5:1 have always been sufficient to let people buy homes; especially considering that more aggressive lending just inflates prices and thereby negates whatever benefit it brings to new entrants. Cautious mutual funds and small investment banks have always been enough to provide liquid financial markets in all the necessary instruments, with the advent of hyper-leveraged speculators bringing no added gain, but causing much loss in the form of instability. And simple derivatives such as futures have always been enough to manage risk, without the need for more complex instruments that actually compound it.

What all of these areas have in common is that benefit to the wider economy as a function increasing levels of financial activity seems to plot as a curve with a slope that becomes gradually flatter – what economists would call diminishing returns. The dangers, meanwhile, seem to compound upon themselves as activity increases.

Thus, if financial controls are set so as to permit the kinds and levels of activity that have always been sufficient historically, while choking-off unnecessary areas such as complex derivatives and leveraged speculation, there will be little adverse effect. This is especially true if we are willing to adjust controls in cases where they are proving to be too tight or too lenient. So, while we should be careful not to design regulations that harm necessary parts of finance, we should also be very clear that the suggestion that well-designed regulation reduces growth rates is essentially bogus – if anything it helps growth by providing a stable environment.

Furthermore, the need to facilitate 'good' kinds of finance, while suppressing 'bad' kinds, shows why multiple kinds of regulation are necessary. Relying on just one set of controls would either leave many escape routes open, or would have to be so draconian as to paralyse some essential aspect of the system. Having multiple controls, and implementing them flexibly, by contrast, closes-off escape routes and avoids the need to put so much pressure on one part of the system that it fails.

## Too Much Money

Another example of bad economic management occurs in cases where the government or its agents are either too zealous in their attempts to counteract a minor downturn through monetary policy, or where they make aggressive use of monetary policy to try and force growth at a rate faster than the physical capacity of the economy can expand. In either case, the result is usually a price surge that then triggers a self-sustaining process of inflation, leading to stagnation and possibly to hyperinflation followed by collapse.

An important consideration here is the idea of full employment. In the terminology of the economics profession this can have varying definitions, but the definition relevant here is that it corresponds to the level of employment that exists at the mid-point of the economic cycle, when the economy is transiently at long-run equilibrium. The unemployment level under these conditions is called the *natural rate of unemployment* (NRU) and, if the labour market is flexible, and benefit systems support and facilitate a return to work, it should stand at no more than about 4-5% of the labour force*.

However, once unemployment falls below this level, it signals that the economy is nearing capacity, and that any attempt to force faster growth and further reductions in unemployment through monetary policy, or through debt-financed increases in government spending, may lead to runaway inflation. In this situation, if money is expanded it may lead to a slight increase in output and employment, but it will also lead to a larger rise in the price level.

Mechanistically, what happens when unemployment falls below the NRU is that workers begin to acquire some bargaining power over firms. And, if the margin by which unemployment is lower than the NRU is significant enough, this triggers a positive feedback loop of increasing wages and spending. This, in turn, has corrosive effects on the economy that cause output and employment to fall back again. Therefore, capacity limitations are reached when unemployment moves somewhat below the NRU, and not at some level of unemployment that is lower-still. Because of the processes outlined here, the NRU is sometimes also referred to as the non-accelerating inflation rate of unemployment (NAIRU)[61].

That this model of inflation and unemployment is correct is evidenced by the Phillips curve; the inverse relationship between inflation and unemployment that is observed over time under conditions where changes in monetary conditions, which might otherwise obscure the correlation, are small. The Phillips curve is clearly visible in data for the period up to the 1950s but, once large monetary changes as part of attempts to manage the economy became the norm, it was necessarily obscured.

Despite the dangers of trying to push unemployment below the NAIRU, it should be noted that the case against trying to over-stimulate the economy in the short run is entirely separate from the role of government spending on things like education and infrastructure in supporting growth over much

---

* In addition, there should be no substantial segments of the population that are outside the labour force because they are, in one way or another, marginalised from society.

longer timescales. Likewise, while the risks associated with attempting to push unemployment below its natural level are real, arguments based on these dangers are often over-stated by bond-holding investors – a group who stand to lose significantly more from inflation than from unemployment – and by the conservative politicians who support them. These groups consistently over-estimate the level of the NAIRU (sometimes quoting numbers as high as 7-8% even for countries with very flexible labour markets) and, when they fear that the NAIRU is being approached, they generally support tightening monetary policy before there is any real evidence that this is indeed the case – instead of adopting the more humane approach of tightening only once there is actual evidence that inflation is set to rise.

Conservatives also underestimate the potential for active policies to succeed in radically reducing the level of the NAIRU. For example, in countries where most people are employed by large corporations or by government bodies, national wage agreements and national collective bargaining arrangements can be used to make very low levels of unemployment consistent with low levels of inflation[62]. In Europe in the 1960s, where such arrangements were the norm, unemployment rates were as low as 1.5% and yet inflation remained under control. Such measures may not be feasible in more fragmented modern economies but, as we shall see, some of the same effect can be achieved by combining flexible labour markets with relatively generous social welfare programmes based on the concept of welfare-to-work.

## Exchange-rate Challenges

Beyond mis-regulation and inflation, other ways in which economic management may be unintentionally pro-cyclical or otherwise harmful to the economy arise from the attempts of governments to manage their exchange rates. Indeed, since foreign exchange is such a complex area of the economy, and is therefore an area in which the most complex errors can be made, it is a topic to which I have devoted a large part of this chapter.

### Aims and methods

Why do governments seek to manage their currencies? As we have seen in Chapter 8, such policies may be based on the misguided idea that short-run exchange rate stability is still beneficial to trade in the modern world. More reasonably, the policies may also derive from the fear that exchange rate instability could develop into an outright currency collapse for less-developed countries faced with economic difficulties. They may also be based on a strategy of continually keeping the national currency at undervalued levels in order to boost exports.

When it comes to acting on these objectives, there are a number of approaches that governments can take to managing exchange rates[63]. The most aggressive possibility, one that is available only to a near-closed economy with little international trade, is the option of simply handling all currency exchange through government agencies and of setting a fiat exchange rate that applies to such transactions.

A somewhat less militant option is a metallic standard based on gold, silver or some other commodity. Under this system, every unit of a currency in existence, or some set proportion of the currency in existence, must be backed by gold reserves held at the relevant central bank; the price of gold in terms of that currency is fixed by law; and everyone has the right to redeem their money for gold. Because the amount of currency that can be issued under such a system is limited to the amount of gold available, it precludes any possibility of general price instability arising from irresponsible government management of the currency. And, the relevant point here, if several countries are pursuing such a system – each fixing the price of gold in terms of their own currency – then these currencies must also have irrevocably fixed exchange rates against one another.

In this system, if there is any downward pressure on one currency as a result of speculative forces, or of relative changes in productivity or in the terms of trade, then foreign investors may tend to redeem their holdings in that currency for gold. This creates a situation where the central bank will have less gold. It will thus be unable to issue new currency to replace that which has been redeemed, and the money supply will therefore be reduced in a process that tends to exactly counteract the downward pressure on exchange rates. Alternatively, the central bank may pre-emptively reduce the money supply to a lower multiple of its gold reserves (a 'multiple' that may be greater or less than one, depending on the details of the system) so as to halt withdrawals and maintain a situation where investors still believe that a unit of the currency is worth its target amount of gold. Either way, exchange rate stability can be maintained under almost all circumstances, as it was in the period before 1914 when a system of this kind operated.

However, this system entails an inability to use monetary policy to counter recession (because it is, in effect, being used instead to maintain a target gold price) and this, together with the need to follow the pro-cyclical option of shrinking the money supply when a recession is underway and foreign investors are withdrawing, leaves economies wide-open to severe deflationary slumps. In addition to this, a metallic standard means that any country that is undergoing consistent changes in productivity, or in the terms of trade, relative to other countries, will see sustained and substantial changes in domestic price levels as its money supply changes. And, finally, if the available supply of the relevant metal does not change in line with economic output, then persistent inflationary or deflationary pressures across all countries operating such a system will be the result.

An inadequate supply of gold contributed to a sustained period of deflation from 1873 to 1896 and this, together with the pro-cyclical effects of a metallic standard, caused the economy to be highly volatile, with many countries experiencing as many quarters of contraction as of expansion over this period[64]. As a consequence, economic historians sometimes refer to the years 1873-1896 as the 'long depression', and they can say that the evidence of these years firmly refutes the claim made by classical economists that price level changes under a metallic standard system would be fully anticipated and would therefore have no real economic effects. In fact, the effects are clearly adverse and it is for this reason that, as one US presidential candidate put it in 1896, a metallic standard amounts to "crucify[ing] mankind upon a cross of gold".

A derivative of the metallic standard is a currency board, where the government of a jurisdiction with a history of excessively loose monetary policy attempts to redeem itself by holding reserves of a more stable foreign currency to back every unit of its own money. Governments pursuing a policy such as this set a fixed exchange rate against the reserve currency and guarantee everyone the right to exchange currencies at this rate if they so wish. In this system, the foreign currency takes the place of gold and the features of the system are almost exactly the same as those of a metallic standard – making it almost equally punitive.

The only redeeming feature of this system is that, if the country whose currency is used as the reserve has an economic cycle that is synchronised with that of the country which is running a currency board, then the latter will at least tend to import a counter-cyclical monetary policy from the former. In essence, if the real value of the reserve currency falls because of a monetary expansion by its central bank, it will now be over-valued against the currency of the country that is using it as a reserve. Thus, people will deposit reserve currency with the central bank of the currency-board country and will take out the currency of that country, which now has greater buying power; causing the volume of this currency in circulation to expand. This process will continue until the real value of the two currencies has equalised. It therefore has the effect of ensuring that the monetary policy of the currency-board country exactly mimics that of the other country. However, this is a beneficial effect only if the economic cycles of the two countries are synchronised. Otherwise, it increases volatility for a country that is presumably weak already.

A less aggressive option than all systems involving rigidly fixed exchange rates, and the option that is usually pursued by countries seeking to manage their currencies today, is for governments to use their central banks to buy and sell domestic currency on the foreign exchange markets in order to approximately maintain some pre-ordained exchange rate.

Under such a system, if a government wishes to keep the value of its currency up, holding it at the ordained level in the face of countervailing forces, then it will use foreign currency reserves or the sale of other assets (such as gold or government bonds) to buy back the national currency, putting an upward pressure on its price. Alternatively, if it wishes to hold the value of its currency down, then it will sell the national currency, either by drawing on existing reserves or by creating new funds, and it will thereby put a downward pressure on the price. Buying back the domestic currency has the effect of causing interest rates in this currency to rise, and selling it has the effect of causing them to fall; effects that may apply either universally, or only outside the country if there are strong capital controls isolating this domain from monetary conditions inside. Either way, this effect reinforces the policy action undertaken by either attracting or repelling foreign investors.

When either of the actions of supporting or suppressing the currency is being pursued, it is pursued on a continuous open-market basis in order to maintain the target exchange rate. If the currency is drifting above the target, the central bank sells it until it comes back down again. And, if it is falling below its target, it buys it until it comes back up again. This is in much the same way as monetary policy that targets a given market interest rate is exercised on a continuous basis in order to maintain that target, even though people only notice the policy when a decision is announced to change the actual target.

When central bankers are supporting the level of their currency, and are using foreign exchange reserves to do so, they may have obtained these reserves from a number of sources. One possibility is that the reserves came from duties and tariffs imposed on imported goods or from gains made on previous occasions when it was necessary to hold the currency down. Another is that the funds were obtained by means of loans from the central banks of foreign jurisdictions, which may be part of a shared bilateral or multilateral system of fixed exchange rates. However, regardless of the source of funds, a central bank cannot continue to rely on such methods forever; if its currency continues to come under downward pressure, it will eventually find itself in a position where it has no more foreign currency to use.

However, this does not mean that a financing limitation on the policy of holding up the domestic currency has been reached at this point. Instead, the central bank, if it is deeply committed to the currency peg, may simply switch to sucking its currency out of circulation by selling gold or bonds from its reserves or by issuing its own bonds in order to draw in cash. But, because this only has an indirect effect on foreign exchange markets, it is generally a slower and less powerful option than using foreign currency, meaning that it has to be done more aggressively in order to succeed, and meaning that it has even greater effects on the domestic economy.

In the converse of all this, if central bankers are holding down the value of their national currency, they have the legal right to issue as much of this currency as is necessary to sell on the foreign exchange markets. There are therefore no financing limitations at all pertaining to this policy.

## Nominal versus real

A further point to bear in mind is that, in the long run, exchange rate management controls nominal but not real exchange rates. For example, if the productivity of a country is growing more slowly than that of others and this is dragging the currency down, then, if the central bank of the country in question is acting to counter this, it will have reduced the supply of the domestic currency compared to other currencies. Assuming there are no capital controls and this reduction in the money supply applies inside the country as well as out, this causes price levels at home to fall and, although the nominal exchange rate will have remained steady, the real exchange rate will have changed once adjustment is made for the change in price levels. Alternatively, if there are capital controls and prices in the home market remain steady, exports will either have to stop, or be made at generally lower prices in order to be competitive, which is still a shift in the real exchange rate.

Similar effects apply to metallic standard systems and currency boards.

However, despite this fact, nominal exchange rate stability may still be considered attractive as a means to encourage international trade (in a situation where there are no other means to hedge foreign exchange risk) or to avoid currency crises of the kind described in Chapter 4. And exchange rate undervaluation may also, as we shall see, still be attractive as a means to boost exports.

## The consequences of pegging

In the long run, the outcome of attempts at exchange-rate management will depend on whether the nominal value of a currency, if left unmanaged, would tend to fall below or rise above its pegged level.

Maintaining a fixed nominal peg for a currency that has a tendency to depreciate necessarily involves shrinking the money supply seen by the foreign exchange markets, and, if there are not stringent capital controls, thereby inducing deflationary pressures in the domestic economy. Indeed, since the nominal exchange rate between two countries can remain stable only if their money supplies, domestic velocities of circulation, economic productivities and terms of trade all move so that the net effect on the exchange rate is zero; maintaining a fixed exchange rate requires that a country with inferior productivity growth, or one that is experiencing deteriorating terms of trade, must tighten its monetary policy continuously compared to other countries. If the country is open to capital flows and this therefore entails inducing deflationary pressures at home, it can slow productivity growth even more and can thereby set-up a positive feedback loop of currency depreciation, tightening monetary policy and further relative declines in productivity growth.

To view all this in another way, a government that is trying to maintain a fixed peg in the face of currency depreciation must try to shrink the stock of its own currency to the point where real prices are in-line with comparable items abroad and downward pressure on the currency abates. However, since the price levels of goods will be slower to shift than the exchange rate would, they will tend to lag and always remain more uncompetitive than necessary if the currency is being pushed down by some ongoing loss in comparative productivity. Much export volume is thus lost. Alongside the effects of deflation, this is another consequence of running an overvalued currency.

If a country does have stringent capital controls and is supporting the value of its currency, while holding the domestic money supply steady, the effects are still adverse. Exports become uncompetitively expensive and the economy suffers. Even if some exports can be marked-down in the international market compared to their price in the home market, the price movement tends to be slower than an exchange-rate movement would, and the domestic economy is still hurt as the volume of exports falls more than necessary compared to the underlying loss of comparative productivity. (However, it would seem that the pain is less than for an economy whose policy mix entails inducing deflation at home.)

When it is eventually recognised that it is destructive to try to maintain an overvalued peg in the face of long-run trends that are pushing the currency down, the peg may suddenly be abandoned. In this situation, if there are not stringent capital controls, there is a danger that the sudden currency fall that ensues will lead to an over-correction and a currency collapse, with all the damage this entails. This risk can be compounded if either the public or private sector was allowed to accumulate foreign-currency debt during the time when the domestic currency was over-valued. This state of affairs may lead to a wave of defaults when the currency fall makes repayment unsustainable and this, as we have seen, may greatly intensify the crisis.

In an alternative process to that which occurs when a currency is over-valued, maintaining a fixed nominal peg for a currency that has a tendency to appreciate necessarily involves expanding the money supply, and thereby running the risk of inflation in the domestic economy if there are not tight capital controls. However, such a policy also results in the accumulation of foreign currency together with financial assets denominated in such currency. Such accumulation is an inevitable consequence of a government continuously expanding the supply of its own currency, using these funds to purchase foreign currency and then converting the foreign currency in question into foreign-currency assets that can be held in reserve so as to earn a rate of return at least commensurate with the rate of inflation in that foreign currency. Over time, reserves accumulated in this way can build up to a level that is equivalent to a substantial percentage of national GDP. Additionally, as we shall see next, an under-valued currency may bring significant trade advantages.

## Competitive under-valuation

Deliberate under-valuation is an option that may be pursued because it results in an increase in export volume that is typically greater than the decrease in export prices that went before. As well as being beneficial in itself; this gives a boost to industry that allows it to establish economies of scale and of clustering that persist even after an eventual upward re-valuation or floatation of the currency[65]. The point to emphasise is that, because exchange rates respond quickly to changes in monetary policy but consumer prices are sticky, there will be a lag before consumer prices adjust to counter an under-valued currency – that is, before real exchange rates return to their long-run level. As a consequence, a country need only expand its currency at a slightly faster pace than others, and target this expansion at the foreign exchange markets, in order to give its exporters a sustained advantage. In effect, by continuously intervening to keep its currency weak, a government makes the short run last indefinitely. And, since the expansion involved need only be mild, any inflation that is induced at home need not be great.

In addition to such gains, running an undervalued currency also has the beneficial effect of making speculative capital inflows less likely and therefore of mitigating the risk of currency collapse that can follow from such inflows. This is because it is known that the government will fight any currency appreciation as soon as it gets going, and because it is more difficult for the currency to gain downward momentum when it was already under-valued.

One drawback to the policy of under-valuation is that, if it is combined with general openness to foreign capital (which is likely to be  mostly beneficial for an emerging economy), it prevents monetary policy being used to manage domestic demand. However, if the policy is successfully producing an export boom, this is not likely to seem like a major drawback – especially given that steady export revenues in a country where export makes up a large part of the economy are themselves a source of stability.

Given its advantages, why do all countries not pursue a policy of under-valuation? The most obvious reasons are that it is logically impossible for everyone to under-value relative to everyone else, and that any attempt to do so would just trigger a series of tit-for-tat under-valuations and a surge in global inflation as money supplies spiralled. In practice, only very poor countries are tolerated to engage in such policies. This is seen as amounting to economic aid that such nations should fairly get; and, even with the extra boost, they represent only a minimal competitive threat.

Furthermore, despite the attractions of currency under-valuation for less-developed countries, this policy can become dangerous to the global economy when the output of such countries grows to a substantial size. There is an unavoidable tendency for the reserves accumulated in maintaining an undervalued currency to be invested in foreign government bonds in order to preserve their value in the face of gradual inflation. This creates extra demand for such bonds and therefore suppresses the interest rate that the governments issuing them must offer. This, in turn, permits banks in the currency zones experiencing the capital inflow to offer less interest on their deposits and therefore to lend at lower interest rates – all of which amplifies the credit-asset cycle and thereby destabilises the economy. Indeed, as we have seen in the recent crisis, which was partially caused by funds that flowed from China to the US in this way, effects like this can ultimately contribute to a global recession and can thereby harm the country that accumulated the reserves in the first place[66].

A tightening of monetary policy by the countries receiving an inflow of funds like this – a form of 'sterilisation' – might or might not be effective in offsetting the speculative effects that follow. Such a policy might just draw in more foreign funds but, if such inflows are already at or close to their practical limit, or are smaller than the domestic banking sector, then it would be the logical way of preventing a credit-asset bubble from inflating.

A more lasting solution, however, might be to create a global reserve currency in which countries accumulating foreign currency reserves (through currency under-valuation or in other ways) could store their funds. This would relieve many of the distortions that arise from the fact of certain national currencies also serving as global reserve currencies. However, leading economies might resist this move because having your currency act as a reserve makes it easier to finance budget and trading deficits and, in order to achieve the best short-run effect, some emerging economies might still feel the need to target their policies of currency under-valuation directly at the currencies of major trading partners.

## The dangers of devaluation

In relation to exchange-rate management in general, governments running managed exchange rates through the open-market operations of their central bank are not usually so foolish as to try and maintain a peg at one unchanging level for all time, despite the disruptive effects this can have when underlying trends mean that the peg is now at an inappropriate level and that a peg at a different level would be more appropriate. Instead, they respond to sustained forces of depreciation or appreciation by devaluing or re-valuing their currencies; changing the target exchange rate and quickly moving to this level, so as to be more consistent with long-run trends. This amounts to a 'fixed but adjustable peg' through which policymakers can partially avoid the dangers and hardships associated with a more rigid system, and it is why I mentioned this approach in Chapter 8 as the least-bad way of managing exchange rates.

In an environment of open capital flows, however, foreign investors can be extremely sensitive to the losses they may incur during a devaluation. If the change is not announced carefully and managed properly, such investors may begin to rapidly withdraw from the country. This leaves the government in question with no option but to sharply tighten monetary policy and defend the new peg, despite its original intention to escape the need for such punitive measures. Such an outcome is likely to be less painful than the more puritanical option of deliberate deflation in defence of the pre-existing peg. But it is nevertheless highly disruptive.

## Softer options

A much softer option to that of a fixed but adjustable peg is a 'managed float' or 'dirty float', where the position of the peg is adjusted at quite short time intervals in accordance with market trends. Alternatively, a country may pursue a different form of dirty floating in which the currency is allowed to float within a relatively wide band and the position of these bands is adjusted over time (fixed exchange rates and fixed but adjustable pegs usually also involve some permissible band but this is, by definition, narrow). Systems such as these supposedly combine the benefits of stability with those of flexibility but, since other means are available to guarantee trade against exchange rate risk, and since they are not much of a defence against 'hot' capital flows, it is not clear that they are any better than just letting the currency float. And they still interfere with the use of monetary policy to manage domestic demand.

Beyond this, as we have seen, when economies have a synchronised business cycle and therefore shift interest rates in a synchronised way in face of the largest movements in this cycle, they are effectively practising a moderate form of currency coordination. They avoid the largest short-run shifts in comparative interest rates and therefore mitigate one potential source of currency instability.

## Floating is better

However, aside from incidental effects such as these, of the three desirables encountered in Chapter 8 – managing domestic demand through monetary policy, achieving short-run currency stability and maintaining general openness to foreign capital – it seems to be currency stability that should usually be sacrificed. Looking again across the different kinds of exchange-rate management; very flexible systems (managed floats of different kinds) serve little purpose, while very rigid systems are deeply counter-productive. Isolation combined with fiat convertibility entails the poverty that results from lack of international integration. And a metallic standard, currency board or permanently fixed peg maintained by open market operations, if the country is open to capital flows, entails a crushingly violent economic cycle, alongside sustained and significant price level changes in the domestic economy whenever its productivity or terms of trade change at a different rate than other countries. If the country is not open to capital flows, rigid systems still entail harm to exports – ironic since some analysts still see supporting trade as one of their benefits.

In addition to this, a policy of continual under-valuation maintained by relatively poor countries is sustainable only so long as such economies remain small and backward; once this ceases to be the case, such a policy may destabilise the world economy or attract political retaliation from abroad. Similarly, a system of fixed but adjustable pegs entails devaluations that, if the economy is open to foreign capital, become ever more dangerous over time as economies develop and these capital flows become larger. It also entails some effects on price indices and trade in the time interval between pressures on the peg becoming noticeable and a decision being made to adjust it.

In general, currency management is practicable only if draconian restrictions are placed on cross-border capital movements or if the country in question gives up the ability to use monetary policy to manage domestic demand. In advanced countries, neither option is advisable. The ability to manage domestic demand is more important than either currency stability or openness to foreign capital. And openness to foreign capital is more important than currency stability. Similarly, in poor countries, openness to foreign capital and the ability to manage domestic demand are usually the priorities, and defence of the currency should only take over from management of domestic demand under certain circumstances when external crisis threatens. In this situation, defence of the currency may be necessary and may be practicable if the country was not previously engaged in active currency management; meaning that the original exchange rate was realistic and that it is only short-run trends that need to be resisted.

## Some exceptions

Overall, there are only a limited number of instances where currency management of any kind is advisable. One such instance, as indicated, occurs in the case of developing countries that are facing the prospect of capital flight. Another occurs in the case of very backward developing economies where currency under-valuation may be helpful for establishing economies of scale in industry, and where the economy is so small that such an action runs no risk of destabilising the world economy. Likewise, frontier markets that have a high risk profile in general for international trade, and where domestic credit is not important, may opt for currency management together with capital openness and sacrifice the use of monetary policy to manage domestic demand.

Beyond this, *ad hoc* joint intervention by a group of central banks aiming to reverse undesirable currency trends at a moment when the markets are amenable to turning may be advisable, as may creation of monetary unions by clusters of trading partners whose business cycles and rates of productivity growth have converged to a very high degree. In the same vein, it may make sense for a small country whose economy is tightly converged with a bigger neighbour to tether its currency to that of its neighbour. But, aside from such cases, floating is better.

## Reckless Spending

Outside of monetary policy, fiscal indiscipline is another way in which politicians may unintentionally harm their economies. This does not mean that we should share the obsession with 'fiscal rectitude' of political conservatives – a group who fail to recognise the benefits of counter-cyclical fiscal policy and who consistently under-estimate the debt capacity of developed-country governments – but instead that we should insist that deficits and surpluses cancel one another out over the economic cycle.

There is, however, an obvious temptation for politicians not to do this. It can seem preferable, rather, to win votes by running deficits even in the expansionary phase of the economic cycle, in an attempt to boost employment and output in the short-run. This temptation can be especially strong given that the majority of the electorate do not really understand economics, and tend to think that government doing 'more for the people', in any form, can only be a good thing. The inevitable consequences of substantial profligacy, however, are inflation, mounting debt, loss of scope for discretionary fiscal stimulus in a severe downturn and perhaps even exhaustion of debt capacity to the point where government cannot run even a cyclical deficit in a normal recession. All of this clearly increases the chances that the normal undulations of the business cycle will develop into more adverse outcomes. It is thus deeply irresponsible.

However, unlike the intricacies involved in matters such as economic stimulus or exchange rate management, this is not a complex problem. It is the simple result of inadequate understanding by voters, and of weak leadership.

Despite this, the solution is not, as conservatives would have it, for politicians to disavow many of their powers to tax and spend. This would do much more harm than having public debt at somewhat higher-than-desirable levels. Instead, the ideal solution is to educate voters better as to how the economy actually works. The essence of democracy is that voters need government to serve their common interests, but that they keep this government under control by voting out politicians that have served them badly. Thus, if voters can be made to understand the basics of fiscal economics a little better, the democratic process can be made to work better in this area. Good management can certainly be achieved (Figure 17). And, even where it is not, unless the profligacy is extreme, the outcome is still far better than the wild swings of an unmanaged economy.

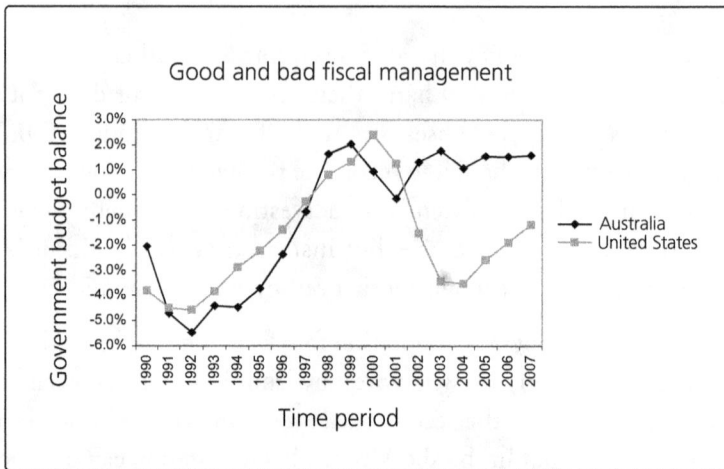

**Figure 17 – Central government budget balances in the United States and Australia from 1990 to 2007.** In the United States surpluses were generally insufficient to cancel-out deficits and federal government debt ended up at 50% of GDP at the end of the period – by no means catastrophic but enough to constrain room for manoeuvre somewhat in a crisis. In Australia, by contrast, surpluses largely cancelled-out deficits and government debt was down to 7% of GDP at the end of the period. What this proves is that good fiscal management is very possible. When considering this data, bear in mind that a given surplus at a later time-point outweighs a deficit of the same percentage of GDP at an earlier time point because GDP itself will usually be higher at the later time point. [Data from the IMF.]

# The Temptation to Protect

A final way in which misguided policy can harm the economy is protectionism: seeking to give advantages to domestic firms and workers and to disadvantage foreign competitors by imposing trade barriers or by intervening directly in the mechanisms through which firms compete. While this might seem attractive, especially in straitened economic times, it is often a spectacularly counter-productive policy that harms both the country which initiated it and many others as well[67].

## Gains from trade

The basic reason for this is that the existence of international exchange boosts global output well beyond what could otherwise be achieved. Countries that trade can specialise, usually at a micro level, in different subsets of activities and then exchange their output with one another. And, because of the economies of scale and the clustering effects that result from such specialisation, together with the fact that overall output will be higher if different groups focus on what they do best (comparative advantage), global output is substantially higher in this situation than in a situation where there is no trade – a familiar phenomenon that is referred to as the *gains from trade*.

It should, however, be pointed out that this phenomenon is not universal. Very poor countries that are trapped in a specialism of exporting primary commodities (especially agricultural commodities) gain little from trade; there is little scope for economies of scale or of clustering in this area, and relying on a few commodities whose price is volatile can be disruptive. However, limitations such as these can be overcome by means of policies designed to stimulate industrialisation, such as currency under-valuation and targeted support for exporters. And, once local industrialisation does take hold, it not only allows economies of scale and of clustering to be established in this sector, but also boosts productivity in the primary products sector as well*. Thus, even for very poor countries, international trade can be of benefit to national income, provided that it is accompanied by policies designed to support the development of industry.

---

\* Indeed, in all historical cases, such spillover effects have been a prerequisite for such primary activities to be a real driver of national prosperity.

## Blind alleys

Despite the global benefits of international trade, for a single country it might still be beneficial to place restrictions on trade while others remain more open. But whether or not this is the case depends on how the policy is executed. If it is carried out by means of giving an advantage to domestic exporters, such as by maintaining an undervalued currency, then it may well be beneficial. But, if it is done by erecting barriers against foreign imports, then all it achieves is to force domestic consumers to buy from domestic firms. And, since such firms will not be able to establish economies of scale in every industry, and will be sheltered from foreign competition, they will necessarily be less efficient than globalised production. As a consequence, real national income will be lower than it might otherwise have been.

Neither can this kind of *import substitution* give a sustained boost to industrial development in the same way as policies designed to encourage exports. This is because, in a less-developed country, the domestic market will simply not be big enough to deliver such an outcome. Likewise, a policy of import substitution does not guarantee jobs to domestic workers very much better than does a globalised economy. The reason for this latter fact is simply that, regardless of whether the economy is national or global, there will be a business cycle where unemployment levels fluctuate around their full-employment equilibrium. It is true that, if trading partners are failing to implement counter-cyclical policies that keep this cycle under control, there may be a compelling reason to reduce trading levels and shelter the domestic population from the effects of a violent economic cycle. However, since all countries have a clear incentive to manage the cycle in a roughly coordinated way, this should not be a long-term argument against international trade.

In any case, the argument that one country might benefit from protectionism while others remain more open is usually beside the point. If any significant economy erected substantial trade barriers to protect itself, or to gain an advantage over the rest of the world, others would follow suit – spurred on by populist demands at home not to be 'left behind' – and there would be a tit-for-tat series of protectionist measures that would reduce global output and leave all countries worse off. In an economic crisis, the likelihood of this would be especially great. And to give an idea of just how harmful this could be, it can be estimated that world output might be 10-15% lower in the absence of any international trade[68]. Thus, if even a fraction of this trade-dependent output were lost for a sustained period of time as a result of protectionist measures, the social consequences would be huge.

## Some better ideas

One argument of the trade sceptics that may contain some truth is that the sheer complexity of a global economy may cause the economic cycle to be more unpredictable, and therefore of somewhat greater amplitude (because the monetary authorities find it harder to react to it), in a national economy open to global forces than in a more closed national economy. Equivalently, a global economy composed entirely of very open national economies may well be significantly less stable than a global economy composed of less-open national economies. This, in turn, creates an argument that national leaders should perhaps agree a common set of trade barriers so as to dampen the transmission of shocks globally. However, the economic benefit of such barriers might well be less than their cost in terms of lost global output. Equally, their existence might just create a temptation to erect yet more barriers. And, in any case, it seems better to impose a habit of cooperation on national leaders by leaving them in a position where they must broadly coordinate their counter-cyclical policies.

Thus, as we have noted, the only cases in which any significant protectionist measures are called for are where a developing country is giving some advantages to domestic exporters in order to trigger industrial development. Such advantages may be needed to accelerate the establishment of economies of scale and of clustering in very poor countries, and they can be tolerated by other nations because any economy that is backward enough to need such measures does not represent a serious competitive threat.

## Global competition and wages

Moving from issues of total global output to issues of the distribution of global income, it should be admitted that integrated global trade can result in the wages of manual workers in more-developed countries being bid downwards as a result of competition from workers in less-developed countries. This process tends to amplify the gap within advanced countries between manual workers and those in more highly-educated professions and it therefore produces the kind of inequality that, as we shall see in Chapter

10, has poisonous effects across the social spectrum. This is a phenomenon that trade unions representing workers in the manufacturing sector repeatedly emphasise and, in advanced countries where union members are electorally significant, it can tempt politicians towards protectionism, even when the economy overall is performing well.

However, this effect of international wage competition is mitigated by the tendency for advanced countries to specialise in high-income service and technology sectors – especially so if workers are well-supported in moving into these areas. And, in any case, such wage loss is an acceptable price to pay for the possibility of lifting millions of people in less-developed countries out of extreme poverty. Protecting the wages of manual workers in more-developed countries should therefore not really be an argument against international trade. We should instead seek to support these workers, and to combat excess inequality in advanced countries in other ways. What these ways might consist of is discussed in detail in Chapter 10.

## Laissez-faire is Still Wrong

None of the potential failures of policy described in this chapter justify the conservative position that government is inherently inept and that all attempts at economic management should be abandoned. The point, rather, of this chapter has been to chart the pitfalls of economic management so that they may be avoided. As said at the beginning of the chapter, taking care to avoid these is, naturally, part of good management.

Doubtless economic management can be inept, but this is not inevitable. The most principled inaction is typically far more inept. This book has shown so far that an unmanaged economy is highly unstable and that sensible means are available to stabilise it, most of which have been well proven in practice. Likewise, in Chapter 10, we shall see that an overly-free market results in inadequate social investment and social insurance; leading to poor growth and an unhealthy society in the long run. Here too, economic management is necessary to avoid highly undesirable outcomes.

# 10. Growth and Inequality as Feedback Processes

onservative ideology portrays the dynamic, 'hire-and-fire' capitalism of the United States as giving it an edge over the more regulated economies of Europe. Unfettered individual enterprise, we are told, allows market participants to direct resources to where they will be used most efficiently and is therefore the best solution for achieving economic growth.

The evidence does not bear this out. Long-run rates of physical investment and capital formation are much higher in Europe[69]. Productivity per hour worked is higher in a number of western and northern European countries than in the US. And rates of business innovation and technology uptake are similar on both sides of the Atlantic[70]. At the same time, when we correct for various distortions, we see that trend rates of unemployment are only slightly higher in Europe than in the US.

It is true that the major eurozone economies of France, Germany and Italy have shown poor trend rates of growth in GDP per capita for more than a decade (1.9%, 1.4% and 1.3% respectively over the period 1995-2005, compared to 3% for the US[71]) but this can be misleading. Over this period, the eurozone economies had to meet monetary and fiscal policy criteria related to the establishment of the euro[72], while Germany also had to meet the costs of reunification[73] and Italy was encumbered by a heavy public debt burden accumulated through political irresponsibility. At the same time, the US was removing controls on its financial system, US residents were borrowing heavily to consume, the Federal Reserve was keeping interest rates low for an extended period after the stresses of 2001-2002, and the US economy was experiencing successive bubbles in shares and in housing – hardly a comparable situation to that which prevailed in Europe.

A slightly more reasonable comparison might be to take the shorter period 2000-2005 and to take the EU-15 (as it stood over the period 1995-2004) as the point of reference. By this definition, Europe experienced a per capita growth rate of 2.6% while the US managed 3.2%[74]. The US still performs better in this analysis, but the difference is less stark and is still skewed by deflationary forces affecting Europe while speculative forces were affecting the US. Overall, US GDP per capita is still much higher than that of Europe (over $40,000 in 2005 versus less than $35,000 for most European countries[75]) but this is mainly due to Americans working almost 30% longer hours than Europeans[76].

The one area where the US does perform noticeably better than Europe is in science and technology. From microprocessors to biotechnology to the internet, the major technological innovations of recent decades have consistently originated in the US and have been adopted by American firms before moving on to Europe. The component of superior US performance in recent decades which is not attributable to speculative forces being underway on one side of the Atlantic, while mild deflationary forces were underway on the other, can be attributed mostly to this technological prowess.

However, even this is not testament to the power of the American free market. It is instead due to the fact that US government spending on research and development is much higher than in Europe, as it has been for many years[77]. In other words, the one regard in which the US truly outperforms its European cousins is one of the few areas where it is more 'statist' than Europe. Little more need be said to prove that the conservative model of growth is nonsense.

## Explaining Growth

The core of a more realistic model of economic growth, while it is quite different from the central arguments of the free market model, is equally simple. It consists of one straightforward feedback loop involving just a few steps, which are as follows:

1. New technology makes it possible to achieve additional output (an increase in economic capacity) with the same amount of inputs as before.

2. The profit motive stimulates firms to adopt this new technology.

3. Overall economic output increases.

4. The state gets control of some of this increased output through its existing tax system.

5. As a result of an unchanged tax system generating additional revenue, there is increased real public expenditure on education and scientific research.

6. This increased spending leads to the development of new technology and of new skills at an accelerated rate.

7.    The experience of previous innovation stimulates firms to adopt later technologies even more rapidly than they did earlier ones.

8.    The growth arising from such adoption facilitates yet more public investment in science and education, causing the whole process to continue and to accelerate.

This basic model has one underlying assumption in common with the conservative model – that the state provides a stable legal, political and physical environment in which to invest – but it also recognises that the necessary role of the state goes far beyond this. Crucially, the kind of spending on education and long-term scientific research that are needed are something that only the public sector has an incentive to support*.


## Catch-up growth

The feedback loop described above refers specifically to growth as it happens in leading countries. However, in lagging countries what occurs is essentially a derivative of this: catch-up growth where adoption of technology from abroad is more of a driver than new innovation.

This process is also driven by feedback but it involves a slightly different series of steps to those which take place in advanced countries. These steps are as follows:

1.    Stimulated by the profit motive, and perhaps by government support, firms import more advanced technology than they currently posess from abroad.

2.    Both overall economic output and export competitiveness increase.

3.    Through expanded exports and real exchange rate appreciation, this makes it possible to import more technology from abroad.

---

* The kind of short-term research that companies are more interested in funding is nowhere near as potent in bringing about fundamental change. The modern IT and biotechnology revolutions, for example, stem largely from research funded, respectively, by the US Department of Defense in the 1950s and 60s and by the National Institutes of Health in the 1960s and 70s. The private sector only became important when these technologies neared commercial viability and, even then, not-for-profit funding remained the main driver of the kind of research that leads to new breakthroughs decades hence.

4.  At the same time, the state gets control of some of the increased national output through the tax system.

5.  As a result of increased tax revenue, there is increased real public expenditure on education.

6.  This increased spending creates new skills that make it possible to absorb more technology.

7.  The experience of previous technology transfer stimulates firms to adopt later technologies even more rapidly than they did earlier ones.

8.  The growth arising from such transfer facilitates yet more technology imports and yet more spending on education.

The important differences in this second process, compared to the process which takes place in more advanced countries, are that imports of technology take the place of innovation as the main driver of growth and that the pivotal role of the state is to support exporters and education, not to support innovators and education (although they should obviously also support innovation). This second feedback process has the potential to generate much more rapid growth than that which relies entirely on new innovation, for the simple reason that it is easier and faster to adopt existing technologies than to develop new ones. However, it should be noted that this process does still involve substantial ingenuity to adapt foreign technology to local conditions. As time progresses, catch-up growth is gradually replaced by growth that is reliant on new innovation. And, in any case, the form of growth that occurs in leading countries is driven by innovation that is shared across countries, not by innovation that is purely indigenous.

## A secular feedback process

The series of steps described in each of these processes consist of a clear positive feedback loop that operates in what economists would call the very long run and which lacks anything resembling a stable equilibrium. However, these processes differ from the feedback loops driving economic cyclicality in that they can usually operate in only one direction – towards ever greater levels of output. The processes driving economic cyclicality can operate so as to either increase or decrease activity in whatever aspect of the economy they relate to but, in the case of secular growth, there is normally no converse process whereby technological know-how is somehow destroyed over long periods of time and the capacity of the economy therefore shrinks.

There may be temporary reversals in growth where, as part of a complex of forces causing a downturn in the economic cycle, firms are disincentivised from investing in new methods and the stock of physical and human capital falls. But, outside of *major* societal collapses akin to the fall of the Roman Empire, the underlying trend towards technological progress cannot itself go into reverse*.

## Technological advances are exponential

One important consequence of the feedback-driven nature of technological and economic growth is that the level of technical ability and material output increases exponentially over long periods of time. Ancient societies certainly did not have tax-funded education and scientific research in the same way we do today. But, even in simple societies, new technology created the wherewithal to develop yet more technology and major historical transitions therefore became more and more closely packed over time. Very approximately, hunting and gathering began over two million years ago; agriculture 10,000 years ago; organised civilisation 5000 years ago; Western oceanic trade 500 years ago; industry 250 years ago; electricity, chemicals, cars and flight 150-100 years ago; electronics 60 years ago and modern biotechnology 30 years ago[78]. Figure 18 shows this same accelerating dynamic in statistical form.

---

* It should, however, be noted that something akin to societal collapse has taken place again and again in many countries on the continent of Africa in recent decades and in other war-torn regions around the globe. In these places, conflict has shattered infrastructure, disrupted key institutions and bred further conflict (an especially unwelcome kind of positive feedback), and all of these have, in effect, cast the process of growth into reverse for extended periods of time.

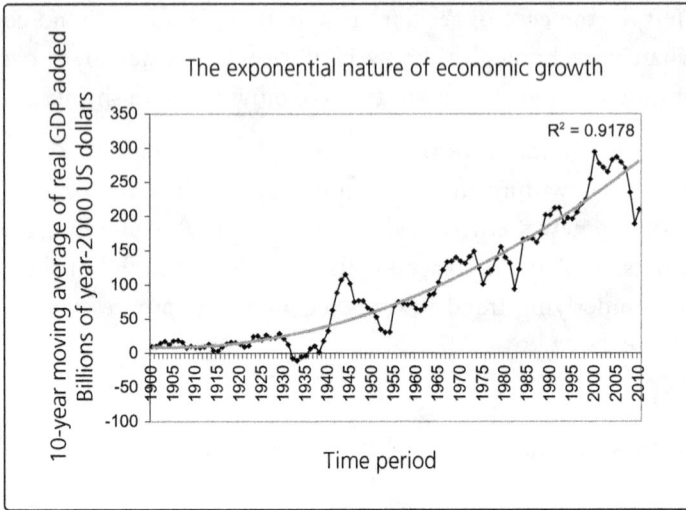

**Figure 18 – Ten-year moving averages of annual real GDP added in the United States, 1900-2010.** The data were processed as follows. Real annual GDP data was taken for the United States for every year over the period 1890 to 2010 (forecast for 2010 and estimates for the earliest years). The amount of real GDP added (or lost), compared to the previous year, was calculated for every year. A ten-year moving average of these real GDP added values was calculated for every year, using data for that year and the nine preceding years, so as to reduce the effect of the economic cycle. And the results were plotted as shown.

This produces a clear exponential trend that shows how technological progress builds upon itself – a positive-feedback process. R-squared shows the goodness-of-fit of the trend line and can have values from a minimum of 0 to a maximum of 1. (Time series analysts will point out that some kind of autoregressive model would be a better way of showing this, but this would be a complication too far for a book such as this.) [Data from the United States National Bureau of Economic Research.]

In the past 60 to 70 years, the self-reinforcing nature of growth has really come into its own as more conscious public investment in science and technology have brought about a whole range of innovations in transport, communications, biomedicine and other areas. Many of these, such as jet aircraft and the microchip, have been spin-offs from defence spending. This still, though, supports the principle that public investment is an essential component of the positive feedback loop giving rise to economic growth. In fact, public investment can only become more important in the future as the development of genuinely new technologies becomes ever more dependent on very lengthy programmes of research, which are unattractive to the private sector.

## Absolute and per capita growth

A complication to the model of growth depicted here is that, just because there is absolute growth, it does not necessarily follow that there is per capita growth. Indeed, for most of human history, mankind has been ensnared in a poverty trap whereby each increase in output – meaning mainly an increase in food output – simply led to an increase in population (up to a limit imposed by famine, disease and war) and little or no growth in output per capita took place.

In effect, there was a negative feedback loop whereby an increase in output per capita led to an increase in population and this increase in population led to a fall in output per capita back to its original level. This insidious process held output per capita constant for most of history, with only slight increases over the centuries. It broke down only when modern industry enabled output to grow much faster than population from the late 1700s onwards and eventually enabled birth control, sanitation and modern medicine, which have made it possible for this situation to become permanent*.

## Explaining Inequality

Along with GDP growth, another secular trend that is observed in economies of a certain type is the tendency for inequality to rise to ever-higher levels†[79] (Figure 19). And, as with growth, this is another example of a process that is driven by positive feedback.

---

* The global population is projected to plateau at 11-12 billion around the year 2100 – a level that is within the ability of technologically-advanced farming and other basic industries to support in relative comfort. Population growth is therefore not, in itself, a threat to our ability to sustain and extend the gains of the past century and a half. Likewise, from a scientific point of view, it is perfectly feasible to indefinitely support our industrial system with low-carbon energy sources and closed-cycle management of key material resources. The only real issue is our ability to cooperate in solving these global problems and, while doing so, to avoid international conflict.

† When inequality is expressed as a ratio of the incomes of those in the top decile to the incomes of those in the bottom, there is no mathematical limit to the extent to which it can rise.

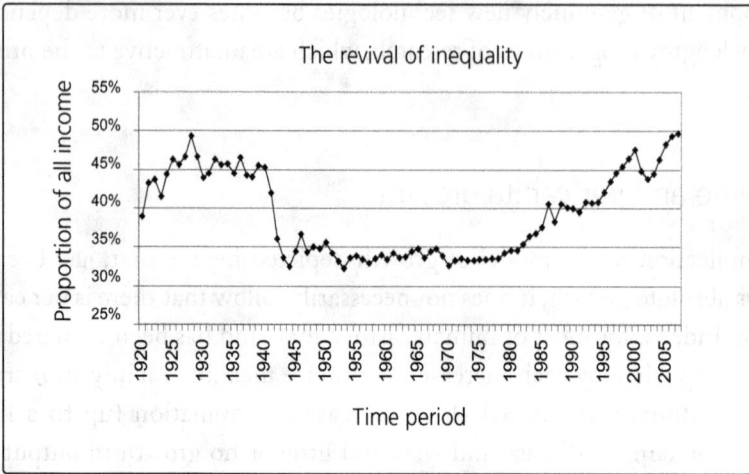

**Figure 19 – The proportion of income going to the top 10% of earners in the United States, 1920-2007.** Inequality fell during the Keynesian-activist era in the mid-20th century and rose thereafter. Indeed, it is notable that inequality surged from about the same time as debt levels and instability – all apparently driven by the same underlying structural changes in the US economy; the aggressive revival of free-market policies. It is equally noteworthy that a degree of inequality in income such as that shown here compounds to a huge divergence in wealth stocks over time, with the top 20% of wealth-holders in the US owning 84% of all assets in 2001. [Data as used in 'Striking it Richer: The Evolution of Top Incomes in The United States', by Emmanuel Saez, University of California, Berkley, 2009.]

The basis of this phenomenon is that, in a free-market economy where there are no countervailing pressures, initial differences in income arising from disparities in ability, motivation or random circumstance leave those upon whom they confer a better status in a position from which they can advance more easily than others. They can afford capital investments, can afford to live under better conditions that are conducive to economic success, can afford to influence political and economic decisions in their favour and can afford to give a better upbringing and education to their children. These things, in turn, lead to a further widening of the income gap and they thereby establish a positive feedback loop that corresponds to the commonplace observation of 'the rich becoming richer'. And, while the initial disparities in income underlying this whole process must, to some extent, be an unavoidable consequence of the need to attract skilled and motivated people into professions that provide highly demanded services, there is no such pragmatic justification for the excessive inequality that eventually results.

This process is not the only source of inequality. Other sources include the inequality that occurs when some investors successfully ride a speculative bubble while others do not; the inequality that arises when those businesses who are the first to develop or adopt a new technology do much better than others; and the inequality that arises when some people in a newly-industrialising economy are inevitably drawn into high-income sectors and positions before others. However, these sources are, in effect, amongst those factors which create the initial disparities in income that positive feedback then sustains and amplifies over time. Indeed, the *only* force that can cause income differentials to remain permanently wide and to widen over time is positive feedback of the kind described here.

This latter fact is obscured in newly-industrialised economies where, once enough people have been fully drawn-into modern sectors, inequality falls. Nevertheless, if we look only within the modern part of the economy, we can still see the tendency for inequality to spiral when there are no countervailing pressures.

## A feedback loop without self-correction

Like the positive feedback driving economic growth, the feedback process driving inequality is also capable of operating in one direction only – towards ever-greater disparities in income. In essence there is no mechanism in an unmanaged economy whereby the wealthy give away a sufficient amount of their income to enable the poor to catch up or to at least keep the gap constant. It can be argued that charity might fulfil this role but the reality is that, in the absence of coercion, the amounts the rich voluntarily give away are insufficient.

## Serious consequences – social *and* economic

Income inequality has far-reaching consequences. Most broadly, because of the diminishing-returns principle that an extra unit of income usually adds more happiness to a less-wealthy person than to a more-wealthy person, it is clear that a society with greater inequality has less total happiness than an otherwise identical society with the same overall income but less inequality. In addition, the sense of exclusion and the poor living standards that arise from very low levels of income can lead to crime, ill health and other problems that represent a huge cost for society as a whole. Likewise, the insecurity and status anxiety associated with wide gaps in wealth and social status seems to trigger stress and ill health across the entire social spectrum. It is for these reasons that, as empirical evidence shows, societies that are more equal almost always perform better on every real measure of living standards than similar societies which are less equal.

Beyond this, high levels of income inequality also seem to undermine many of the foundations of productivity growth in the economy[80]. Indeed, if rates of educational drop-out, teenage pregnancy, drug abuse, incarceration and other problems are elevated, it becomes obvious that productivity must suffer. Along with higher rates of physical investment, the control of problems such as these explains how the social market economies of western and northern Europe are able to achieve equal or greater labour productivity compared to the United States.

A final problem with inequality is that greater disparities in income can compound the problem of economic instability inherent in a lightly managed economy. Large pools of accumulated capital make for financial markets that are more systemically important. And, if the less well-off see others consuming more than they are allowed to consume themselves, they may try and increase their consumption through borrowing (facilitated by the bank deposits of the wealthy). This is obviously not sustainable but, in the bubble conditions that can arise in an unregulated market, this may either not be realised or loan salesmen may have no incentive to be restrained. Large amounts of low-quality debt can thus accumulate and, when the economic cycle eventually turns, default rates may be especially high as those on low incomes cannot repay what they have borrowed. This intensifies the downward phase of the credit-asset cycle and drives the economy towards a deeper recession than would otherwise have been the case[81]. A process of this kind seems to explain the credit card binge that occurred in the United States and United Kingdom over the middle years of the period 2000-2009. It can thereby be said to have contributed to the current global recession.

## Policy responses

Given all of this, what policy responses to the phenomenon of self-sustaining inequality should governments pursue? And how do these responses compare to the policy actions that are necessary in the cases of economic growth and economic cyclicality?

In the case of economic growth, the positive feedback that takes place is desirable and, in order to execute its responsibility of managing the economy in the general interest, the role of government must be to do whatever it can to intensify the feedback. Indeed, since the government necessarily plays an intrinsic role in the processes that underpin growth, all it needs to do is to take something in which it is already inextricably involved and play its role better. In the case of inequality, however, things are different. It is feasible for the government to have little involvement with the processes affecting this aspect of the economy if it so decides and, if it does get involved, since the feedbacks that take place are undesirable, its role must be to do whatever it can to dampen out the processes. In this sense, the appropriate policy responses to inequality resemble the policy responses to economic cyclicality, many of which also aim to dampen-out undesirable feedback effects.

The key public policy measures needed to dampen-out the rise of inequality consist of government spending to provide universal access to health, education, unemployment cover, social housing and other basic elements of social investment and social insurance – all of which has been obvious for more than 60 years. Provision of such services exploits economies of scale that only the state can achieve, and it guarantees those born into disadvantaged circumstances, along with those who have suffered misfortunes in their lives, both a minimum standard of living and a platform from which to compete[82].

There is much evidence that such policies work, both in terms of maintaining a basic standard of living and in terms of providing a base from which to compete. In terms of living standards, income inequality and social exclusion in European societies today is far less significant than in the Europe of the 19th century or in the United States of today. And, in terms of providing a competitive base, levels of social mobility in contemporary Europe are also much higher than in the Europe of the past or in the US of today[83, 84].

In addition, the comparatively high taxes needed to support such systems do not have any adverse effect on overall economic output. The evidence shows that high taxes seem not to create any general disincentive effect (Figure 20) and implies that firms and their employees just work up to their normal capacity regardless of tax rates. Indeed, given that businesspeople usually have a strong profit motive, given that ordinary people need to work to earn an income and given that employers usually demand full effort from their staff, it would probably take very high rates of taxation for market participants to give up on work to any significant extent*.

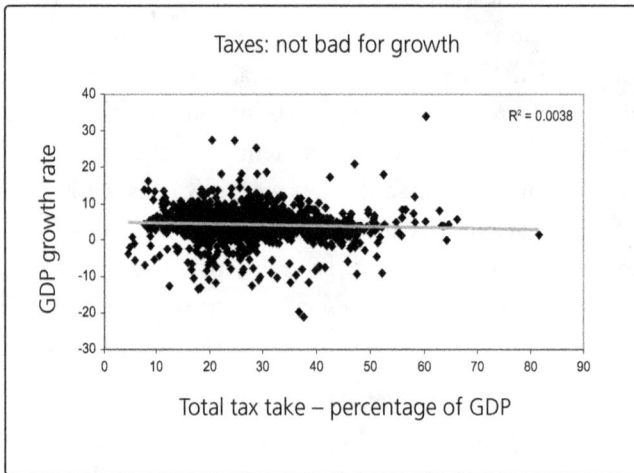

**Figure 20 – Comparison of GDP growth rates to general rates of taxation for 1346 country-year data points over the period 1962 to 2007.** This data shows no evidence for the traditional conservative idea that higher taxes are bad for growth. Similar results are obtained looking at 3-, 5- and 10-year moving-average tax take. And, when we look at moving averages of changes in tax takes over the same time horizons, there is actually a faint hint of a positive correlation, with an R-squared of 4-6%; something that may perhaps reflect the beneficial effects of a newly-activist state in certain countries. All countries and years for which data were available were included. R-squared shows the goodness-of-fit of the trend line and can have values from a minimum of 0 to a maximum of 1. [Data from the IMF.]

---

* Countries that have set themselves up as financial centres may be something of an exception to the principle that higher general taxation does not harm economic growth. Since portfolio capital, and the people who manage it, are exceptionally mobile, activity is likely to shift elsewhere if tax differentials are great enough.

This observation that high taxation does not adversely affect trend rates of growth differs from the specific disincentive effect that applies to sectors targeted with higher rates of taxation than others. In this case, there is an observable tendency for resources to be moved to other areas of activity. It also differs from the cyclical effects of changes in taxation and government spending. In this situation, when the government spends above its tax take and borrows to fill the gap, there is a short-run stimulus effect. And, when it taxes above spending and uses the funds to pay-down debt, there is a short-run cooling effect. In other words, tax-funded expenditure simply redistributes spending within the economy, whereas counter-cyclical fiscal policy changes the level of spending in the short run.

## Weaknesses of the European social model?

Despite its advantages, however, the European social model is not perfect and its main weakness is unemployment. Generous unemployment cover seems to give people an incentive not to return to work (or not to enter work in the first place) until they find a highly attractive job, and this seems to lift the level of the natural rate of unemployment (NRU) across Europe. For the EU-15 (as it stood in the period 1995-2004) unemployment levels over the years 1990 to 2005 moved in the range of 7.6% to 10.5%. In the United States, by contrast, they moved in the range 3.8% to 7.8%, if we define unemployment in the same way as in Europe[85].

However, a number of factors distort this comparison. First, as we have already seen, Europe was experiencing mild deflationary pressures over the 1990s and early 2000s while the US was experiencing speculative pressures. It is thus fair to say that the EU-15 probably has a structural NRU somewhere in the region of 7.5-8%, whereas the US has a structural NRU around 6%. This is still a difference of up to 2.8 million people employed in the US who would not be employed in Europe. But it is not as wide a gulf as conservatives would have us believe.

Second, the pattern of labour force participation is very different in the US and Europe. The US has larger areas of deprivation and incarcerates a number of people equivalent to 2.1% of its labour force, compared to about 0.4% in Europe[86]. As a consequence, non-employment rates amongst young men seem to be roughly the same in the US as in Europe (11.9% in the US versus 11.7% across France, Germany and Italy[87]). The US has been much more successful than Europe at getting women into the labour force but this is again distorted by the fact that women's liberation came earlier to America than to Europe and is therefore not a fair comparison of economic systems. Thus, given the facts as they are presented here, it is not at all clear that the US makes any better use of its human resources than does Europe. However, given the disincentives that can be associated with generous unemployment benefits, it is highly plausible that the US would still have somewhat lower levels of formal unemployment even if its excluded groups were active in creating and seeking jobs.

## Improving unemployment cover

Either way, it is clear that an NRU of more than 7% leaves room for improvement and one can think of various adaptations to the basic concept of unemployment cover that should be able to deliver such a result. The goal, in essence, is to re-structure these policies so that they minimise benefit dependency – a process that actually perpetuates inequality – while still providing a secure platform to those who need it. In this regard, simply reducing unemployment benefits to a low level or making them highly transitory is not an option; all that such a move would achieve would be to increase the risk that people drawing on benefits would fall into a poverty trap while failing to support the living standards, in the transient period where they need it, of those who do bounce back out of the social safety net.

Short-sighted policies like this might even increase the state's benefits bill in the long run by creating more dependents and more social problems – as may have been the case in the UK from the 1980s. And they definitely increase costs in health and law enforcement.

Instead, in order to reduce the level of the NRU in economies with a good system of unemployment cover, two things are needed. Firstly, unemployment assistance should be structured either as welfare-to-work or, in certain cases during a serious downturn, as subsidies designed to allow basically healthy firms to retain staff, thereby keeping up both output and demand. In this context, welfare-to-work should consist of training and robust support in job-seeking for those who need it, combined with credible penalties every time a suitable job is refused, perhaps involving a step-wise reduction in benefits down to some tolerable minimum level.

And, secondly, labour markets should be sufficiently flexible that employers can hire and fire as the please, so long as there is a reasonable business case for doing so and so long as there is no discrimination on the basis of gender, ethnicity and so on. These arrangements give firms a more powerful incentive to recruit and, if combined with incentives for reticent workers to take jobs as described above, they should go a long way towards reducing and holding-down the level of the NRU in economies with generous unemployment cover.

Beyond this, in countries where unemployment cover is not generous, it should be increased, in lock-step with measures to cut dependency (admittedly, not an easy task), as this is likely to be the most cost-effective option, socially and economically, in the long run.

## Social Democracy: a Coherent Package

In this book, we have now discussed three kinds of economic policy. In Chapters 6-9 we looked at policies designed to reduce the amplitude of the economic cycle, their limitations and the ways in which they can be executed poorly. And, in the current chapter, we have looked at policies designed to support economic growth and at policies designed to counterbalance the rise of excess inequality. What we have not looked at, however, is the question of how these three sets of policies interact with one another. Do they clash or are they complementary?

In terms of fiscal policy at least, the same basic set of policies – taxation and spending on health, education, infrastructure, scientific research, social housing and unemployment cover – dampen out economic instability and inequality while at the same time supporting economic growth.

In narrow terms, it might seem that the priority of supporting economic growth would focus on paying for education, infrastructure and scientific research. Likewise, that the priority of fighting inequality would focus on education, health, social housing and unemployment cover. And that the priority of fighting instability would not care where public money was spent, so long as government spending stabilised total spending.

This, however, is an excessively narrow focus. Growth is less likely to develop into speculation and instability if it is based on the right kinds of investment and is inclusive – in essence, if the state plays a full role. Similarly, equality supports growth by improving the quality of human resources, and promotes stability by reducing the incentive for debt-financed consumption. And economic stability supports both growth and equality by providing an environment where businesses invest in capacity because they have confidence in their future; by avoiding damage to the productive capacity of the economy in deep recessions; by avoiding situations where people are driven into destitution; and by making it easier to plan-out taxation and spending.

Beyond this, fiscal stabilisation works better when it is targeted at the less affluent. The security provided by public services and unemployment cover make people more willing to spend consistently. And, because the poor have no choice but to spend a greater proportion of their income on consumption than the rich, the automatic stabiliser effects that arise from increased payments to the unemployed during a recession are more effective than any payment to the wealthy (such as discretionary fiscal stimulus implemented as a tax rebate)[88].

Economic regulation also benefits growth, stability and equality. General business regulation designed to prevent abuse of workers, consumers, the environment and the political process clearly supports each of these objectives. It supports growth by being essential for the economy to function at all. It supports stability by providing some constraints on the extent to which firms can change their behaviour. And it promotes equality because the consequences of each of these forms of abuse would be most adverse for those who are less well-off. Likewise, regulation targeted specifically at financial services promotes growth by improving the balance between leveraged speculation and long-run backing of real physical investment. It promotes stability for all of the reasons we have already discussed in Chapter 6. And it promotes equality by making it more difficult for successful speculators to make stellar returns from market volatility that have little justification in pragmatic economic terms.

In the case of monetary policy, the picture is somewhat more clouded. By dampening inflation, speculative bubbles and the severe downturns that can follow from these, monetary stabilisation prevents long periods of lost output, damage to productive capacity and the disincentivisation of physical investment that can follow from volatility. It is therefore good for both growth and stability. In the case of inequality, however, it is difficult to say whether monetary stabilisation is a net help or a net hindrance.

Loosening of monetary policy during a recession reduces the return to wealthy bond-holding investors and corrodes the real value of certain illiquid interest-paying investments. But it also supports the value of other asset classes such as equity and housing, and involves placing new funds into the hands of large investors first. At the same time, such a loosening reduces the return to ordinary people living on private pensions and corrodes the buying power of a fixed nominal wage. But it also makes it possible for more people to be drawn back into employment, and thereby counteracts inequality. Similarly, when monetary policy is tightened, the converse of all these effects takes place and it is equally difficult to say whether the process exerts a net pressure for or against inequality. All we can say is that, if monetary policy is successful in bringing stability, this is also of benefit for equality.

## State provision or outsourcing?

Aside from being generally complementary, a further point that needs to be made in relation to all these policies is that they can only be implemented by a strong state. If we define the state as a central body tasked with coordinating society that should be headed by democratically-elected representatives, then it becomes clear that only the state can make coherent decisions on society-wide issues; only the state has an incentive to act in the interests of the electorate generally; only the state can have the legal authority and monopoly on force needed to make its decisions binding; and only the state can achieve the economies of scale needed to make public services efficient.

In some cases, the state can subcontract its activities to the private sector; using tax revenues to pay private firms to provide specific services to the public. And, in cases where the activity in question is sufficiently granular (small-scale in individual cases) to induce firms to compete on the basis of costs and performance; where borrowing costs are not a significant factor; where the dangers associated with cost-cutting are acceptable; and where the activity is not something central that underpins the entire power of the state, then this approach can improve efficiency and quality of service overall.

However, there are a whole host of areas where these criteria do not hold. In the case of building and operating public infrastructure, for example, there will be large borrowings whose associated interest cost is determined by whether or not they have explicit state backing. And, because each project is effectively a local monopoly, and because the threat of a new operator taking over in a number of years is not a credible deterrent, companies can demand higher returns from a government that is ideologically committed to privatisation.

As a consequence, when funding, construction, maintenance and operation of public infrastructure are subcontracted to the private sector, the result is often a greater cost to the taxpayer[89]. The correct solution in this case is thus for funding and operation to be handled by the state, while construction and maintenance are subcontracted to the private sector on a somewhat more small-scale and short-term basis. This would drive real competition and would make the process work better.

Likewise, the provision of health and educational services involves serious risks to quality of service if costs are cut too aggressively – risks which may not become obvious until a substantial amount of time has passed and their full impact has materialised[90]. Thus, it seems best if operation of these services remains with the public sector; and, as with public infrastructure in general, if the role of the private sector is limited to constructing and maintaining the associated facilities.

## No race to the bottom

Despite the need for significant state involvement if the economy is to function well, for much of the era of neoliberal globalisation that has prevailed since about 1980 there has been real cause for concern that international competition would make this impossible. This concern goes beyond the challenges for counter-cyclical policy mentioned in Chapter 8, and relates to the fact that, in a globalised world, trying to maintain the taxes needed to fund an activist state could conceivably be highly problematic. In essence, capital might be withdrawn from high-tax jurisdictions and invested instead in low-tax jurisdictions, where investors can retain a greater share of the returns that are generated. This process might cause growth to slow or even reverse in high-tax countries and might trigger tax competition between governments; a 'race to the bottom' that would tear the foundations out from under essential state activities and eventually undermine the entire global economy[91].

However, this outcome has yet to materialise, and there are many reasons to believe that it will not. First, governments everywhere know that drastic cuts in public services would be hugely unpopular, and they thus have a powerful incentive not to get drawn into competition over taxes. Second, extensive social investment and the concomitant creation of physical and human capital produce a favourable business environment that counterbalances the effects of higher taxes on private returns to business investment. Third, even highly-skilled workers are usually less mobile than financial capital and much of the investment in skills made by the state therefore stays at home. Fourth, the clustering effects that have been built up by advanced economies allow them to remain attractive in the face of competition from emerging economies with lower tax rates. Fifth, economies with lower taxes often have more civic problems and therefore pose a greater risk to capital. Sixth, and finally, since most business investment is financed by retained earnings[92], and since most businesses are still national[93], there is still much private capital that is not internationally mobile.

Thus, while international capital mobility may have some adverse effect on the ability of the state to fund itself through taxation, this effect is much weaker than some have feared[94]. And, in terms of policy, the conclusion reached in Chapters 8 and 9, that openness to international capital flows generally brings benefits that outweigh those of currency stability, still stands. It is possible that some structural changes in the economy might alter this position in the future, opening up greater scope for tax competition between governments and therefore necessitating significant rollbacks in international capital mobility. However, given that many of the forces that stand against such a trend are essentially permanent, there is good reason to believe that this will not come to pass.

## Social democracy

Everything I have said in this section amounts to recommending a complete package of policies along the lines of what is normally referred to as social democracy. And, as I have alluded to, it has been fairly clear for more than 60 years that policies such as these are a pragmatic necessity for achieving a well-functioning economy and society.

Indeed, if governments did not engage in polices of this kind, the result would be gradual environmental degradation, economic disruption and social unrest to the point where the entire social structure was eventually undermined. In fact, the incipient signs of such events are often what bring activist governments to power in the first place and they are why, despite the neo-conservative onslaught, most advanced countries today still follow policies that are basically social-democratic.

# 11. Conclusion:
# The Need for Change

For decades, free-market economists have told a consistent story. Markets are rational, efficient, stable and fair, and even volatile financial markets should be left mostly to their own devices. Governments, meanwhile, should seek to maintain basic institutions but should otherwise 'stay out of the way' of market forces. This is supposedly the only route to prosperity, and is even held to be the only economic system consistent with human freedom. From the late 1970s, one government after another was influenced by this perspective and a distinctive era of 'neoliberal' capitalism was born.

But the free-market ideology is a dangerous one. It creates great financial and economic instability, as demonstrated by the severe crises that have taken place over the past two years in the developed world, and over the past 30 in the developing – a pattern that could eventually undermine the democratic, mixed-economy systems in which we live. Market fundamentalism also undermines the material foundations of long-run growth, which requires an interplay of private and public sector, and it unleashes a great deal of excess inequality.

This book has aimed to begin exploring a better alternative to classical economics, starting with the scientific principle of building theories on observation, and with the specific observation that feedback effects dominate all network systems (of which the economy is one).

## The Feedback Perspective and its Implications for Policy

The argument presented in this book rests on the empirical principle of taking the evidence of reality as the ultimate arbiter of truth. In doing so, it finds that that the economy is a network like many other material systems and that it is therefore governed by feedback effects whereby downstream elements affect the level of activity at upstream elements, leading to several specific patterns of behaviour.

## Types of feedback and their effects

Of the two most general patterns of behaviour that emerge in this way, one is negative feedback, a process whereby a change in the level of activity at some node in a network sets in train consequences that eventually attenuate that change. The other general pattern is positive feedback, a process whereby a change in the level of activity at some node in a network sets in train consequences that eventually amplify that change. Negative feedback leads to relatively stable levels of activity in the nodes of the economic network to which it applies. Positive feedback, by contrast, leads to either continuous rises or to continuous falls in activity, or to alternating periods of rising and falling activity.

In some cases, the level of activity at a reference node that is subject to positive feedback is, under all normal circumstances, capable of changing in only one direction, with the result being a secular trend in activity that continues over the very long run. In other cases, the level of activity at the reference node is easily capable of changing in either direction (an increase or a decrease) and the result is a cyclical fluctuation where periods of increasing or decreasing activity alternate with one another. In this process, the reversals of direction that occur between the activity-increasing and activity-decreasing phases arise either as a result of exogenous shocks or because negative-feedback forces build up that transiently overwhelm the positive feedback and cause the system to go into reverse.

## Long and short run

The secular trends that arise when positive feedback can occur in only one direction must, by definition, play out over the very long run. By contrast, the cyclical up- and down-swings that arise when positive feedback can operate in either direction play out over what economists call the short run. (The time period where several such cycles have taken place, but there has not been time for much secular movement is called the 'long run'.) Thus, in cases where a node has cyclical positive feedback effects overlaid on secular positive feedback effects, the result is an undulating trend of the kind that is observed for GDP and certain other macroeconomic variables.

## Desirable and undesirable

The feedback effects that occur in the economy may be desirable or undesirable depending on the node they apply to and the form they take. The secular trend that affects economic output in a mixed economy with access to technological innovation, for example, is usually considered desirable. By contrast, the cyclical effects that also affect economic output are undesirable, as is the secular trend that affects inequality in a very free-market economy. In essence, while the classical paradigm of economics assumes that individual actions are consistently rational and that this leads the market to produce desirable outcomes overall, the feedback perspective recognises that there is such a thing as unintended consequences. It recognises that, even where actions are individually rational (which is not always the case), the collective outcomes they produce may be irrational. Dumping assets in a falling market or hoarding cash in a deflationary environment, for example, may make sense for the individual but, as collective social choices, they are deeply irrational and destructive.

## No private sector without the public sector

As a model, feedback can explain all kinds of change in the economy. The feedback effects that drive economic growth, for instance, involve a single, relatively straightforward, feedback loop. This process involves the following steps:

1. New technology makes it possible to achieve additional output with the same amount of inputs as before.

2. The profit motive stimulates firms to adopt this new technology.

3. Overall economic output increases.

4. The state gets control of some of this increased output through its existing tax system.

5. There is increased real public expenditure on education and basic scientific research.

6. This increased spending leads to the development of new technology and of new skills at an accelerated rate.

7.   The experience of previous innovation stimulates firms to adopt later technologies even more rapidly than they did earlier ones.

8.   The growth arising from such adoption facilitates yet more public investment in science and education, causing the whole process to continue and to accelerate.

In less-advanced countries, a variation on this process operates whereby adopting new technology from abroad using the funds generated by previous growth largely takes the place of new innovation, but the basic logic is the same.

Thus, unlike the simplistic conservative and classical model where the private sector is seen as the sole driver of growth and advancement, in the feedback model the public and private sectors have equally vital parts to play. In essence, the process driving ongoing economic expansion involves links that no business has an incentive to sufficiently maintain. It relies on long-term scientific research to produce a continuous stream of new technological ideas for the commercial world to exploit. It relies on providing individuals with 12 to 20 years of education each in order to be useful in an advanced economy. It relies on a national and international infrastructure of transport systems, communications, power and other utilities. And it relies on medical care and public health measures to keep workers at their most productive. Only governments have the incentive to guarantee these things, although there is some room for variation in how they are financed and delivered.

A system in which government retreats from these responsibilities may continue to generate growth for several years as there will be a pool of technological ideas and educated workers that will persist for at least this long but, eventually, it will stagnate.

## Momentum of cycles – the need for management

The feedback effects that drive economic instability in a market economy are more varied than those driving growth. In each of credit, asset prices, overall price levels, employment, overall output and sometimes also commodity prices, a fall in price or activity tends to lead to another fall and a rise tends to lead to another rise. This produces cycles in all of these things and, because the processes involved are all interlinked, the cycles tend to become synchronised so as to produce an overall business cycle that has a great deal of momentum.

From a policy viewpoint, financial regulations can be enacted so as to limit the propensity for credit levels and asset prices to rise under speculative forces, therefore stabilising the economy overall. At the same time, fiscal policy can be set so as to have a natural tendency to drift into surplus in boom times and deficit in recessions, acting as an automatic stabiliser on levels of economic activity. Monetary policy can be adjusted so as to stabilise consumer and asset prices. And, finally, in a deep enough crisis, discretionary fiscal stimulus, large-scale monetary injections, bank rescues and other special measures can be pursued so as to prevent a deflationary collapse – although such drastic measures should not be needed in the first place in a well-managed economy.

## Inequality – the need for management

Persistent inequality, like economic growth, is driven by a single relatively straightforward positive feedback loop. Initial differences in income arising from disparities in ability, motivation or random circumstance leave those upon whom they confer a better status in a position where they can afford capital investments, can afford to live under better conditions that are conducive to economic success, can afford to influence political and economic decisions in their favour and can afford to give a better upbringing and education to their children. These things, in turn, lead to a further widening of the income gap and they thereby establish a positive feedback loop that corresponds to the commonplace observation of 'the rich becoming richer'. And, while the initial disparities in income underlying this whole process must be an unavoidable consequence of the need to attract skilled and motivated people into professions that provide highly-demanded services, there is no such pragmatic justification for the excessive inequality that eventually results.

Growing inequality is destructive in that it is at odds with the 'diminishing returns' principle of how to maximise social happiness, as mentioned in Chapter 10, while it also fosters status anxiety across all economic classes, leading to health and social problems on a wide scale. At the same time, it creates an excluded underclass whose condition drags-down the average well-being of society, which is a source of many problems and social costs and which represents a wasted pool of human capital. It is thus clear that policy measures are needed to counterbalance the rise in inequality that takes place in an overly-free market. These measures must consist of public services that give the underprivileged a base from which to compete and which are funded by taxes that take a greater proportion of income from the more-well-off than from the less-well-off.

A further vindication of all the policies advocated here is the fact that the objectives of economic growth, economic stability and the avoidance of excess inequality are all highly compatible. These objectives are themselves mutually-reinforcing and each of the main areas of economic policy – regulation together with fiscal and monetary policy – further all three.

## Ethical Imperatives

Humans are ethical animals. This might seem surprising when we consider the violence and selfishness we see on the daily news, and in the pages of history as it is usually written. But to focus on these things is an example of what statisticians would call 'selection bias'; it is to latch-on to specific examples that are dramatic enough to stand out, whilst ignoring the rest of the evidence.

The reality is that humans evolved to live cooperatively, as part of a group, and are utterly dependent on the instinct to work together, and to show a great deal of consideration for one another, in order to survive. If we did not have this instinct, mankind would have perished long ago and neither you nor I would be here to consider the matter[95]. Thus, the barbarities of the daily news, and of conventional history, are just one extreme of the distribution of human behaviour; the great bulk of the distribution is made up by ordinary people behaving in ethical ways most of the time, and there is also another extreme composed of those saintly individuals who show an unusually high degree of consideration for others.

All of this disproves the ethical individualism that is inherent in certain kinds of free-market thinking. Instead it shows, unsurprisingly, that we are motivated by, and must be motivated by, an interplay of individual and social imperatives.

It is true that people can show less consideration for those outside their own communal, ethnic, national or class group. But our moral instincts nevertheless seem to be universal; they even extend to other sentient beings, and sometimes (absurdly) to beings that are not sentient. And, in the educated and interconnected world of today, people have both a greater interdependence and a greater ability to understand this interdependence. Thus, while the spectacle of 24-hour news might create an impression of a 'world gone mad', our moral instincts are in fact more inclusive than at any point in the past.

## An intellectual journey

However, we still have the question of how to achieve ethical outcomes in a complex society. This has inspired a huge volume of literature over the centuries, including in economics; where leading thinkers have always recognised that the subject must have both analytical and ethical aspects.

Keynes, for example, described economics as a "moral science" and, in our own time, Nobel Laureate Amartya Sen has made a sustained effort to preserve this outlook[96]. Likewise, Adam Smith, founder of the original school of classical economics with *The Wealth of Nations* in 1776, was actually a professor of moral philosophy who earlier published *The Theory of Moral Sentiments* and who viewed all economic inquiry as ultimately serving a moral purpose.

In pursuing this purpose, economic thought has weaved through different outlooks over time[97]. In the 19th century, the idea of laissez-faire dominated, with the view that government should take care of little more than law and defence and should leave almost everything to the market. This view, while it left the poor to sink into destitution at the same time as it benefited many at the top of society, was, in the minds of intellectuals, based on honest philosophy. The thinking was that allowing market forces to operate freely in all regards would direct resources to their best use; that this would maximise total wealth and that any state help for the poor would just encourage them not to work, and worsen their condition.

The barbarities of this era inspired a Marxist school of thought that saw all economics in terms of class warfare and recommended collective control, by the industrial working class, over the means of production. However, the economic structures Marxism implied turned out to be invalid. Marxism never became dominant in the leading industrial countries, but it did gain sway in Russia and elsewhere, leading to a concentration of power, together with a failure of central planning in the face of great complexity and distorted incentives, that produced outcomes even more perverse than laissez-faire.

Instead of Marxism, it was Keynesian economics that displaced laissez-faire in advanced countries, after the latter was discredited by its role in the Great Depression of the 1930s. This led to an era of extensive taxation and government spending, investment in growth, national wage bargaining, counterbalances against inequality and a combination of financial regulation and automatic stabiliser effects that kept economies stable. There was an unhelpful system of fixed exchange rates, together with perhaps too much state involvement in industry, and a tendency for governments to over-use 'stimulatory' fiscal policy in contexts where it could never work. But, overall, the decades after the Second World War were the most economically progressive that leading countries have yet experienced. (Progress was helped by post-war rebuilding, favourable demographics and the availability of a back-log of technologies whose adoption was delayed in Europe by the disruptions of 1914-1945; but this cannot explain why such full use was made of this potential, why rapid growth continued into the early 1970s, or, most especially, why growth was accompanied by marked improvements in stability and equality.)

In the 1970s, inflation triggered by a policy framework that was not well-enough attuned to it, by debt-financed spending on the Vietnam War and social programmes in the US, by the collapse of fixed exchange rates in 1971, and by the oil price shock of 1973, wracked major economies. This caused economists, who were also motivated by seeking theories amenable to mathematical purity, to over-react and abandon the entire Keynesian paradigm – a decision that dovetailed with various political trends at the time, especially in the United States. Economists went back to something very like the thinking of the 19th century and called for much smaller government budgets, together with deregulation of finance and other areas. This had some benefits – such as floating currencies, greater care for inflation and greater opening to trade in developing countries (advanced countries had already opened significantly in the Keynesian era) – but, even though it has only achieved part of its aims, the free-market revival has generally had an adverse effect on social investment, equality and stability.

The 'neoliberal' era that began around 1979 or 1980 ultimately culminated in the crisis of 2007-2009, and this gives us an opportunity to start again. In terms of an intellectual framework, this book suggests one way of doing so. The challenge is not easy; even as the economy is just recovering, there are already those who are pushing for no change so that they can continue to profit as before. But, if they do succeed in delaying progress, it just means that there will be an even bigger crisis in five or ten years from now, showing again the dangers of lax supervision. Either way, provided we do not somehow destroy ourselves first, reason must eventually return to economics.

# References

[1] The observations of one prominent market participant on the equilibrium-centric theories of modern economics are to be found in 'Can Europe Work? A Plan to Rescue the Union', George Soros, *Foreign Affairs* (September/October 1996).

[2] Any mainstream economics textbook will give a good overview of these ideas. I would suggest *Economics*, Michael Parkin, Melanie Powell and Kent Matthews (Addison-Wesley, 2007).

[3] For a more technical overview of feedback and its implications see *Feedback Systems: An Introduction for Scientists and Engineers*, Karl Johan Astrom and Richard M. Murray (Princeton University Press, 2008).

[4] For a description of this pattern see *Macroeconomics*, Rudiger Dornbusch, Stanley Fischer and Richard Startz (McGraw-Hill, 2004).

[5] For a discussion of the interaction between recessions and real inequality in lightly-managed versus well-managed economies see 'Unequal Growth, Unequal Recession?', A. B. Atkinson, *OECD Observer* (December 2008).

[6] See *Animal Spirits: How Human Psychology Drives the Economy and Why it Matters for Global Capitalism*, George A. Ackerlof and Robert J. Shiller (Princeton University Press, 2009).

[7] For details of the economic and social 'golden age' that prevailed in developed countries from approximately 1949 to 1973 see *Age of Extremes: The Short Twentieth Century 1914-1991*, Eric Hobsbawm (Abacus, 1995).

[8] For details of Britain's travails in the early 1990s over the sterling-deutschmark peg, see *The European Economy Since 1945: Coordinated Capitalism and Beyond*, Barry Eichengreen (Princeton University Press, 2007).

[9] For an overview of the assumptions and methods that underpin this specific school of thought, see *The New Classical Macroeconomics*, Kevin D. Hoover (Wiley-Blackwell, 1990).

[10] A review of the ways in which classical economic assumptions about human behaviour are at odds with reality is provided in 'How Mainstream Economists Model Choice Versus How We Behave, and Why it Matters'; Peter E. Earl, in *A Guide to What's Wrong With Economics* (Anthem Press, 2004).

[11] This desire of economists for their subject to be like physics is mentioned in 'Can Mathematics Be Used Successfully in Economics?', Donald Gillies, in *A Guide to What's Wrong With Economics* (Anthem Press, 2004).

[12] Cited in 'How Economics Lost Sight of the Real World', John Kay, *Financial Times* (21 April 2009).

[13] This viewpoint originated in 'Econometric Policy Evaluation: A Critique', Robert Lucas, *The Philips Curve and Labour Markets* (January 1976).

[14] Any standard economics textbook will cover these foundational principles quite well; I would again recommend *Economics*; Michael Parkin, Melanie Powell and Kent Matthews (Addison-Wesley, 2007).

Such texts, however, tend to underemphasise the importance of economies of scale and of clustering in explaining the success of developed economic centres. For a more detailed coverage of this, I would recommend *How Rich Countries Got Rich and Why Poor Countries Stay Poor*; Erik S. Reinert (Constable, 2008).

[15] An overview of the scientific method is presented in *The Scientific Method: An Historical and Philosophical Introduction*, Barry Glover (Routledge, 1996).

[16] An overview of these facts is presented in *Kindness in a Cruel World: The Evolution of Altruism*, Nigel Barber (Prometheus Books, 2004).

[17] International wage data shows that wage differentials, before taxes and transfers, are substantially lower in egalitarian societies such as Sweden and Japan than in individualistic societies such as the United States. Likewise, the results of experiments based on economic games show clear cross-cultural differences between individualistic and egalitarian societies.

[18] For a discussion of the importance of institutions in economics see 'Roots of Development', *The Economist*, 3 October 2002.

[19] An example of this debate is 'Can Economics Start From the Individual Alone?', Geoffrey M. Hodgson, in *A Guide to What's Wrong With Economics* (Athena Press, 2004).

[20] For an overview of where this field of research currently stands see *An Introduction to Behavioral Economics*, Nick Wilkinson (Palgrave-Macmillan, 2007).

[21] These results are presented in 'Endogenous Steroids and Financial Risk Taking on a London Trading Floor'; J.M. Coates and J. Herbert, in *Proceedings of the National Academy of Sciences of the United States of America* (6 November 2007).

[22] Much of this research is considered as belonging to the field of complexity theory. An overview of this field is presented in *Complexity: A Guided Tour*, Melanie Mitchell (Open University Press USA, 2009).

[23] Presented in *The (Mis)Behaviour of Markets: A Fractal View of Risk, Ruin and Reward*, Benoit B. Mandelbrot and Richard L. Hudson (Profile Business, 2004).

[24] An excellent discussion of the circumscribed usefulness of mathematics in economics is provided in 'Can Mathematics Be Used Successfully in Economics?'; Donald Gillies, in *A Guide to What's Wrong With Economics* (Anthem Press, 2004).

[25] A farsighted recognition of this cyclicality and its effects on the wider economy is presented in *Stabilizing an Unstable Economy*, Hyman Minsky (Yale University Press, 1986).

[26] For more on this history see *Manias, Panics and Crashes: A History of Financial Crises*, Charles Kindleberger and Robert Z. Aliber (Palgrave-Macmillan, 2005).

[27] For a robust and accessible critique of the efficient market hypothesis see *The Origin of Financial Crises: Central Banks, Credit Bubbles and the Efficient Market Fallacy*, George Cooper (Harriman House, 2008).

[28] For a reprint of the classic 1936 work outlining these processes see *The General Theory of Employment, Interest and Money*, John Maynard Keynes (Prometheus Books, 1997).

[29] For a snapshot of the quantity theory of money see 'The Quantity Theory of Money', Yi Wen, in *Federal Reserve Bank of St. Louis Economic Synopses* (2006).

[30] An account of how this can occur in the case of crude oil is provided in 'Bubbling Crude: Crude Oil Price Speculation and Interest Rates', Eduard Gracia, *E-Journal of Petroleum Management and Economics* (29 June 2009).

[31] For an example of futures market activity feeding through to real commodity prices see 'Insight: Commodities Swamped in Rush to Safety', David Roche, *Financial Times* (17 March 2008).

[32] For details of some of these effects see *Commodity Speculation: The Risk to Food Security and Agriculture* (Institute of Agriculture and Trade Policy, 2008).

[33] An in-depth analysis of how downward pressures in the financial system and downward pressures in the wider economy can reinforce one another is provided in *The Holy Grail of Macroeconomics: Lessons From Japan's Great Recession*, Richard C. Koo (Wiley, 2008).

[34] Descriptive statistics on these events in 'Economics Focus: Diagnosing Depression', *The Economist* (30 December 2008).

[35] For details of an economy in deflation see *Essays on the Great Depression*, Ben S. Bernanke (Princeton University Press, 2004).

[36] Details of how external crises of this kind can unfold in less-developed countries, together with the policy issues that surround them, are to be found in *Globalization and its Discontents*, Joseph Stiglitz (Penguin, 2002).

[37] For details of the basic dynamics of bank runs and how they are intrinsic to a fractional reserve banking system, see *The Origin of Financial Crises: Central Banks, Credit Bubbles and the Efficient Market Fallacy*, George Cooper (Harriman House, 2008).

[38] One article that tentatively asked in the early stages of the current financial crisis what the ultimate consequences of CDOs and CDSs might be was 'The Alchemists of Finance', *The Economist* (17 May 2007). More robust and far-sighted comments came from the legendary investor Warren Buffet who, in 2003, expressed the view that "derivatives are financial weapons of mass destruction, carrying dangers that, while now latent, are potentially lethal".

[39] For arguments in favour of such an expansive definition of banking see *The Return of Depression Economics and the Crisis of 2008*, Paul Krugman (Penguin, 2008).

[40] For details of some bouts of hyperinflation in recent history see 'The Realities of Modern Hyperinflation', Carmen M. Reinhart and Miguel A. Savastano, *Finance and Development* (June 2003).

[41] For details of Japan's 'growth recession' see 'The Incredible Shrinking Economy', *The Economist* (2 April 2009).

[42] A concise and lucid account of these events is provided in *The Return of Depression Economics and the Crisis of 2008*, Paul Krugman (Penguin, 2008). Another excellent, if somewhat controversial, account is provided in *Globalization and its Discontents*, Joseph Stiglitz (Penguin, 2002). A quite dispassionate account is provided in *Globalizing Capital*, Barry Eichengreen (Princeton University Press, 2008).

[43] Perhaps the most high-impact analysis of what went wrong and how to fix it is *The Turner Review: A Regulatory Response to the Global Banking Crisis*, Adair Turner (2009). Another excellent account of how the crisis originated is to be found in *Fixing Global Finance*, Martin Wolf (Yale University Press, 2009).

[44] Data discussed in 'Community Reinvestment Act Had Nothing to Do with Subprime Crisis', Aaron Pressman, *Business Week* (29 September 2009).

[45] Data in 'World GDP', *The Economist* (17 December 2009).

[46] For a detailed introduction to monetary policy see *Monetary Economics: Policy and its Theoretical Basis*, Keith Bain and Peter Howells (Palgrave-Macmillan, 2003).

[47] For an overview of current systems of financial regulation see *Global Financial Regulation: The Essential Guide*, Howard Davies and David Green (Polity, 2008).

[48] For an overview of how fiscal policy can be used to manage the economy see *Current Thinking on Fiscal Policy*, eds. Jerome Creel and Malcolm Sawyer (Palgrave-Macmillan, 2008).

[49] Data from the OECD and IMF show that the majority of countries with a comprehensive set of public services have public spending in this range.

[50] For an example of how even publications that are normally staunchly free-market support bank rescues under sufficiently adverse circumstances see 'Inside the Banks', *The Economist* (22 January 2009).

[51] For a discussion of the time-lag effects inherent in fiscal stabilisation see 'The Case Against The Case Against Discretionary Fiscal Policy', Alan S. Blinder, *CEPS Working Paper Series* (Princeton University, 2004).

[52] An extensive review of time delays, liquidity traps and other issues relating to the use of fiscal and monetary policy to manage aggregate demand is provided in 'Weapons of Mass Distraction', *The Economist* (26 September 2002).

[53] An analysis of different approaches to pollution control is presented in 'Instrument Choice in Environmental Policy', Lawrence H. Goulder and Ian W.H. Parry, *Resources For the Future Discussion Paper* (April 2008).

[54] Analysis presented in 'Minimum Wages and Economic Outcomes in Europe', Stephen Machin and Alan Manning, *European Economic Review* (April 1997).

[55] For an account of the various aspects of globalisation see *Globalization: A Very Short Introduction*, Manfred Steger (Oxford University Press, 2009).

[56] For an account of how the fortunes of more- and less-developed countries can differ in the face of an economic crisis, see *The Return of Depression Economics and the Crisis of 2008*, Paul Krugman (Penguin, 2008).

[57] For an account that describes this issue in stark relief, but which is quite pessimistic about it, see *False Dawn: The Delusions of Global Capitalism*, John Gray (Granta, 2002).

[58] A realistic and accessible introduction to exchange rate economics is provided in *Macroeconomics: Understanding the Wealth of Nations*, David Miles and Andrew Scott (Wiley, 2004).

[59] For an acknowledgement that this kind of volatility is observed empirically, see 'Exchange Market Volatility and Securities Transaction Taxes', *OECD Economic Outlook*, 2002.

[60] For a discussion of this trilemma, see *The Return of Depression Economics and the Crisis of 2008*, Paul Krugman (Penguin, 2008).

[61] For a technical discussion of this principle see 'The NAIRU Concept – A Few Remarks', Karl Pichelmann and Andreas-Ulrich Schuh, *OECD Working Papers*, (1997).

[62] Extensive discussion of such arrangements can be found in *The European Economy Since 1945: Coordinated Capitalism and Beyond*, Barry Eichengreen (Princeton University Press, 2008).

[63] An overview of these possibilities is presented in *Exchange Rate Regimes: Fixed, Flexible or Something in Between?*, Imad A. Moosa, (Palgrave-Macmillan, 2005).

[64] For information on the United States in this period see 'Business Cycle Expansions and Contractions', *National Bureau of Economic Research* (retrieved 27 August 2009).

[65] For the views of one prominent economist on this matter see 'An Undervalued Currency Gives Value to Economies', Dani Rodrik, *Taipei Times* (14 August 2007).

[66] The capital flow from China to the United States arising from the undervaluation of the Chinese Renminbi, and how it contributed to the financial bubble that inflated from the early 2000s, is described in detail in *Fixing Global Finance*, Martin Wolf (Yale University Press, 2009).

[67] For details of the upsurge in trade protectionism during the Great Depression see 'The Slide to Protectionism in the Great Depression: Who Succumbed and Why?', Barry Eichengreen and Douglas A. Irwin, *NBER Working Paper* (July 2009).

[68] For the United States, an economy that needs foreign trade less than most because of the size of its internal market, research puts the extra income added by trade opening since the Second World War at 7-12% of GDP. This analysis is presented in 'The Payoff to America from Globalisation', Scott C. Bradford, Paul L.E. Grieco and Gary Clyde Hufbauer, *The World Economy* (July 2006).

[69] For data see 'Employment, Growth and Taxation in Industrial Countries', Francesco Daveri and Guido Tabellini, *IGIER Working Paper* (November 1997).

[70] Data from the OECD, IMF and Economist Intelligence Unit (EIU).

[71] Data from the OECD, IMF and World Bank.

[72] Data on the consequences of this in *OECD Economic Outlook* (June 2001).

[73] Data in *OECD Surveys – Germany* (May 2001).

[74] Data from the OECD and IMF.

[75] Data from the IMF.

[76] Data in 'Why do Americans Work More Than Europeans?', Claudio Michelacci and Josep Pijoan-Mas, *CEPR Policy Insight* (September 2007).

[77] Even though European corporations spend more on R&D than American corporations, the extent of public funding in the US is enough to ensure that total R&D investment stands at 2.6% of GDP, compared to 1.9% in the EU-15 as it stood until 2004. Data on this are presented in *Federal Support for Research and Development*, Congressional Budget Office (June 2006).

[78] For details of the trajectory of technological development over the course of human history see *Technology: A World History*, Daniel R. Headrick (Oxford University Press, 2009).

[79] For a tacit acknowledgement of this see 'The Rich, The Poor and the Growing Gap Between Them', *The Economist* (15 June 2006).

[80] Evidence that this is the case, with an emphasis on how widely-distributed asset ownership benefits growth, is discussed in 'Economic Growth and Income Inequality: Reexamining the Links', Klaus Deninger and Lyn Squire, *Finance and Development* (March 1997).

[81] Data supporting the view that high levels of inequality promote high levels of consumer borrowing and thereby lead to economic instability are presented in 'The Household Debt Bubble', John Bellamy Foster, *Monthly Review* (May 2006).

[82] The general principles of public service provision are reviewed in *Economics of the Welfare State*, Nicholas Barr (Oxford University Press, 2004).

[83] An historical analysis of social stratification and social mobility is provided in *Social Mobility in the 19th and 20th Centuries: Europe and America in Comparative Perspective*, Hartmut Kaelble (Berg Publishers, 1985).

[84] Statistical analysis shows that income inequality is lower, and that almost every aspect of social performance is better, in Northern European societies that are social-democratic in orientation compared to societies such as the US and UK that are more free market in orientation. An example of such analysis is presented in *The Spirit Level: Why More Equal Societies Almost Always Do Better*, Richard Wilkinson and Kate Pickett (2009).

[85] Data from the OECD and IMF.

[86] For an in-depth discussion of these issues see *The World We're In*, Will Hutton (Abacus, 2002). See also *False Dawn: The Delusions of Global Capitalism*, John Gray (Granta, 1998).

[87] Data presented in 'Do Employment and Income Security Cause Unemployment? A Comparative Study of the US and the E-4', Robert Buchele and Jens Christiansen, *Cambridge Journal of Economics* (1998).

[88] An in-depth discussion of different approaches to fiscal stimulus is provided in 'Assessing The Macro-Economic Impact of Fiscal Stimulus 2008', Mark M. Zandi, *Moody's Economy* (January 2008).

[89] Evidence for such a conclusion in the case of UK hospitals is provided in 'PFI in the NHS – Is There an Economic Case?', Declan Gaffney, Allyson M. Pollock, David Price and Jean Shaoul, *British Medical Journal* (July 1999). Similar effects are reported in other areas of public infrastructure.

[90] For evidence on the effects that private sector provision can have in healthcare see 'Downsizing of Acute Inpatient Beds Associated with Private Finance Initiative: Scotland's Case Study', Matthew G. Dunnigan and Allyson M. Pollock, *British Medical Journal* (April 2003).

[91] For a very pessimistic discussion of this possibility see *False Dawn: The Delusions of Global Capitalism*, John Gray (Granta, 1998).

[92] Data across several countries provided in *UK Investment and the Capital Market*, Stephen B. Bond, HM Treasury (2000). Comments on the eurozone in *Business Investment in the Euro Area and the Role of Firm's Financial Positions*, ECB Monthly Bulletin (April 2008).

[93] Small business accounts for just over 50% of GDP in the United States. This result is shown in *The Small Business Share of GDP 1998-2004*, Small Business Administration (retrieved 27 August 2009). Such a result also implies that, since many medium-size businesses will also be national as opposed to multinational, the GDP share of multinationals must be well under 50%. This is consistent with figures showing that big industrial firms accounted for 17% of GDP as of 1998 but, it should be borne in mind that some multinationals will fall outside the definition of "big

*industrial* firms". The latter datum is presented in 'Big is Back', *The Economist* (29 August 2009).

[94] One article noting the fact taxes have not fallen in the face of neoliberal globalisation is 'Is Government Disappearing?', *The Economist* (27 September 2001).

[95] This is discussed in much more detail in *Kindness in a Cruel World: The Evolution of Altruism*, Nigel Barber (Prometheus Books, 2004).

[96] The most recent example of this is to be found in *The Idea of Justice*, Amartya Sen (2009).

[97] For a detailed account of this intellectual journey see *The Penguin History of Economics*, Roger E. Backhouse (Penguin, 2002).

# Index